SECRETS OF THE SNO CONE LADY

ANGELA'S STORY

ROMOX

Good Luck + Best Wishes
Angela R. Mattox
TEL: 314-845-3669

SECRETS OF THE SNO CONE LADY

ANGELA'S STORY

ANGELA MATTOX

Sno-Biz Books

Secrets of the Sno Cone Lady: Angela's Story
Copyright © 2008 Angela Mattox
Published by Sno-Biz Books

Although this book represents the whole truth and nothing but the truth, some of the names have been changed to respect the privacy of certain individuals. Other characters are nameless as a consequence of the atrocious pain and suffering which led me to obliterate their identities decades ago. These persons will always remain anonymous.

I offer my heartfelt apologies, if the Greek words and names are incorrect or errantly written due to memory repression and/or a challenging alphabet.

For more information, please contact:
www.sno-bizbooks.com

Book design by:
Arbor Books, Inc.
www.arborbooks.com
19 Spear Rd.
Suite 301
Ramsey, NJ 07446

Printed in the United States of America

Secrets of the Sno Cone Lady: Angela's Story
Angela Mattox

1. Title 2. Author 3. Memoir/Biography

Library of Congress Control Number: 2008905486

ISBN 10: 0-9818590-0-3
ISBN 13: 978-0-9818590-0-2

To the Veterans

From the Two World Wars to the Iraq War
Those among us and those who rest in peace
In honor and in glory

You are the real heroes
The pulse of America

Table of Contents

ACKNOWLEDGMENTS

My gratitude is extended too all those wonderful individuals who played a part in making this book the realization of another dream.

I owe a debt of gratitude to Al Becker and his parents for giving me the opportunity to flee my devastating past and begin a new life in the United States.

Special mention to my devoted husband and life companion, Gary Mattox; as a result of his unwavering love, support and encouragement my dream came true. Thanks to Gary I became an American citizen, and a well respected, successful entrepreneur selling millions of sno cones.

I express my heartfelt gratitude to my loyal customers for their extraordinary love and devotion. The source of my prosperity, they are my beloved family and most treasured friends.

Special thanks to Nancy Genovese for her talents, guidance and hard work. Without her exceptional editorial and writing skills this book would not have been written.

Thanks to Melissa Singleton for all her help, communicating with the folks at Arbor Books so that this book could become a reality.

Thanks are also due to the American people who planted in me invaluable seeds of trust. Their generosity, kindness and love through out the decades has been a precious and unforgettable gift. They gave and give me "life."

I am grateful for my faith in God. Without Divine Intervention in my life I would not have made it.

PROLOGUE

"I am not an Athenian or a Greek, but a citizen of the world."

—Socrates

Although people of faith are taught that suffering is a pathway to salvation, undoubtedly, it is neither gratifying nor uplifting to live in constant strife, be it emotional, spiritual or physical. Add maternal rejection at birth, abducted innocence, relentless abuse as well as poverty in post-war Greece and the scenario becomes hopeless, beyond any understanding of redemptive torment.

Yet, despite the agonizing beginning and equally painful first two decades of my life, I would not permit the austere environment to either penetrate my spirit or quench my thirst for happiness. Instead, I searched for answers, questioning why I was unloved and unwanted, and why I was always so painfully ashamed of my Greek heritage. What was really behind this frustrating feeling of shame?

I struggled to come to terms with who I was and what was so awful about me to warrant dismissal from my family at such an early age. Why had I been banished so cruelly? An infant, a toddler, a child—what terrible sin could a youngster ever commit to be so harshly penalized? For years I wondered if I would ever find a response, knowing in the core of my being I would not yield until I did.

Thankfully, much is said about the merits of learning to accept unalterable circumstances over which there is little if any control. However, sometimes, far too few words are spent discussing the extraordinary strength, determination and persistence of those unwilling to accept a destiny of repeated persecution. Not only do they vow to alter the course of their lives, but undaunted by even the most ruthless obstacles, they forge ahead until triumphant, they walk away from their demons.

This was the substance of my dream. But in my mind, it was more than a little girl's fantasy; it was about making a commitment and honoring it with unwavering loyalty. It was about walking away from defeat and holding my head up triumphantly.

I remember the pain. Vicious and stabbing, it was ever-present until one day, I realized the thorn was no longer embedded in my side. Though a minute consolation, I knew that if I wanted the throbbing to cease, I needed to face the healing process—not only for myself, but for countless others entrapped in agonizing situations. Only then would I gain and merit the inner quiet I was yearning for.

I just wanted it all to stop—the doubts and confusion, the questions and the burning quest for answers, the pain and frustrations, the inner chaos that was such a part of who I was as a child and for years thereafter.

Still, it doesn't end here. Decades later, I'm impassioned with the desire to protect all children from the disfiguring experience of rejection, abandonment and abuse. I want to eradicate the unsightly scars and lifelong consequences that if left unattended, will blemish any possibility of serenity.

Thus was born Martyrdom of the Sno Cone Lady: The Whole Truth and Nothing But the Truth. Into its blank pages, I poured all the love and nurturing I was denied as a child. I blended in my fears and pains, my disappointments and anxieties, my doubts and insecurities, in addition to the many miserable episodes of my personal tragedy.

As the pages turn, the course of events changes, as do the circumstances of my life. From the blood of martyrdom are born my victories—and for the first time in my life, all my sorrows are unveiled to deliver hope and healing to others.

For a long time, I felt as if I were imprisoned in a windowless dungeon. Would I ever get to see the light? Would I enjoy the warmth of a ray of sun dancing along the contours of my face? Would someone think me worthy of a hug? Was being Greek so awful that no one could possibly love or want me?

Realizing there had to be a reason for such a famine of emotional bonding in my life, I felt impassioned to discover the secret.

What I wanted to overcome was the fear of being asked, "Where are you from?" I'd shudder at the mere sound of those words. A paralyzing silence would leave me voiceless.

Years ago, in my childish imagination, I fantasized that I could receive the question with a smile and a dignified response. But before I could be proud of my heritage, I had to be willing and able to cast aside the tears of self-pity that overshadowed any speck of self-respect I could possible visualize. However, more importantly, I had to move beyond telling my story; I had to relive it moment by moment, staggering through the dark labyrinths as if it were my maiden voyage.

This book recounts my journey—a tortuous expedition plotted with thwarted events, circuitous routes and unexpected impediments. However, while searching for closure, I hope the reanimating of my memories will cleanse the anguish that lives within, gnawing away at the inner quietude I fought so long and hard to acquire.

But if my tears and suffering help even one soul in agony, I will feel it was not all in vain. Perhaps entwined in the crevices of my physical and emotional anguish sits an important purpose—the significance of my life.

This book is a testament to the strength of will and an unwillingness to accept defeat as part of the human condition. It is about relentless persistence in overcoming the shame attached to an imposed stigma that destroys like a malignancy. It is proof of the power of faith—not only in God, but in myself.

Secrets of the Sno Cone Lady: Angela's Story is also a special tribute to the disabled veterans at Jefferson Barracks Hospital in St. Louis, Missouri, but more importantly, it is the expression of my heartfelt gratitude to one American serviceman who I firmly believe was God's emissary—a man who made the dream I designed in my fantasy become a reality the day I landed at Kennedy International Airport in New York.

I journeyed through the intricate maze of an earthly hell. But the trip back into yesterday allowed me to put my today in perspective while helping me chart my personal metamorphosis from Avyrini Judis, an illegitimate child of shame, to Angela Mattox, wife, step-mother, successful entrepreneur, friend, confidant and humanitarian—loved, cherished, respected and admired by all who chance upon her.

I have traveled far and long, crossing national and international boundaries. I have braced physical and emotional tempests. I have escaped from the confining box into which I was stuffed and locked, freeing myself from the shackles that once upon a time kept me from taking flight. I have reached my destination.

Today, it is no longer about where I am going but how I am getting there. Yes, I'm proud of my Greek origins, though I consider myself a woman of the world. I'm comfortable with who I am wherever I am, and have in my heart a deep love for the United States of America.

I look back from time to time, to put my today in perspective and to render thanks for the abundance of blessings received. I'm always mindful of how essential it is to pause amid the daily chaos of life and just say "thank you." I am also aware that often, our pain and suffering make us better human beings.

After the martyrdom of Christ came the redemption and salvation of all humanity. There is a purpose to suffering; sometimes, it just takes a lifetime to discover it. Thankfully, I did—in time to save myself and hopefully others.

PART I

Τραγωδία
TRAGEDY

"He who learns must suffer. And even in our sleep pain that cannot forget falls drop by drop upon the heart and in our own despair, against our will comes wisdom to us by the awful grace of God."

—Aeschylus

FIRST EPISODE

"Upon the conduct of each depends the fate of all."
—Alexander the Great

Late one afternoon in early May of 1946, just minutes before the dwindling sunset cast the day into total darkness, a petite, slender girl from an affluent, Greek family met one of the boys from the village. The young man, a tall, handsome fellow with a penetrating gaze, never made a secret of his crush on her.

Hand in hand, Maria Souliou and Spiros Judis strolled along a gravel path, stirring up sand-colored clouds of dust in their wake like a couple of children too engrossed in their own world to either realize or care that they were soiling their shoes.

The early evening's stillness was shattered by the crunching echo of two sets of dragging footsteps in chorus with a loud, husky voice discussing the latest tactics of the EAM-ELAS Εθνικό Απελευθερωτικό Μέτωπο - Ελληνικός Λαϊκός Απελευθερωτικός Στρατός—the Communist National Liberation Front-National Popular Liberation Army.

"Maria, you will see," Spiros blurted without lifting his gaze from the ground. "The Civil War is not over—the Communists will win. They will overtake the right-wing royalist Greek government. It's time—and it will happen. We won't have to wait much longer. I will head the insurrection. I will bring Communism to Ktismata!"

Politics was an alien language to Maria. She did not have the faintest idea what Spiro was speaking about or why he was so red-faced and excited. All she knew was that his attentions pleased her, and his politically agitated temperament was electrifying—even if in a mysterious way.

Elevating her glance to meet his, she smiled shyly. This was her response, and the only one he would get. Although it conveyed neither agreement nor dissension, it was politely appropriate for a child. How could she possibly contradict him?

Disturbed by her silence, Spiros jumped in front of Maria, interrupting her pace. Placing his two hands firmly on her shoulders, he pulled the startled, young girl close.

"Did you hear what I said?" Spiros questioned.

Maria felt the warmth of his breath on her face. Wincing from the pungent odor of the garlic he'd ingested at lunch and the cigarette he had just smoked, she dared not inhale. It was nauseating, and she did not want to wretch like a child in front of him. It would be far too embarrassing.

The realization that if she held her breath, she would not have to smell the traces of his midday meal mixed with the tobacco was a strategy Maria learned early on to keep her stomach from somersaulting. The Greeks loved garlic, and they were predominately chain smokers, disbelieving in any moderation philosophy.

Maria shrugged, nervously licking her lips. Gazing into the handsome boy's deep-set eyes, she nodded her head. Of course she had heard his heated words.

Barely thirteen, Maria was a child filled with schoolgirl dreams and romantic fantasies. Her gracious, carefree personality gave her an innocent, endearing charm that was far too enticing to resist.

Spiros, just several months shy of twenty, was a visionary with grandiose political ideas for his country. A determined manner of speaking and strong convictions gave him an adult bearing. Maria admired his self-confidence and grown-up demeanor. In return, Spiros was attracted to her fresh, unmarred beauty, and the special way in which she looked up to meet his eyes when he spoke, slightly tilting her head. It made her seem captivated by his words—or so he liked to believe.

However, what seemed like an enjoyable teenage rendezvous turned into a tragic escapade that designed the destiny of one little girl not yet born—a child who would be fated to carry the burden throughout her life.

After the post-dawn sunrise the following morning, the thirteen-year-old's virtue was violated, her innocence stolen. Though unknown to her, Maria was pregnant. The young man, on the other hand, had forfeited his honor. The perpetrator, Spiros, was a man of ill-repute—a conniving rapist.

Upon completion of the crime, the deflowered girl returned home, crawled into bed and erupted into uncontrollable sobs. The pain, emotional and physical, was excruciating.

Maria lived with her parents, in a comfortable house with all the conveniences available in the late '40s. A government official, her father was an eminent figure in the village, revered for his professional and familial merits. However, his distinguished position left him open to criticism and judgment. Therefore, any breach of honor or morality on his part or that of his family would be an intolerable and unpardonable indignity. It was the price of respect and prestige in Ktismata.

The village way of life was simple and traditional. Children grew up, attended school, became self-sufficient, chose a life companion from among the other eligible townspeople, and married. Individuals from reputable families did not stray from this course. It would be far too embarrassing and humiliating to dishonor their parents with any kind of unacceptable behavior.

Sundays were reserved for church. The family would attend the service together, profess a belief in Jesus Christ who died on the cross to redeem mankind, and try to live a life free from sin and corruption so as not to offend the Savior. Children learned the commandments at an early age and were expected to honor their parents and demonstrate respect for sacred law. However, sometimes, the recklessness of youth leads to terrible mishaps.

Spiros, with the egocentricity and unthinking mind of a restless teen, focused on his mission to turn a peaceful, existing government into a Communist monopoly. A member of the Russian Communist Party on a crusade to overthrow the Greek government, he believed he was invincible. When he wasn't feeding his political obsession, he was looking for prey to satiate his physical passions—selfishly, of course.

There was no romancing, no sweet words or endearing declarations. Instead, there was a rapacious appetite and a man unwilling to consider the feelings, well-being or reputation of a young girl from a prominent family.

The sexual encounter between Maria and Spiros was violent, wicked, injurious and not without devastating consequences—for her. Physically ravaged and emotionally traumatized, Maria was left permanently tarnished.

Keeping her dark secret buried in her heavy heart, the young girl realized that sooner or later, as the pregnancy became visible, she would have to endure the wrath of her parents. She also knew that children born out of wedlock, as well as their mothers, were scorned and disowned. Consequently, she and her family would be the objects of gossip and ridicule. Furthermore, due to the scandal, Maria's father would risk the forfeiture of his high-level position in the government.

Unjust or otherwise, the entire family would be liable for her unfortunate brush with a cruel destiny. But worst of all, there was an additional price to pay; another innocent life would be marred—the undesired child she was carrying in her womb.

To conceal the beginning bulge of her new, rotund silhouette, Maria dressed in clothing several sizes larger than her petite frame required. She looked sloppy and unkempt. Neatness was obviously not a primary concern. It was of little importance. She had to keep her gloomy secret intact as long as possible.

"Maria," her mother said one morning, glancing at the young girl as she was leaving for school. "You seem to be gaining weight. Maybe you'd better limit some of the sweets you eat. You're not very tall, and you don't want to get fat. It's terribly unattractive."

Feeling her heart thump in her chest, Maria took a deep breath, purposely avoiding her mother's eyes.

"OK, Μαμά," she lied. "I'll be more attentive to what I eat."

Once outside the door, Maria broke into irrepressible sobs. How could she tell her mother she was expecting a baby with a soldier who would never accept paternity? How could she admit that the man who had fathered her child had immediately and without warning left Kitsmata?

Spiros was a young, political reactionary who had no intentions of accepting responsibility, let alone of asking for her hand in marriage. Maria had to face the truth—she was on her own to deal with the brutal after-effects of his terrible crime.

Eventually, with the passage of time, Maria's tremendous weight gain could no longer be camouflaged behind loose-fitting garments or implausible fibs about over-indulging at the table. It was too much too soon, and it was becoming rather obvious.

Realizing the inevitable, Maria prepared to tell her parents. After supper, she lingered in the dining room waiting for the right moment.

"Maria," her father asked, lifting his eyes from the newspaper, "is everything all right?"

"Yes, Μπαμπάσ," she mumbled, obviously unconvinced of her own response.

"You seemed exceptionally quiet at dinner," he said, removing his glasses to rub his eyes. "Are you sure something isn't wrong?"

Listening to the father-daughter exchange of words, Maria's mother walked over to the young girl, totally unprepared for the life-shattering news she was about to receive.

"If something is wrong at school," she said, sliding her hand down her daughter's long, dark hair, "you can tell us."

Unable to contain herself, Maria burst into tears. The painful secret was far too big for her to conceal any longer.

"Μαμά, Μπαμπάσ," she sobbed, gasping for air. "I'm έγκυοσ!"

The room fell into a funereal silence. Maria's mother dragged her chair along the marble floor, creating a scraping sound as piercing as her daughter's desperate cries.

"How can that be, Maria?" she shrieked, burying her head in her open palms. "How can you be pregnant?"

Rising from his chair, Maria's father looked dazed. His olive skin paled. Tiny beads of sweat decorated the perimeter of his brow, enhancing the pallor of his complexion. A tiny, blue vein protruded from the side of his slender neck. Gasping for air, he seemed to have trouble catching his breath.

"How could this happen, Maria?" he questioned, repeatedly wringing his hands. "Do you realize you have disgraced the family? Do you know what you have done—to yourself and to all of us?"

Falling to the floor in hysteria, Maria shouted, "He forced himself on me, Μπαμπάσ. I begged him to stop. I said I didn't want to do that awful thing. But he wouldn't listen. Μαμά, Spiros raped me and then he just disappeared!"

"Maria, do you realize what a serious problem this is?" her mother asked, neither waiting for nor wanting a response. "The entire village will ridicule us. We will be dishonored. And your father...your father will loose his position! We're ruined."

"But it wasn't my fault," Maria repeated as her mother's cold palm slapped her across the face. The crackling sound of her hand striking her daughter's cheek echoed in the stillness.

That evening, Maria went to bed but was unable to sleep. Restless and distraught, she rubbed a trembling hand over her protruding stomach. Unlike most expectant mothers, it was not a loving caress to reassure the unborn child that everything would be OK. It was instead a regretful gesture—a wish that the child would just disappear like its father. The mother-to-be harbored feelings of resentment for her infant, an unwanted baby of ill-repute that should never have seen the light of day.

On February 10, 1947, during the second phase of Ελληνικός εμφύλιος πόλεμος,

the Greek Civil War, Avyrini Souliou was born to fourteen-year-old Maria in the northern Greek mountain village of Ktismata, after a long, grueling labor.

The young girl cried out in agony for hours, writhing in pain, without any comfort or support from her mother. Instead of administering an anesthetic or some reassuring words, she was repeatedly chastised for her heinous sin. With every tortuous contraction, the young mother-to-be was reminded of her atrocious deed.

"Suffer!" Maria's mother shouted at her daughter, who was about to make her a grandmother. "You deserve to suffer. This is your punishment for putting yourself in the position of inviting a man to use you for his own pleasure. You could have stopped him—but you didn't. Now you will pay the consequences, just as we all will. Your reputation is ruined. Once the news is out in the village, no decent man will ever want you."

The last part of the outrage was drowned out by a blood-curdling scream, as Maria gave the gift of life to a brand new soul. But in lieu of bringing joy and celebration, the out-of-wedlock infant was immediately repudiated by a patriarchal society that stigmatized illegitimate children pitilessly.

Branded an insignificant product of dishonor, Avyrini, which in Greek means "morning star," brought shame on her family. Would the child born of an "unknown" father be forced to pay for her own notorious crime, even if she were without fault? It would not take long for the question to be answered.

In fact, it took neither a judge nor a jury to decide the verdict. Of course there was no clemency—undoubtedly, born in disgrace, I would be held accountable and harshly penalized for my mother's sin. February 10 was not a day of happiness. It was an occurrence of sorrow and shame.

Immediately after my birth, my grandmother snatched me from my mother, who was far to exhausted to protest. Hurriedly, she carried me into her room. Swaddled in a wool coverlet, I spent the rest of the night with my grandparents, deprived of the initial mother-child contact that starts the bonding process. Although far too tiny to understand, I had my first bitter taste of rejection. Hence, I reacted accordingly.

Newborn babies cry and fuss. Helpless and vulnerable, it is their only means of communication. Newborn infants also miss their mothers, from whom a separation after nine months in the womb is traumatic.

Apparently, I felt scared, feeling neither the security of loving arms cradling me nor the delicate touch of a maternal hand caressing my face. Then, there was the cold silence, the missing laughter, the absent smiles and the hushed whispers; there was an eerie quietness, shattered only by the muffled voices pronouncing incomprehensible words.

Left alone in a corner of the room, I was isolated from any human contact. So I cried—loud and long, believing, like all infants, that it would gain me some attention. It did. Irritated, my grandmother approached. Extending a pair of gelid hands, she shook me violently.

"Keep quiet and go back to sleep," she shouted, as if a day-old child could respond to her command.

I didn't. Exasperated, she reached into the crib and took me in her arms. Her brisk, almost violent movements served to accelerate my wails. Fear, though unknown to me, was brewing inside.

"Stop it, you λίγοσ μπάσταρδοσ!" she shrieked, calling me a "little bastard."

Maria heard her mother's rage and trembled. Recognizing anger in her mother's voice brought terror to her heart. However, still too weak to leave her bed bed, she covered her ears with her hands, to muffle the terrorizing duet of piercing screams—her child's and her mother's! Turning over, she buried her head in the same damp pillow which hours earlier, she had cried into.

Years later, I was told that I did not cease my wailing. The louder my grandmother yelled at me to hush up, the more volume I gave to my screams.

Crimson-faced and drenched in tears, my grandmother grabbed me by the heel of my left foot. Tightening her grasp, she pulled me from my reclining position with a swift, yanking movement. Dangling upside down, I was carried across the room like a clucking chicken ready to be skinned. However, even my agonizing yelps did little to either warm her icy heart or interrupt her evil intention.

With a calculated thrust and the premeditated will to destroy, my grandmother flung me into the air, aiming my fragile body toward the still-smoldering fireplace. Landing head-first in the searing embers, I broke my toes and foot upon impact. The burning logs scorched the tender skin on my arms, legs, face and torso.

"Burn, λίγοσ μπάσταρδοσ," she ranted, her furor enhanced by the odor of charred flesh. "Die and free us from this shame!"

Thankfully, I didn't break my neck or incur a serous head injury. God was certainly watching over me that day.

Although I survived the burning, I carry the scars from my mangled foot. Left untreated, the bones, tendons and ligaments did not develop properly, causing me to walk with difficulty and a noticeable limp. The burns healed, leaving hardly any traces except for on an area of my face, near my eyebrow.

When I learned about my initial years of torture and disdain, I discovered that the resulting emotional wounds would be forever a part of me. Exceedingly more agonizing is that these are undoubtedly almost impossible to cure.

Denied any contact with her infant, my mother was nursed back to health. Far from the doting attentions of a happy grandmother, she was treated as an outcast—fed and attended to in an almost mechanical manner, with neither warmth nor compassion.

Alone in her bed, the new mother drifted between the peaceful dreams of her darling baby—the perfectly formed, miniature hands and feet; the sweet, almost circular face framed by a mass of dark hair—and a seared conscience that rolled all her guilt for having dishonored her family and herself into an ugly burden wedged in her heart.

She longed to cuddle her baby. She yearned to kiss the soft, pink cheeks and sing the infant to sleep, reassuring her that everything was OK. But it was prohibited. Everything was not OK, and Maria knew it.

Realizing her life had been forever altered, my mother contemplated her future, questioning what destiny could have planned for her. Fearful, she tried to escape the reality of her situation, imagining how sweet it would have been had she given birth as a married woman. Sadly, the Greeks just did not look kindly on either illegitimate children or the shameful women who gave them life. I was as my grandmother had said—I was just a little bastard!

Two days following my birth, my grandmother, disappointed that I had not died in the flames, emerged from the bedroom. Nestled in her hand was a double barrel shotgun. Pointing it in my mother's face, she yelled, "Maria, since you will not consent to marrying Spiros, I want you and that λίγοσ μπάσταρδοσ out of here right now. If you don't leave Ktismata today, I'll kill you both. Take your bastard and go as far away as possible. We don't want to see you ever again. You mortified your father and me. For us, you are dead!"

Terrified for her life and mine, my mother wrapped me snugly in a wool shawl, rummaged around her room, gathering several of her belongings, and headed for her maternal aunt and uncle's house in another village.

Aunt Cynara and Uncle Evan, an elderly couple, were not as fortunate as my mother and did enjoy the luxuries of an affluent lifestyle. On the contrary, theirs was a life of poverty and misery—so aptly reflected in their demeaning and cruel personalities.

Situated in Ιωάννινα (Ioannina) Village, Aunt Cynara and Uncle Evan's house, unlike my grandparents', was a Spartan shack built without electricity, plumbing or running water. A stale, musty odor permeated the air. It was often unheated, and mold crawled along the walls, creeping up to the ceiling in dark patches. Furnishings were sparse, of rudimentary quality and apparently mistreated. Every piece of furniture was scratched, dented, chipped and stained. Worst of all, there was very little concern for personal possessions.

My mother's arrival was without welcome. Several grunts, and a finger pointed to an area located in the farthest corner of a dark, humid room, introduced my mother to her living quarters. Though it was not a very accommodating ambiance, she believed she was at least safe from her own mother's furor.

A short, frumpy woman, dressed in tattered garments and obviously unaccustomed to the daily rituals of personal hygiene, Aunt Cynara was decidedly overweight. Indisputably unattractive, her square face was designed with a total lack of symmetry. Deep-set eyes glared instead of glanced. A relaxed chin line and deep jowls framed her mouth. Midway between eyes and chin stood a prominent nose, far too large and bumpy for a woman of below-average height.

Her husband, Uncle Evan, was a well-suited spouse. Tall and slender with stooped, rounded shoulders, his beady eyes focused intently on the objects of his attention. A series of horizontal lines etched between his bushy eyebrows betrayed a mean-spirited nature. Far from making a fashion statement, Uncle Evan dressed in oversized trousers and large shirts that refused to stay tucked into his waistband. Resolute, he knew what he wanted—and he was more than adept at getting it.

Neither husband nor wife was capable of love or affection. On the other hand, their niece was a shunned woman with an out-of-wedlock baby.

Settled on the bare floor in the icy shack, my mother was offered neither a blanket nor a pillow to rest her head on. Thankfully, emotional and physical exhaustion, like a sweetly sung lullaby, escorted her into a deep sleep.

The following morning, a breakfast of overripe berries and two empty buckets awaited her. If she wanted water, she would have to fetch it herself. Walking over to the well in the backyard, shivering from the raw, winter cold, Maria drew just enough water to splash her face and quench the parched feeling in her throat. I would have to remain in my soiled diapers—it was far too cold to undress a tiny infant without risking a bout of pneumonia.

A short time thereafter, I've been told, my mother, unable to bear the burden of shame, abandoned me and headed for Athens to seek employment. Disheartened by the devastating living conditions and embarrassed by the incessant outrage of her family for the scandal of birthing an illegitimate child, she believed this was the right path to follow.

"Μαμά will come back for you, my sweet Avyrini," she whispered, bending over to kiss my forehead. I hoped… I prayed… But I never again felt the warmth of her moist lips on my cheeks, and I never again heard her soft, almost whispering voice call out my name—"Avyrini, my darling Avyrini!"

SECOND EPISODE

"And what law of heaven have I transgressed? Why, hapless one, should I look to the gods any more, what ally should I invoke, when by piety I have earned the name of impious? Nay, then, if these things are pleasing to the gods, when I have suffered my doom, I shall come to know my sin; but if the sin is with my judges, I could wish them no fuller measure of evil than they, on their part, mete wrongfully to me."

—Sophocles, Antigone

Although memories of the first three years of my life remain somewhat muddled, remembrances of a penetrating sadness are almost impossible to cancel from my mind. For a rejected toddler, distanced from her mother not long after birth, there can be no joy.

Unaware of my repudiated status, parental love was an unknown to me. Since Μαμά was a stranger, I did not miss her presence in my life. There were no endearing moments, no sweet voice, no cherished kisses and no familiar scent. Aunt Cynara and Uncle Evan were all I had—two miserable individuals who seemed to have an aversion to children. This probably explains why, thankfully, they were childless.

It was 1951 and at four years of age, I was old enough to understand the harsh words uttered in my direction. Still ignorant of the fact that other children were loved, nurtured and coddled, I was often surprised when I scratched my head and caught my fingers in a tangled mass of knotted hair.

Even a small child eventually realizes something is wrong when she is left cold, hungry and dressed in soiled garments until the lack of hygiene causes an incessant itching. Never spoken to, I was always yelled at. I cried often and for long periods of time, but if someone had ever taken the time to ask me why, I would not have been able to given a reason. Too young to know any better, I did not have the vaguest clue that I was living in misery.

"Avyrini, Uncle Evan and I are having breakfast," Aunt Cynara shouted with her mouth full of food. "If you're hungry, go outside and pick some berries."

Of course I was famished, and the aroma of fresh, scrambled eggs gave rise to a pool of saliva in my mouth that made my stomach growl with desire.

Glancing sideways at the platter of fluffy αυγά ομελέτα, I wondered what it would be like to place some of the soft mound on my tongue. "What do αυγά taste like?" I often questioned.

Judging from the purrs of utter contentment coming from my uncle's lips, I imagined they were delectable morsels. Maybe one day, I too would be able to feast on the eggs.

"Hurry, Avyrini," Aunt Cynara said, interrupting my fantasy. "Go get some berries before the birds beat you to it. Then you'll just have to stay hungry."

"OK, θεία," I responded turning on my bare heels and heading for the door. Once outside, I ran over to the berry bush, dropping on all fours, lightly skinning my knees.

There were berries everywhere—succulent, dark berries glistening under the first rays of the early morning sun. There were squashed berries, which had stained the long, un-mowed blades of grass different shades of blue and crimson with bright, bold strokes, as if an artist had delicately hand-painted each strand with miniature brushes.

There were berries that had been targeted by the birds and later discarded. Apparently overripe and fermented, they were disappointing. However, these rejected fruits were surrounded by a swarm of sap beetles crawling in circles, eager to get some of the oozing juice.

With my left, hand I chased away the beetles and buzzing bees that invaded from the actual plants, clearing the way for my right hand to snatch a handful of berries. Without checking to see which berries I had grabbed, I shoved them into my mouth, splattering dark juice over my face and shirt.

No longer plump and sweet, the berries tasted bitter in my mouth. And as I crunched down in a frenetic attempt to appease my appetite, I felt the crackle of sand between my teeth. I guess that in my frenzy to snatch the fruit, I paid little heed to the granules of dried sod I was collecting between my fingers.

What I was eating really didn't matter, as long as I calmed the dull ache in my stomach. Satiated to the point of nausea, I returned to the house. Later, I would deal with the unpleasant after effects of my feast. Doubled over with cramps, with my intestines in rebellion, I would lie awake, crying. However, my options were extremely limited. This less-than-nutritious menu was the source of my nourishment for many years. It was my main staple—un-rinsed, overripe and often rotten fruit, leftovers snubbed by the birds and insects.

"Avyrini," come here a moment," Uncle Evan mumbled one afternoon, puffing on the lit cigarette perched on the corner of his lips. Open-hand slaps and belt beatings were already common practice; therefore, fearing his violent wrath, I obliged. Lifting myself from the floor, I scrambled over to where he was seated.

The late afternoon rays shadowed half his face, giving him an uncomplimentary, austere look that made him seem even older than his fifty years.

"Come on, hurry up," he blurted. "Get over here."

As I neared his chair, he reached over and pulled me onto his lap. "You're awfully dirty," he snarled, lifting up my badly stained dress. "What did you do Avyrini—did you soil yourself?"

"No, θείοσ," I responded, "I did not."

"We will see about that," he grunted, pulling down my panties.

Unaware of what was about to take place, I felt uneasy. Suddenly, I felt his cold hand on my flesh. I shuddered, pulling back. Firmly enclosing my shoulder in his hand, he yanked me toward him.

Uncle Evan's breathing was heavy, and the stench of garlic and tobacco caused my stomach to capsize. His face was so close to mine, I had little choice but to hold my breath and hope the stench would go away. It didn't. And neither did the sudden, sharp pain I felt, which caused me to gasp. It seemed as if something had been roughly thrust into me, pulled out and thrust in again and again.

"θείοσ, σταματώ αυτό- με πονάs! Uncle stop it! You're hurting me!" I cried, squirming in pain. Jarred by my screams, he shoved me off his lap.

"Don't tell anyone about this," he whispered in my ear, "or something bad will happen to you! Did you hear what I said, Avyrini?"

I knew this was a question I could not avoid. I knew I had to answer. Terrified, I nodded my head and ran out the door as fast as I could. Every step sent a shooting pain through my body. Gazing down, I noticed a narrow stream of blood trickling along my legs. It splashed to the ground in iridescent blotches.

Of course I was too young to understand that I had just been sexually molested by Uncle Evan. Violated, I was left emotionally vulnerable and helpless in my loneliness. I did, however, realize that I couldn't tell anyone what had happened. On the other hand, I had no one to confide in. Nobody cared about an illegitimate child. It was as if I did not exist.

Terrified, I retreated to my allotted space in the corner of the room. Curling myself into a ball, I drew my knees up to my chin. Fearing repercussions, I buried my head in my arms, desperately trying to stifle my sobs.

It seemed like an eternity before I saw a faint trace of light invade the gloom. Another day had begun.

Aunt Cynara was not a working woman. Her life was at home, and within those four dreary walls she remained, awaiting Uncle Evan's return from his government job at day's end. In most instances, this lifestyle should have left her plenty of time and energy to focus on me. But Aunt Cynara followed another script. Caring neither for my personal needs nor her own, she emanated a strong body odor both summer and winter, which actually made me happy that she kept her distance.

Both my aunt and uncle bathed exclusively on Saturdays.

"Avyrini, your uncle wants to take a bath. Get the pail and draw some water from the well." I did what I was told.

I knew this would take a while because at five years of age, I was neither tall enough to walk at a quick pace nor strong enough to carry a full bucket. My best strategy was to fill the pail half way and return repeated times. I knew that if I followed this plan, I was certain not to trip or spill the water.

Most of the morning was dedicated to this task—and all before my overripe berry breakfast. If I did not execute this mission with absence of error, I would face a severe punishment.

As I grew older, I became more vocal and curious about my surroundings. Like all six- and seven-year-olds, I asked questions and ventured outside not only to use the hole-in-the-ground bathroom facility to take care of my needs, but to get away from the dark, humid shack.

Once again, my early morning experience was greeted with a revolting odor of waste products. Powerful, the stench would penetrate the cement walls. In the evenings, it would remain trapped inside. Every few months, a sanitation truck would pull up, clean out the odorous, foul waste materials and chemically sanitize the area. For a couple of days, the air would be agreeable, until the mess built up again.

In Aunt Cynara's mind, as time passed, I became more uncomfortable to deal with. My childish chattering was an unbearable annoyance, and my growing, questioning mind, instead of delighting her, bothered her. Evil-intentioned since my arrival, my aunt began to incorporate brutality in her child-rearing strategies.

"θεία, why can't I go to school like the other children?" I asked one morning. Silence and a glare that cut through me was her response. Unsatisfied, I repeated my question, putting a bit more volume in my voice, perhaps believing she had not heard what I'd said. Instead of waiting for her reaction, I blurted, "I want to go to school."

Exasperated beyond her fragile endurance, she marched over to where I was standing. "λίγοσ μπάσταρδοσ, be quiet," she screamed, reaching for my arm. Terrified of her wrath, I lowered my eyes and stopped speaking. Knocking me off my feet, she dragged me across the dirt floor. I thought my arm was going to break loose from her violent jerking.

"θεία, please stop. My arm hurts," I sobbed, gulping air.

"Didn't you hear what I said, λίγοσ μπάσταρδοσ ? I don't want to hear your annoying voice. Little bastards don't go to school. Now stand up and stop all that fussing."

Before I was at full height, she whacked me across the face, causing me to lose my balance and topple over. The unexpected violence left me gasping for air. I coughed to clear my throat and suddenly felt a tight collar being fastened around my neck. At the end of the collar was a chain-link leash.

"Now you will learn to keep quiet and be still, λίγοσ μπάσταρδοσ," Aunt Cynara sneered. Wrapping the chain around her thick waist, she had me restrained like a harnessed dog. In fact, my range of motion was no wider than several feet. Trapped, my only option was to crouch down on the floor.

The shack was poorly heated. A coal stove was lit to keep my aunt and uncle warm during the evening hours. However, the fuel was not sufficient to reach my area. Given neither a blanket nor a sheet or pillow to sleep on, I soon discovered that if I curled myself into a fetal position, what little body heat I had would eventually protect me from shivering to death. So I huddled into a tight ball and rocked back forth. My nose and the tips of my ears burned from the cold. But my fingers were too stiff and painful to offer any relief.

Fastened to Aunt Cynara, I was not permitted to leave the premises. It was forbidden even to make a trip to the outdoor hole in the ground, to take care of my needs. I had no choice but to soil myself or burst. At six, I opted to relieve myself beside my aunt's feet. The berries always caused intestinal distress, and I did what I had to do.

Obviously, my deed did not go unnoticed.

"What did you do, λίγοσ μπάσταρδοσ?" Aunt Cynara shouted as soon as she realized what had just taken place. "Did you dirty yourself again?" She glared down at me, her icy blue eyes ripping through me like a pair of sharp-edged daggers. It was a wicked look, far scarier than her outrageous verbal rages. But what alternative do I have? I wondered silently. Chained to this nasty, obese woman, I was restricted like a wild animal.

"Did you hear what I said?" Aunt Cynara persisted. Out of the corner of my eye, I could see the huge, purple vein on the side of her neck. It was inflated. Early on, I'd learned the warning signals; this meant that she was dangerously angry! This, of course, translated to serious trouble for me.

"Yes, θεία," I responded, "I heard. But I couldn't go outside to do it. I really had no choice and I had to go badly."

I could only fantasize about understanding or compassion. It was just not a factor in my life.

Wincing and moaning, she dragged her huge body from the chair. The loud squeak from the old, dilapidated piece of furniture told me that overweight Aunt Cynara had little respect for herself.

She approached with several heavy steps. I knew I would be the focus of her wrath. However, I wondered what to expect this time.

Taking my face in her burly hands, she drew me close. I could both smell and feel her putrid breath waft across my face. I shuddered, holding my breath.

A split-second later, I felt the sting of her saliva splash into my eye.

"Don't you ever dirty yourself again, λίγοσ μπάσταρδοσ," she howled, shoving me down on the floor, right into the terrible mess I had made. "Now I have to clean you up."

Although being spat at was definitely unpleasant, I was not old enough to understand the demeaning significance of Aunt Cynara's vile action. It was an emotional and psychological assault at a most humiliating level.

Rummaging though a stack of old newspapers, Aunt Cynara ripped off two large sheets. Crumbling the pages in her fist, she walked back to where I was standing. Extending her free hand, she inserted her fingers into the neckline of my dress and pulled me toward her.

"Take off those filthy clothes," she demanded. "I have to wipe up the mess you made."

Never daring to disobey, I undressed, trembling as the cold rattled my bones. I was a rather frail and exaggeratedly scrawny child, which was not surprising, considering the nutritionally deficient diet I was being raised on.

"Stand still and stop that shaking," Aunt Cynara growled through half-clenched teeth. "How do you expect me to clean you if you're fidgeting all over?"

Again I obliged, and froze like a marble statue, leaving myself vulnerable to whatever she had planned. With a sudden, brisk movement, she raised her arm. Suddenly, I felt the crumbled newspaper rub against my face. Her pattern was a hurried up-and-down, then sideways and then in circles—all with dry newspaper. I felt my cheeks burn. It seemed as if she were trying to scrub my skin off, to expose my bones. The more I flinched, the faster and harder she scoured. It seemed as if she were scrubbing an encrusted frying pan after burning the eggs.

The clean-up obviously did not end with my face. Returning at various intervals to her supply of newspapers, she crumbled more sheets, came back and proceeded to buff up the rest of my body. No water, no soap—just abrasive sheets of dry newspapers that left traces of black ink on my irritated flesh. This was Aunt Cynara's child hygiene method whenever I was "fortunate" enough to be cleaned.

Uncle Evian concerned himself neither with my well-being nor my upbringing. He was egotistical and for him, I represented a convenient means of gratifying his sexual appetite. During those lurid moments, I was the center of his attention. Afterwards, I was left crying, bloody and in agonizing pain, always threatened into silence with promises of additional violence. He would use and abuse me at will, escalating the frequency and severity of his attacks with the passage of time.

Initially, Aunt Cynara was a hushed accomplice, feigning ignorance of the crimes and injustices committed under her own roof. After the fact, the evidence was scrupulously removed with her newspaper dry-cleaning process. And although the outward traces were soon gone, I always wondered why I was constantly in pain and bleeding all the time. But at six years of age, I was incapable of finding the answers.

When I wasn't in my dog collar, chained either to Aunt Cynara or the dining table, or playing unwilling host to Uncle Evan's lascivious yearnings, I was expected to single-handedly assume responsibility for all the domestic chores. This meant that I had to clean the house every day, wash and sweep the mud floors, dust off the battle-scarred furniture, and make certain my aunt and uncle's bedroom was fresh and neat. Unlike me, they had a bed available for their nightly repose and after they awakened, I was ordered to pull off the bedding, straighten the sheets and fluff the pillows.

The job description did not end there. I was also the πλύστρα, the laundress. Given a heavy, wooden washboard that was almost my height, I was instructed to fill a large basin with water. After several trips to the well, I had part one of the task completed.

Next, I took a bar of soap from a squeaky, old cupboard, the door of which was held in place with two badly rusted hinges. In the beginning, until I wore it down by scrubbing it, the rectangular bar of soap was far too large for my hands. One morning, it slipped from my grip and fell to the floor.

"What are you doing, λίγοσ μπάσταρδοσ?" Aunt Cynara yelled, sliding the last morsel of pancake into her mouth. "Now you got the soap all dirty. How do you expect to get the clothes clean with that muddy piece of soap? Bring it over here right now!"

Obedient for fear of stirring her wrath further, I handed her the soap. Unable to predict that she was intent on swatting me across the face, I met her extended arm halfway. When our arms clashed, the soap tumbled to the floor. Enraged, she grabbed me by the ear, yanked me over and whacked me first with her open palm and then with the back of her hand.

"This little bastard," she muttered under breath, "can't do anything right."

Empowered by her own irrational rage, Aunt Cynara felt that I was not properly punished for the wrongdoing I had committed. Still rambling incoherently, she pushed her chair away from the table and stood defiantly.

Although my aunt's severe overweight condition left her with slowed reflexes, it unfortunately did not interfere with her strength. Crossing the room, she headed over to the counter upon which was placed the collar and chain that restrained me.

I shook all over, fully aware of her plan. When I felt the cold chain whip across my bare legs, I knew I would be bruised and sore for at least a week. I also knew I would not sleep that night or the following night. And, I was fully aware that despite the beating, I would have to finish doing the laundry.

I turned on my calloused, bare feet. Suffocating my sobs, I picked up the soap, walked outside to the well, drew a pail of water and rinsed off the mud spots.

Cut and blistered, my toes hurt from never wearing shoes. They were just not part of my wardrobe—even if every other child wore them.

I returned to the shack, limped over to the already filled basin, grabbed one of my uncle's badly soiled shirts and dipped it into the icy water. I watched as it soaked in the water and sunk to the bottom. With both hands, I lifted the washboard and set it down in the basin. Fishing in the water with my left hand, I pulled up the shirt, placed it against the corrugated panel and held it while I grabbed the soap with my free hand.

For the next hour, I rubbed and scrubbed up and down the ridges, trying to dissolve the greasy food and dark yellow perspiration stains that covered more than half the surface of every article of clothing.

My fingers hurt from the constant friction, especially since my nails were so brittle; they chipped easily and were worn down into my flesh. When I noticed a few drops of blood ooze from my finger, I knew I should remove my hand from the water or I would risk staining the laundry.

I pulled it out and put in my mouth to stop the bleeding. Aunt Cynara, who never missed a move I made, focused her eyes on me. She knew I was in pain. I knew she was ready to verbally blast me. An eerie hush invaded the room. Tension mounted.

"If your mother would have married your father," she sneered, twisting her lips to the side, "no one would mistreat or be mean to you. We can't love you—we can't treat you like other children because you don't deserve it. And you don't deserve it because you're nothing but a little stinking bastard. That's enough laundry for today—now come here. I have to chain you to the table, λίγοσ μπάσταρδοσ!"

I wriggled away in terror—needlessly.

THIRD EPISODE

"He who commits injustice is ever made more wretched than he who suffers it."

—Plato

I remember the dull ache I carried in my stomach from morning until night. It was a gnawing feeling arising from the repetitive swing between hunger and the actual gratification of my appetite with the exaggerated consumption of overripe and often rotten fruit. It was also more than obvious that I would have relished a decent meal and a sweet treat from time to time.

Uncle Evan, recognizing my yearning for food, converted a basic need for nourishment into an illicit strategy in which he enticed me for his own selfish gain with promises of sweets. To a starving child, candy was like manna in the desert after endless days of abstinence. Therefore, when Uncle Evan dangled goodies in my face in exchange for sex and silence, I was obliging.

By the time I was seven years old, he was treating me as a man treats his wife—without the violent approach, of course.

"Get over here, Ayvrini," he said hoarsely, clearing his throat. "Come spend a little time with Uncle Evan."

Upon hearing his voice, I spun around, fear rising. I knew it would not be fun when he lifted me and forcefully threw me down on the dining table.

"Are you coming, Avyrini?" he persisted.

Taking a few hesitant steps in his direction, I nodded. Lunging forward, he grabbed me around the waist, dragging me toward him until I felt the impact of his body against mine.

My mind rummaged through the repercussions born of yesterday's acts of defiance. Fearing his wrath, I obeyed; fearing his disciplinary punishment, I surrendered, assuming once again the role of a violated child.

Gratified, Uncle Evan dug deep into his trouser pocket and pulled up a small, white, paper bag filled with candy. Fumbling, he opened the top and shoved the treats under my nose.

"They smell good, no?" he said, grinning. "Well, they taste even better." He swirled them around my face teasingly. "Would you like to eat one?"

His question encouraged me to reach out with my hand to accept the offering. My gesture was a reason to taunt me. Instinctively, he pulled away, hiding the goodies behind his back. Bending over, he whispered, "You can have the candy if you promise to keep our little secret."

Before I could nod, he forced a bit of sweet nut toffee between my lips. With a swift movement of my tongue, I carried it into my mouth. The taste was delightful—like nothing I had ever experienced. I crunched down. The echo of crackles continued until my remaining milk molars ground the candy to powder. I swore I would not breathe a word about Uncle Evan's "games," even if they hurt, leaving me bruised and bleeding.

Unable to sleep, I opened and closed my little bag of treats, promising myself I would not eat them all at once. Instead, I would savor one tiny piece at a time until I got a new bag.

After the deed, Aunt Cynara greeted me with the threatening glance of a whippet sight-hound coursing its prey. Drawing my gaze away from her somber face, I avoided any reprisal—at least this time.

"λίγοσ μπάσταρδοσ, go get some water," Aunt Cynara grumbled, not bothering to remove her attention from the newspaper she was reading. "I've got black ink all over my hands and it's Saturday—time for my bath. The pail is in the kitchen. Take the larger one so you can get more water and not waste time."

"OK, θεία," I said, scurrying to get the bucket. Such commands were just daily happenstances. By then, I was accustomed not only to receiving and executing orders, but to the severe repercussions for disobedience. Obedience, on the other hand, was an irrevocable law, just like corporal punishment.

Grabbing the bucket with both hands, I darted out the door. The rough-edged gravel underfoot irritated my feet like the rubbing of salt in an open wound. No longer reacting to insignificant pain, I hobbled over to the well. My right foot bore the scars from my flight into the hearth; therefore, my gait was noticeably affected.

Although the air was damp following the early-morning storm, the newly risen sun was intent on defeating the humidity by midday. Still, I trembled as the rawness seeped into my bones.

The well was just a few steps away. Hugging the wood bucket, I reached for the cord and fastened it to the handle. Even if I did it almost daily, I still had trouble tying the knot. Knowing the consequences of failings, I had to be certain I wouldn't loose the bucket in the well. That would warrant a serious beating, or worse.

With the bucket firmly attached to the cord, I stepped onto the large, jagged, tipped-stone slab that Uncle Evan had positioned beside the well since I was not tall enough to reach the opening. Placing the free end of the cord in my clenched, right fist, I pushed the bucket over the edge with my free hand. Water levels varied according to the season and the amount of rainfall on any given day.

Unable to discern if the bucket reached the water, I stood on my tiptoes and leaned over the side of the well to catch a glimpse of the pail. With the majority of my body weight gravitating toward the edge, I lost my balance, slipped and tumbled head-first into the well.

The flesh on my arms, legs and back was scraped raw, as if I had been repeatedly rubbed along the corrugated edges of a cheese grater. Scared and in pain, I paddled frantically, desperately trying to keep from sliding under the ripples. I knew that if I wanted to survive, I had to keep my head above water. My arms and legs stung from the bitter cold. Every breath I took produced agonizing pain.

"θεία," I shouted, barely keeping my head above water. "Help me! I fell into the well. Come get me out!" I paused just long enough to catch my breath and then resumed my blood-curdling howls.

Although Aunt Cynara was unresponsive to my wails, God was with me that day. Hearing the ear-shattering ruckus, the neighbors ran over to the well.

"It's Avyrini," a man shouted. "The child has fallen into the well. We have to get her out before she drowns or freezes to death."

Several neighbors ran from their doorways to join the concerned man, who was focused on pulling me out of the well.

Thankfully, the rescue mission was successful. Swaddled in a big blanket like a newborn infant, I was carried back to the shack. After I explained, through chattering teeth, how the mishap had occurred, the kind townsfolk departed, leaving me in the care of Aunt Cynara. She had remained stoic throughout the unraveling of the drama. However, once the neighbors had departed, she became livid.

Sneering like the devil incarnate, she yanked off the blanket with one brisk whisk of the hand.

"Give me that," she snarled, "and get undressed. Take off those wet, mud-soaked clothes before you dirty the whole place." The order was followed by a series of offensive obscenities that I did not understand.

Knowing Aunt Cynara, I had an inkling about what was going to happen, though I prayed I would be in error this time. I wasn't.

"Hurry, λίγοσ μπάσταρδοσ. Get out of those clothes," she yelled. I did as I was told, though every bone in my body ached and rattled from the cold. Naked and bleeding from the torn patches of flesh on my arms, legs and back, I walked up to her.

She seemed to lust after the sight of my agony.

"Turn around, λίγοσ μπάσταρδοσ," she shrieked in a tone I had not heard before. "I don't want to see your ugly face."

I turned just in time to feel the cold chain links across my back. It didn't end there. In fact, it seemed as if each splash of my blood, every new tear of my flesh and every painful cry enraged her further, empowering the brutality from which her character was formed.

"I wanted you to die, λίγοσ μπάσταρδοσ," she chanted over and over as she repeatedly lifted her arm to lash me. "Why didn't you die in that well?"

The force of the chain hitting my frail body caused me to topple over.

"Stand up, λίγοσ μπάσταρδοσ," Aunt Cynara growled. Realizing I had absolutely no strength to rise to my feet, she gave me a kick, sending me spiraling across the floor until I hit my head against the cement wall, breaking my spin. Too weak to cry, I remained there, making it my resting place for the night.

No one applied pressure to my cuts to stop the bleeding. No one washed or dressed my open wounds. No one gathered me in their arms to ease my fright or comfort my hurts.

It was a long, frightening night; it was the night I learned the truth. Terrified and badly injured, I was abandoned to my own fears and left with the bitter reality that I was unwanted, unloved and wished dead!

When Uncle Evan heard about my accident, he admonished Aunt Cynara for further mistreating me.

"You didn't have to beat her," I heard him say. "I'm sure she learned a lesson after falling in."

Then, he screeched, as he too felt the ire of her madness the moment his own back was pelted with the chain. However, as an adult, he was more equipped to escape than a small child left at the mercy of an overwhelming force.

In silence, perhaps not to fuel her anger, he fumbled in his pocket, grabbed his pack of cigarettes, slapped it against his wrist, extracted the one that showed its head, lit up, drew a puff and walked outside. Hesitating a moment, he gazed up at the sky and sighed. It was a suffering sigh. This time, the scent of tobacco was comforting; it meant that someone else was in pain.

Since I was restless and wide-eyed all evening, I mulled over the day's events, focusing my attention on the parade of Blessed Virgin Mary statues Aunt Cynara had positioned in various places around the shack. In front of each icon was a lighted candle. Was this devotion, or another symptom of her irrational folly?

Although we attended church on Sundays, Aunt Cynara did not live a life in tune with Christian principles. The priests often delivered homilies centered on the truth that God expected us to love one another and treat children with dignity. Quoting from Mark 10:17—"Let the little children come to me, and do not hinder them for of such is the kingdom of God"—they spoke about how the disciples were chastised for reprimanding those who tried to bring the children to Him.

Even with my seven-year-old mind, I understood the meaning of being loved and treated with kindness. I also knew that my aunt didn't love me. Opting for free expression, Aunt Cynara never made a secret of her hatred for me.

However, despite her defiance of the Lord's teachings, she was fanatical about her Blessed Mother statues. In fact, I had to be absolutely sure that there was a candle lit in front of each one every day.

This was not always an easy task because in order to reach the statue on the fireplace mantle, I had to drag over a chair, climb up and light the candle, making certain not to drop anything and above all, not to topple over.

Although the statues were a sweet representation of the Virgin Mary, the ambience with all the flickering candles was somewhat eerie. Consequently, instead of offering solace, they made me restless.

At the time, I was too young to define Aunt Cynara as a hypocrite, but looking back at her behavior, it is more than apparent that she had adopted a double standard in her life.

On one hand, she condemned my mother's sin, and on the other, she offended God by abusing one of His innocent creatures, rendering judgment on a matter that was beyond her jurisdiction. Even if the Greeks socially condemned illegitimate births, it did not give anyone the right to torture the innocent. What guilt did I have? What did I do to warrant such vicious reprisals?

FOURTH EPISODE

"Those who can make you believe absurdities can make you commit atrocities."

—Voltaire

The dining area in my aunt and uncle's shack was rather scant; space was so restricted, I sometimes became stiff trying to curl into a ball. A tattered, faded curtain separated the bedroom from the living part of the house. Hanging limply, it seemed to have been wrung dry of any energy. Whenever a breeze from an opened window caused it to sway, it secreted an overpowering odor of mold. Its reason to be was to ensure privacy by keeping me out of my aunt and uncle's sight during the evening hours.

When daylight did not peer through the bare windows, the ambiance was dreary and insufferable. Although the candles standing at attention around the living room still flickered in the early-morning glow, the flames were hardly powerful enough to eliminate the dismal feeling.

Standing near the coal-burning stove, Aunt Cynara was preparing breakfast for Uncle Evan. It was an icy morning and she was generously layered with oversized wool shawls and hand-knitted sweaters, a look that accentuated her girth, giving her the appearance of an overdressed Sumo wrestler.

Uncle Evan was still dressing in his room and I could hear his first-thing-in-the-morning smoker's cough as he tried to rid his lungs of the previous day's nicotine toxin. The echo of his gagging was pronounced in the early dawn stillness, and not silenced until he successfully dislodged the buildup of phlegm in his trachea. When he spat, I knew he was ready to come out, sit down to breakfast and satisfy his hunger. Uncle Evan was all about the instant gratification of his appetites.

The aroma was sumptuous—a combination of butter and cream mixed with the fragrance of fresh-brewed καφές. Aunt Cynara had the μπρίκι, the coffee pot, on the fire. From where I sat, I could see the foam forming on the top in tiny, crystalline bubbles. When the coffee was finally poured into the espresso cups, the grounds settled on the bottom, creating a very rich, dense and flavorful drink.

Never permitted to partake of the aromatic specialties, I often wondered what these piping-hot provisions tasted like. In my mind, I tried to fantasize, but ignorant of any palatal sensations apart from fruit, nuts, rice, milk and bread, I could not imagine the experience of savoring eggs or meat. But they certainly smelled tantalizing.

Usually, breakfast for my aunt and uncle consisted of αυγά, κουλουράκια (butter cookies) or μια τηγανίτα, a pancake. After Uncle Evan feasted on the sizzling-hot pancake and deep, dark coffee he reached for the stained, white, linen napkin and rubbed it across his lips several times. Dropping it on his plate, he pushed his chair from the table, stood and left for work without uttering a word. Once the door slammed shut, Aunt Cynara cleared the table and returned to the stove.

From the corner of my eye, I could see that she was whipping up another batch of pancakes.

"Avyrini, come here," she called as the pancake hit the griddle. "I want to give you a hug." Surprised, I inched myself toward her, unsure of what to expect. Never one to give affection, it seemed like such a strange request on her part.

Before the thought was finished, and before I had any time to question its validity, I felt a thumb and index finger close tightly over my earlobe. A sharp pain suddenly knocked me off balance.

"Sit on my lap," she murmured, tugging on my ear.

My heartbeat accelerated. My pulse raced. The ray of sunlight furtively stealing its way through an opening in the dirty window momentarily blinded me.

In a decidedly less than graceful move, I was catapulted flat across her soft thighs. My face settled between her legs in a rather uncomfortable position. I dared not move.

"Avyrini, I'm going to make you a nice, big pancake," she said, loosening her grip on my ear. "Would you like to taste a pancake?" Her question was conspicuously out of character. However, I had to admit, it was a tempting invitation.

"Yes, θεία," I responded, fearful she would change her mind if I didn't answer quickly enough. "I'd love to eat a pancake."

"OK, Avyrini, go sit at the table. I'll let you know when it's ready."

I did as I was told; I walked over to the table, pulled out a chair and sat down, full of expectations. Even my throbbing ear couldn't stifle my excitement.

Aunt Cynara lifted herself from the chair with noticeable difficulty, emitting a muffled groan as she hobbled over to the stove. Years of excessive weight had affected her knees and feet, slowing her down. Apparently, arthritis had weaved its way into her joints.

As she whipped up the batter and threw it onto the searing griddle, the scent of melting butter teased my nostrils. Famished, I was delirious, and could hardly sit still. Squirming in my seat, I tried to imagine what a pancake could possible taste like. Would it be sweet like the pieces of candy Uncle Evan sometimes gave me when I made him happy? Or would it have the tart bitterness of the squashed berries I picked off the ground?

Glancing toward the stove, I watched as Aunt Cynara lifted the skillet. With a quick jerk of her wrist, she flipped a circular, golden-brown pancake several inches into the air. I knew it wouldn't be long. I would soon have it between my teeth—assuming, of course, she didn't drop it.

Thankfully, she maintained full control. Placed on a white, chipped plate, the pancake was set down before me. Afraid to even blink, I watched with glaring eyes as Aunt Cynara submerged the circular delicacy in dense, brown syrup. The meandering liquid, with its own exotic perfume, spread graciously along the entire surface of the plate.

Extending my hands, I lifted the gooey pancake, tore off a chunk and shoved it into my mouth, dripping the sticky syrup down my chin. The experience was unimaginable, almost incredible. I was totally unprepared for such a delicious treat. Never tasting anything so scrumptious, I giggled as the pliable, almost spongy consistency tickled my tongue.

I was living an exhilarating moment, but like all moments, it was short and fleeting. Before I swallowed the last morsel, Aunt Cynara approached.

"Did you like the pancake, Ayvrini?" she inquired.

"Oh ναί! θεία," I answered feeling pleasingly gratified for the first time in my life. "Yes and ευχαριστίεσ—thanks."

Suddenly, I felt a slight pressure on the back of my head. If I moved, it actually hurt. Aunt Cynara had crept up from behind, gathered my hair and tightly enclosed it in her fist. In a split second, I was ejected from the chair, dropped on the floor and propelled across the room in a fast, sweeping motion. Petrified, I let my limbs go weak, recalling from experience that the least resistance resulted in less pain and injury.

Thrashed under her feet, I was eventually lifted by the hair and pulled over to the coal stove. I felt the heat of the simmering flames. Breaking into sobs, I tried to draw back.

"Stop it, λίγοσ μπάσταρδοσ," Aunt Cynara yelled. "Stop that annoying shouting." I knew something bad was about to happen but I didn't know why. What could I possibly have done to warrant this outburst of anger?

"You little bastard, stop that infuriating crying or I'll kill you right now!" she sneered, dragging me right in front of the stove. With a brusque slam of her palm on the back of my head, she shoved my face onto the searing coals.

The pain was excruciating. Terrified, I shut my eyes just as the bright yellow and blue flames were smothered by the pressure of my head hitting the grill. I was unprepared for the burst of agony when the blistering burner scorched my face. Too petrified to scream, I feared for my life.

The haunting aroma of my charred flesh nauseated me. But when I heard the crackle of my eyebrows and eyelashes crumbling into ashes, I keeled over, unconscious.

I awakened to Aunt Cynara's violent diatribe. Leaning over me with the demented glance of a Dr. Jekyll, she violently shook me. "Why don't you die, λίγοσ μπάσταρδοσ!" she screamed. "I want you dead. You are nothing but a dirty, stinking bastard. We don't want you here. You bring shame on this family. It would better for everyone if you were dead."

In unbearable physical pain from my parched face, I was in shock and too emotionally numb to be hurt by her tirade. From the mad look in her eyes and the ferocity of her atrocious words, I understood that she was serious in wishing me dead.

"It's too bad you came back, little bastard," she hissed, distancing herself from me. "I really thought I was rid of you for good this time."

Gazing at her contorted face through blurred eyes, I choked on my own saliva, hardly able to swallow without suffering excruciating pain. Even though I was too young to know about God's promise of finite retribution for evildoings, I later imagined it was a preview of infernal damnation—a burning in the fires of hell.

That evening, despite my tormenting pain, I was approached by Uncle Evan. "Tomorrow we'll spend some time together, Avyrini, OK?"

he muttered, sliding the tips of his fingers across my blackened forehead. "I have some sweet treats for you. I think you'll really enjoy them."

Looking back, I wonder how he could have been so oblivious to the savage, deranged way in which his wife treated me. Such cruelty should have alarmed any man.

For a few weeks, I was left alone to heal my bruises. Believing Uncle Evan had forgotten about his desired "play" time, I actually started to count my blessings. Not for long, though; one day, he unexpectedly grabbed me by the arm and escorted me into his bedroom.

Quickly undressing me with clumsy hands, he once again satisfied his carnal urges, unmindful that I was a seven-year-old child. As my tiny body writhed in pain, Uncle Evan went through his lurid routine.

I learned to expect the constant trickle of blood that came afterwards, though I was unable to understand what was happening. In fact, my most vivid recollections of childhood include being covered in soot, feeling pain in one or more areas of the body and always, the sight of blood. It seemed to be everywhere—on my hands, on my clothes and running down my legs.

Pulling up his pants, Uncle Evan lit a cigarette, took a long, slow drag and went outside to relieve himself. I dressed myself, slid off the bed and limped past Aunt Cynara, who was standing near the stove, heating some of the water I had drawn from the well earlier. I guess she knew her husband would need a bath.

I tiptoed across the room, careful to neither interrupt her thoughts nor divert her attention.

"You dirty little bastard," she screeched out of the corner of her mouth. "What were you doing in there with my husband?"

I could see the transparent beads of perspiration glide across her rutted brow. I knew they would eventually slide down her cheeks. They always did when she was angry.

I was certain Aunt Cynara was enraged, and I knew that she knew exactly what Uncle Evan had done. However, though she was fully aware beyond any doubt of the repeated sexual abuse, she never tried to quash it. An accomplice, she held her tongue until it was time to conveniently lash out at me, inculpating me for her husband's evil deed.

The accusatory tone confirmed my thoughts. First, she allowed the predator to violate me—then she admonished me, denying in her mind that I was just a helpless child, an innocent victim of his violence.

The madness did not end with a verbal outburst. Infuriated, Aunt Cynara ran into the bedroom. I heard the sound of drawers opening and shutting—she was searching for something. Her breathing was heavy and quick, almost the panting of an overheated dog. When she returned, I noticed she was cradling a thick rope. Scared to death, I sat still, unwilling to even imagine what she was about to do.

Dragging her feet on the dusty floor, she staggered over to the table and plopped her oversized derrière down in the chair. Muttering incoherencies under her breath, she made two unsuccessful attempts to tie a noose.

Suffering from osteoarthritis in her hands, Aunt Cynara's fingers were visibly deformed. Red and swollen or a pale ashen hue, the dexterity was gone. Frustrated by her inability to succeed, she dropped the rope. It met the ground with a slight swoosh and was quickly retrieved, and a third attempt was made.

Sneering, she tugged several times on the noose, proud of her accomplishment. An all-encompassing aura of angst permeated the room with the swiftness of fog veiling an entire city. I shuddered, witnessing the gradual but steady shattering of my nerves. Overcome with fear, I felt ever muscle in my body tighten.

Aunt Cynara was incarcerated in the silence of doom. This could not be good. Something was simmering in her mind. I knew she was furious with me for "playing" with Uncle Evan, but I had no idea just how insane her anger had grown.

Rising from the chair, Aunt Cynara hobbled over to where I was seated, Indian-style, on the floor.

"Get up! Get over here," she ordered in one breath, with the harsh tonality of a prison warden summoning a death-row inmate to his final destiny.

Trembling like a newborn foal trying to stand for the first time, I obeyed her command. A pair of cold, clammy hands slipped the noose around my waist. With a jerk of her arm, she tightened it. I could hardly breathe from the pressure on my ribs.

Binding my arms and legs, Aunt Cynara hurled the free end of the rope in the air with a wide, sweeping movement. It tumbled as quickly as it soared.

On the third try, it reached its target, catching on one of the rafters in the vaulted ceiling. Seizing the moment, she hung on to the rope with all her weight, frantically tugging and pulling. I felt a series of piercing pains. I was dangling several feet above the ground! I realized Aunt Cynara was trying to hang me. Holding my entire body weight, my wrists burnt and throbbed. The rope was cutting into my flesh.

Screaming and yelling in both fear and agony, I baited her rage.

"You stinking little bastard," she ranted, crimson-faced and panting. "If you go anywhere near my husband one more time, I'll kill you!"

Thank God, I fainted. I came to while she was cutting me down. I dropped to the floor like a bag of potatoes, and she yanked me to my feet by the hair.

"Get up!" she shouted, covering my face with a spray of foul-stinking saliva. I suffered two dry heaves.

Dizzy and sick to my stomach, I once again did as I was told. As soon as I was on my feet, Aunt Cynara whacked me across the face with a fast, rhythmic double slap. Again I lost my footing and crumbled into a ball on the floor.

"I don't know why you don't die," she blurted. "I can't seem to get rid of you."

Sleeping on the hard, mud floor without heat or a pillow intensified the wounds Aunt Cynara had inflicted. It was impossible to find a position comfortable enough to help me enjoy a restful night. Consequently, months would pass before the mental and physical pain would subside.

The neighbors were frequently horrified by the repeated echoes of my blood-curdling screams. Witnessing, especially during the seasonally warm months, the huge welts and dark black-and-blue marks that decorated my arms and legs like a sailor's tattoos, they began to feel sorry for me. Although unwilling to confront Aunt Cynara or Uncle Evan on my behalf, everyone realized that I was not being treated appropriately.

One kind-hearted lady, who lived next door, unexpectedly dropped in one Saturday afternoon.

"Hello, Avyrini," she said, smiling. "How are you today, honey?" Flustered, I looked down at my feet, unable to respond. I was so unaccustomed to smiles and sweet words, I didn't know what was required of me. Feeling ill at ease, I shuffled over to where she was standing. Bending over, she gave me two kisses—one on each cheek. I felt a surge of blood rush to my face. I had never been kissed before!

"Come see what I brought you," the gracious woman cooed, motioning for me to come closer. I walked over as she unwrapped a beautiful, hand-knit dress. The crinkled, torn paper slipped down to the floor. Mumbling an apology, she picked it up.

I had never before seen anything so stunning. Could it possibly be for me? I questioned silently. It was a delicate pink with strong, sky-blue designs in a unique pattern.

"Come on, Avyrini," she whispered, "let's try it on. I want to see how pretty you look in it."

Excited, I pulled my soiled, torn smock over my head and waited for her to slip on the dress. It was a perfect fit and felt so soft against my skin.

"Oh, Avyrini, you look absolutely gorgeous. Tomorrow is Easter Sunday. You can wear it to church."

She gazed over at Aunt Cynara, who seemed oblivious to it all. Stone-faced and lethargic, she reacted with a nod. I breathed a sigh of relief; it was a confirmation that I would be going to Easter Sunday Mass all dressed up like the other children. For once, hanging my head in shame would not be a justifiable act. Surprisingly, I would even get to wear the one pair of shoes reserved for special occasions.

Ironically, in this den of evil deeds, where Satan seemed to rule, religious holidays were commemorated. Furthermore, for some inexplicable reason, Aunt Cynara seemed to honor these sacred occurrences with an armistice. There were neither violent reprisals nor the shouting of belittling, derogatory comments on Easter and Christmas. And certainly, there was no demeaning name calling. I was just Avyrini, a little, vulnerable seven-year-old who began to pray that God would make every day a holiday. Could Aunt Cynara possibly fear the Lord? I wondered. She certainly had a valid reason to.

Given a warm, soothing bath, my long, dark hair was un-matted and shampooed with anti-lice soap. Once I was dried off, the beautiful new dress was slipped over my head. Stepping into my black, patent-leather shoes was a mite bit irritating because of my toe blisters and calluses, but I was so happy to be pretty, I ignored the discomfort.

The walk to church that Sunday was joyful. I smiled at the other children and actually skipped along the way, to keep up with Uncle Evian's brisk step. Aunt Cynara, on the other hand, lagged behind. Her obesity and resulting diabetes prohibited her from moving at a normal pace.

Once in front of the church, Uncle Evan took a photo of me. No one had ever paid that much attention to me before. I was living a fairy tale. I had no idea that this photo would be the sole souvenir of my early childhood.

Children were laughing and giggling, chasing each other and enjoying the warmth of early spring. I watched from the sidelines, not a participant but a mere observer.

Once inside the church, I tried to sit as still as possible and not fidget. The last thing I wanted to do was upset Aunt Cynara.

Overcome with the aroma of incense, I looked toward the altar. It was ablaze with a kaleidoscope of color. The lilies were tall and stately. Their huge, white heads were lifted in tribute to the holiday. Each was placed in a wide, bronze urn together with various multicolored flowers, most of which I was unable to identify.

The organ music was thunderous and practically overpowered the voices raised in song. When the singing subsided, the priest climbed the narrow steps to the pulpit and addressed the parishioners, chanting, "Καλό Πάσχα, Χριστός ανέστη"—"Happy Easter, Christ is risen!"

I giggled silently, lowering my head and covering my mouth with my hand, when his footsteps squeaked while he slowly ascended the creaky, wood steps of the pulpit. He carried the paschal candle and lit the flame to symbolize the resurrection of the Son of God and the salvation of mankind. I sat on the edge of the pew, not wanting to miss a minute of the celebration.

The homily was centered on suffering, salvation and love. I listened to the comforting, encouraging words, wondering about God. Who is this God? I questioned. Would this loving Creator help me if I asked Him to? Would He rescue me from my suffering? Would He take me away from Aunt Cynara and Uncle Evan? Would I be saved? Could I possible be free of this dreadful torment?

FIFTH EPISODE

"Let us all be brave enough to die the death of a martyr, but let no one lust for martyrdom."
—Mohandas Gandhi

Oddly, before every meal, Aunt Cynara and Uncle Evan bowed their heads, shut their eyes, joined hands and thanked the Lord for blessings received at their table. Uninvited to share their abundance, I observed this ritual from my post on the floor, incapable of understanding how they could be people of faith and such brutal sinners. In a sense, they defaced the glory of Christianity. Didn't they have consciences?

It almost seemed as if reciting a few words several times a day in a trance-like state acquitted them of all the vicious emotionally and physically macerating crimes they committed against me. They spoke of God with awe and admiration and addressed Him in prayer with requests and petitions—then, they turned around and tortured one of His creatures.

After a while, this constant "devotion" left me wondering if I too could ask God for assistance. Would He be my emissary? Would He speak to Aunt Cynara on my behalf and tell her to halt the agonizing and devastating attacks? Would He approach Uncle Evan and urge him to stop the painful and humiliating sexual abuse? Could this be my salvation? Could it be the answer to my torment?

After my face was scorched, I had never been visited by a doctor. My wounds were stiff, raw and insufferable, and left unmedicated. There was no compassion and certainly no remorse. After all, Aunt Cynara was serious when she told me, "I want you dead." And I feared she would continue her terror strategy until she succeeded.

She lived to torture me—it was her reason to be. It started every morning when I opened my eyes and ended when I laid my head on the mud floor and tried to fall asleep. Then, making the sign of the cross, with her lips parted in prayer, she believed she made amends with God. Thus, she was bleached of every trace of guilt.

On Sundays, the priest would sermonize about loving one another, doing good deeds and respecting others. Yet, though they were committed churchgoers, neither Aunt Cynara nor Uncle Evan ever demonstrated either love or respect for an innocent child. Something was very wrong. The hypocrisy was rampant. The mistreatment was appalling. Consequently, I began to fear for my life.

Still not old enough to fully comprehend the severity of my situation, I did have the certainty, from the chronic name-calling and the recurring threats, that I was unloved and unwanted, and all because my mother had me without marrying my father. There would be no reprieve and no hope of a pardon for the responsibility I was forced to carry because of the sin of another. Furthermore, as long as I lived in the shack with Aunt Cynara and Uncle Evan, mine would be an experience of demeaning domination and oppression. It was as if my fate were sealed in my own blood.

Thinking about God and repeatedly musing over the Sunday messages I heard in church, my mind would often wander through wishful daydreams in which I envisioned myself in the role of a happy child—happy like the children I met in church.

Unlike me, these children had loving, doting parents whose hugs and affectionate glances announced feelings of nurturing and caring. These children had bright, healthy complexions and clean, proper fitting clothing. Their faces were decorated with broad, genuine smiles and glistening eyes. But most of all, their individual personalities bubbled. They chatted among themselves animatedly, almost nonstop, about school, teachers and their companions. Knowledgeable and able to read and write, they talked about so many things of which I was totally ignorant.

Theirs was such a different world from mine—a world I yearned for, a world I was entitled to as a child created in the image and likeness of God. This was how the Reverend defined human beings. Yet, despite growing up in Christian surroundings, it was a world I was unjustly denied.

Many evenings, anxious and scared, I would twist and turn on the hard floor, either shivering from the bitter cold or sweating from the torrid heat, contemplating the horror of my life. The pain and stiffness of my bruises always intensified during the motionless hours of the night and not having a mattress to buffer my injuries, the discomfort intensified.

Drifting in and out of a restless sleep, I would try to imagine how life would be with my mother. Certainly she would not beat me and burn my face on a searing griddle. Surely she would cradle me in her arms and love me—even if I destroyed her life by coming into the world unwanted. I wondered if she would be happy to see me. Would she welcome me with kisses?

I imagined she would throw her arms around me, squeeze me real hard and swing me off my feet, whispering ever so sweetly, "Avyrini, little darling, I love you." I would see other children on Sundays giggle with delight as they were kissed and twirled around by their parents—so why not me?

Instead of affectionate kisses, I got beastly lashings. And as an alternative to school, I was frequently bound and punished, when I wasn't being sexually abused.

The following day, the Easter truce was annulled. Aunt Cynara saw it fitting to admonish me once again for being an illegitimate child.

"Get over here, you little bastard," she blurted. "I hate your mother for leaving you here with us. We don't want you."

I ran, unwilling to suffer the consequences of noncompliance. As an unworthy recompense, I received her open palm across my face. Basing my decision on a serious error of judgment, I cried out in pain, drawing my hand up to my smarting cheek to ease the sting.

"Get in the closet right now," Aunt Cynara yelled, "and stop that annoying carrying on." Before I could obey her command, she grabbed me by the hand, dragged me over to the closet and threw me in. With a violent slam that caused two chips of wood to rain down on my head, she locked the door.

It was cold and dark in the closet; the only bit of light that was visible was a narrow, yellow beam peeking out from under the door. I knew that if I screamed or cried, she would yank me out, whip me and shove me back in to nurse my wounds. Therefore, after careful reasoning, I opted to abandon that strategy. Instead, I sat cross-legged on the floor and prayed that God would come to my rescue.

In the meantime, I was destined to spend three days in this bleak prison without any bathroom breaks. Twice a day, Aunt Cynara opened the door to throw some stale bread and berries at me.

I didn't know what to do. I felt so powerless. Sometimes I thought my crying would soften her up, but through trial and error, I eventually learned it had the opposite effect. If I was quiet, I had a better chance of getting out with less bloodshed.

After a while, the walls seemed to move closer and closer, stealing what little breathing space was available. To compensate, I rolled myself into the tightest ball possible, until every muscle and tendon in my body ached. My breathing became shallower. There was no other alternative but to wait for a reprieve.

I began to seriously consider the possibility of running away. In my fantasy, I created vivid scenarios of a daring getaway. Realizing that if I no longer lived with Aunt Cynara and Uncle Evan I would not have to be a subservient, pitiable victim of their maliciousness, I made up my mind to devise an escape plan.

I believed the best strategy was to climb on the roof and wait until the first gloaming ray of sun snatched away the darkness. Once I was able to see clearly, I would head for the street and run as fast as my little legs would carry me. I was convinced that my plan was perfect.

That evening, I put it into action. Uncle Evan's thunderous snoring and Aunt Cynara's rattled breathing were the indication that both had drifted off to slumber. What a relief; this was the only time they were actually tolerable.

Not having any possessions, clothes, blanket, pillow or toys, I had no luggage to pack or to slow me down. What I slept in was what I wore all day except on Christmas, Easter and Sundays, when I accompanied my aunt and uncle to church. When it became noticeably tattered and filthy beyond usage, it was replaced. This was the pattern—this was my life with Aunt Cynara and Uncle Evan.

I'd made up my mind, and it was time to follow through. Quietly, I stood up and tiptoed toward the front door. I prayed, "Please, God, don't let it squeak when I pull it open."

The ruckus from the bedroom was so loud, I actually doubted that they would awaken even if the door slammed. However, it didn't. "Oh, ευχαριστίεσ Θεός, thank you, God," I prayed.

I peeked outside, just to be certain that the neighbors were securely tucked in their own beds and not roaming around. It was important to be careful because if I bungled the escape and got caught, I risked a severe punishment—perhaps even death. This was a serious decision, but I was desperate. After Aunt Cynara had burned my face and tried to hang me, it was a life-or-death situation.

I walked out the door and into the misty evening air. Although the sky was ablaze with stars, the stillness was almost eerie. However, I focused on following the plan I had designed in my head just a few hours earlier, realizing that I had to get it right the first time. I knew there would be no second attempt.

The καλύβα was a one-level, low-lying shanty with rotting windows. Nearby, there was an easy-to-mount olive tree with wide, spreading branches. I walked over, curled my arms around a thick branch, climbed up and dragged myself over the flat roof. Scraping my elbow, I drew a few drops of blood.

Though the shack was rather weathered and dilapidated, surprisingly, the slate roof was smooth except for scattered mounds of sooty ash from the chimney and large bird droppings.

I stepped carefully, so as not to dirty my shoes. They were special, and I was allowed to wear them only on holidays and to church. My only provisions were two packages filled with nuts and some overripe berries. This would have to sustain me until I reached my destination.

Settling myself down on a relatively clean area of the roof, I drifted off to sleep. My plan was to awaken at dawn and begin my journey toward freedom. All I wanted was to find my mother and be happy—nothing more, nothing less. However, perhaps detained by my dreams of leaving Aunt Cynara and Uncle Evan behind, I overslept.

With the sun splashing its scorching rays along the contour of my body, I opened my eyes. My flesh seemed to glow like the sea beneath a cloudless sky.

Lifting myself to a sitting position, I squinted in the brightness of day, unwrapped one of the untidy newspaper packets, grabbed a handful of nuts and shoved them into my mouth. Repeating the gesture with the second package, I ingested some of the soured berries.

Breakfast consumed, I rose to my feet, walked over to the edge of the roof and peered down. I had to be certain that Aunt Cynara and Uncle Evan were not around. My breathing became irregular as butterflies pirouetted in my stomach. Things were decidedly different in the daylight. This was no longer just an idea, a pretense—it was for real. I was actually escaping.

I ran to the north side of the roof, gauged the distance between my aunt and uncle's καλύβα and the neighbor's shack, backed up and ran with all my might until I neared the edge. Then, shutting my eyes, I jumped onto their roof.

My feet came crashing down hard and mercilessly. Although I was wearing shoes, the leather soles did little to buffer my landing. A razor-sharp pain ran from my heels up to my knees. Losing my balance, I instinctively latched on to the electrical wires crossing directly in front of me. In my eight-year-old mind, it was an ingenious solution to keep me from falling off the roof.

I felt a stinging bolt of current run through my hands, up my arms and down my entire body. I quivered and vibrated in uncontrollable movements, like the earth in the midst of an unforgiving earthquake. Paralyzed from the fright of a terrifying unknown and from the live wires holding my hands captive, I let out a series of blood-curdling screams.

I was trapped as the fitful shaking intensified. My eyes were glued open, making it impossible to blink. Bits and pieces of slate had come loose from the friction of my trembling body. Once again, the now-familiar odor of charred flesh reached my nostrils—my palms were seared!

The current continued coursing through my body, causing repeated shock waves. Then, my vision blurred. I could see the wires and my trembling hands, but they seemed faded and distorted. Dizzy from the convulsive spasms and racked with pain, I gasped and screeched until my voice went silent.

Hearing my howls, the neighbors ran into the street. Catching sight of my gyrating body with my hands attached to the wires, one of the women, a registered nurse, ran into the house and switched off the power. Her quick thinking saved my life. I was later told that I'd been minutes away from death by electrocution.

The electrical power interruption released my hands from the wires and propelled me off the roof. The fall to the ground knocked me unconscious.

"Oh my God! This child has to be taken to the hospital immediately," the nurse shouted, bending down to see if I was still breathing. "She needs immediate medical attention."

I gained consciousness just as Aunt Cynara blurted, "No, she doesn't have to go to the hospital. I will take care of her. She will be just fine in a day or two." Approaching me, she yelled, "Evan, help me carry Avyrini into the house."

Uncle Evan ran over, lifted me in his arms and brought me into the shack. I was still trembling both from fright and from the wrenching pain of my bruised body and severely burnt hands. Each step he took irritated my wounds.

"Put her over there," Aunt Cynara commanded, gesturing to my designated spot on the floor. Perhaps indebted to his wife for closing an eye on his sexual exploitation escapades, he obliged without ever questioning her judgment.

"Evan, I'll take care of Avyrini—she'll be OK."

Uncle Evan glanced at me, flashed a shy smile, slipped on his jacket and left for work. I was alone with Aunt Cynara and I was in tears.

She abandoned me for several hours without any medical consideration. She did not cleanse my wounds or give me food and water. I was simply ignored. Even my whimpering did little to attract her attention. It was as if I were a savage animal caught in a trap, bleeding but destined to be destroyed for the dangerous threat I represented.

At first, she seemed satisfied to see me helpless and ailing. She threw me a sneering glance from time to time when she passed my spot.

Then, like a chameleon, her eyes bulged and rotated. Using her gnarled hand as a tong, she picked up Uncle Evan's horse whip. Moving ever so slowly, with a swaying gait, she approached. I held my breath.

Flipping into malicious mode, she commanded me to stand up.

"Take off your dress," she ordered hoarsely. "And I don't want to hear a sound out of you, or you'll get more lashings. Do you understand, λίγοσ μπάσταρδοσ?"

"Yes," I lied, unable to understand why I was the victim of such torment.

Believing I should be punished for my evil deed, Aunt Cynara swung the coarse leather whip into the air and brought it down across my back—twice. It crackled as it dug into my flesh. Satisfied with the new welts, she changed direction and targeted my legs.

"θεία Cynara, σταματώ αυτό—με πονάς," I cried. "Aunt Cynara, stop—it hurts," I shrieked, just seconds before I threw up and fainted, crashing down flat on my face. God had heard my prayer.

No longer able to gain pleasure from viewing my face contorted in anguish, and hearing the echoes of my suffering whimpers, Aunt Cynara dropped the whip, kicked it under the dining table, walked over to the faded curtain, swept it aside and retreated to her own sanctum, where, for eight hours, I was non-existent. It didn't matter that I was an eight-year-old child, bleeding, unconscious and lying in my own vomit.

Eventually, my physical wounds healed, leaving a legacy of ugly scars on the palms of my hands and along the perimeters of my wrists.

Once I was fully recuperated, I made several more attempts to run away from Aunt Cynara and Uncle Evan's madness. Choosing the church as my asylum, I thought I could seek refuge from the atrocities at home among the holy priests who always preached about love and forgiveness. However, whenever they found me on the monastery's doorstep, they calmly escorted me back to Aunt Cynara, despite my visible scars and the undisputed awareness of my abusive circumstances.

It was the mid-1950s and child abuse was not a relevant issue in Greece. Social Services was a non-existent entity and Ελληνική Στρατιωτική Αστυνομία (ΕΣΑ), the Greek Military Police (ESA), would never interfere in family situations for any crime less than murder. Furthermore, I was an illegitimate child, neither worthy of a dignified identity nor human rights. This was who I was.

Several months later, after numerous futile escape attempts, Aunt Cynara called me into her bedroom.

"You're going away, little bastard," she said, tying my few measly belongings together before slipping them into a small piece of luggage that was about as old as she was. "I'm finally getting rid of you. Take off that dirty dress and put on your pink and blue one."

Puzzled by this unknown and unexpected eventuality, I did as I was told, realizing that any protesting on my part would only secure me a nasty beating.

Dressed in my pretty pink outfit and with my Sunday shoes on my feet, I was escorted outside. In front of the door was a horse and carriage. The driver jumped down and opened the door, graciously helping me climb in, then helping my aunt and uncle after me. Still very confused, I asked, "Where am I going, Aunt Cynara?"

"You're going away, Avyrini, far away from me and Uncle Evan. I'm finally getting rid of the little bastard!"

By now, my relationship with God was quite strong. Amazingly, Aunt Cynara had planted seeds of faith in my mind, teaching me about Jesus Christ and the twelve apostles. On Sundays, I had heard the parables and had always looked forward to Mass so I could listen to more beautiful stories.

Throughout the day, I evoked God's help multiple times, getting down on my knees to beg for a reprieve from the torture.

"Oh, God," I begged, with my eyes shut so tightly, my forehead furrowed like the brow of a centenarian, "please let this stop. I'm tired of hurting. I'm sick of being beaten and locked in the dark closet. Why can't I be happy like other children?"

Seated in the carriage, I prayed again, asking God to help me.

"Maybe you're sending me to my mom," I whispered with the unsoiled naïveté of a vulnerable, young child. "Are you, God? Am I going home to my mom?"

SIXTH EPISODE

"But we exult in tribulations also, knowing that tribulation works out endurance, and endurance tried virtue, and tried virtue hope. And hope does not disappoint..."

—Romans 5:3-5

The spine-tingling thrill of riding in a horse-drawn carriage, all gussied up in my favorite pink and blue dress, was overshadowed by the disquieting feeling of uncertainty mixed with a fear-based apprehension. Coerced into an unfamiliar situation, I was unable to maintain even a light grip on reality long enough to size up the events and decipher what was happening. I knew I was leaving my aunt and uncle's house, but why remained a mystery.

Unsettling the bits and pieces of mislaid gravel scattered along the path, the rhythmic click-clock of trotting hooves kept my mind focused and my pulse racing. Although I dared not vocalize either my confusion or nervousness, the absence of luggage except for my own tiny, weathered suitcase encouraged me to wonder where I was going—and why alone.

Aunt Cynara and Uncle Evan were exaggeratedly quiet. Seated like two wide-eyed owls opposite each other, they ping-ponged several whispered words between them, more occasionally than regularly. Always rather boisterous, whether focused on scolding me or admonishing Uncle Evan for some random misdeed, committed or alleged, Aunt Cynara's new tranquility left me fidgety and on the edge of the seat. It was a different situation, and it left me uneasy.

I sat lost in my own fantasy, no longer intent on decoding the baffling mystery of the day, until the carriage came to an abrupt halt. The reins jangled, the hooves were silenced and the horse neighed in response to the carriage driver's long, drawn-out 'Whoa!' Immediately, I was jolted back to reality.

We had arrived in Ιωάννινα—Ioannina—a city in northwestern Greece several hundred meters above sea level, with Lake Pamvotida as one of its main attractions.

Leaning over to peer out the window, I noticed that we had stopped in front of a rather desolate area of parched, discolored land, populated by a series of arch-shaped steel structures. Their appearance was odd; I noticed that they had no windows.

"Come on—get out, Avyrini," Uncle Evan said, cutting into my thoughts. Reaching for my hand, he helped me exit the carriage. My heart skipped a beat—was I going back home to my mom? Was she here, amid these ugly buildings? Was God finally answering my prayer? Were they bringing me home?

Excited, I stepped down and onto the ground. I focused my glance on the nun who was quickly approaching. Uncle Evan took me by the hand and escorted me toward the mysterious lady in black, whose long, flowing robe ballooned in the wind with every step she took.

"This is Avyrini," he said dryly when our paths crossed, "the child I told you about."

In a high-pitched, almost shrill voice, the nun greeted me with a brusque "Γειά σου—hello."

Uncle Evan dropped my hand while Aunt Cynara stood beside him, gazing down at her shoes. Her blank expression confirmed that she was an uncaring woman deprived of any sensitivity, even for a sweet, innocent child who wanted nothing more than to be loved and treated like the other happy children. However, her propensity for distancing herself from a creature she deemed a shameful consequence of a sinful deed gave this decision an unwavering status.

The final goodbye was cold. Without the vaguest trace of emotion, Aunt Cynara and Uncle Evan turned on their heels, obliterating the vision of my scared, questioning face from their lives forever.

I, on the other hand, was in tears—not from having to leave them behind, but from a very raw fear of the unknown. There would be neither pining for the wretchedness that characterized my life so far, nor nostalgia for my wicked aunt and uncle. In a sense, this was a blessing—or so I mistakenly thought.

"Avyrini, collect your belongings," the nun said, "and come along with me."

"Where are we going?" I blurted, almost regretting my impatience as soon as I finished the question. In my heart, I was unsure if I really wanted an answer. Using my own fantasy, I had learned early on, was certainly a great deal more reassuring, if not more comforting, than the reality of my life. Furthermore, I could find solace a bit longer in imagining that I was going to meet my mom. However, my childish curiosity pushed me past any daydream.

"Avyrini," she said, quickening her gait, "you are going to the ορφανοτροφείο."

Silently, I repeated it several times. It was such a monstrous-sounding word, I could hardly pronounce it. "What's an ορφανοτροφείο?" I asked.

"It's a place for children who have nobody—orphans who lost their parents in the war, children who are all alone in life and have no place to go."

"But I have a mom," I exclaimed, unable to understand why I had to go to an orphanage.

"Avyrini," she said dryly, "your mother does not want you, and your aunt and uncle have had enough of you. You are disobedient and defiant—a troublemaker. They can't and absolutely refuse to deal with you any longer. You will be living with other children who are alone and abandoned like you."

What I did not realize at the time was that I was under the wing of the Greek government. Once I was rejected and abandoned by my aunt and uncle, the state was, in a sense, acting as my legal guardian. Consequently, it had the authority to make decisions regarding my welfare.

The prejudicial social attitudes of the day concerning the condemnation of illegitimate children, together with my mother's abandonment and my aunt and uncle's rejection, signed my fate—I was an orphan.

My chest tightened as a large lump swelled in my throat. Unable to fully grasp the significance of this life-altering moment, I felt anxious and fearful. The nun patted me on the head. "You'll be settled in soon and you will be able to meet the other children," she murmured almost inaudibly.

I was surprised to see a series of Quonset storage huts. I was told that was where I would be living with the other girls. They were odd looking buildings, so unlike the shacks in Ktismata. Tall, arched structures constructed of corrugated steel, they bore a striking resemblance to greenhouses.

I later learned that the Quonset storage huts had been commissioned by the US Navy both as storage and to house troops. Easy to transport and equally uncomplicated to assemble, they were cost-effective and suitable for many uses.

Surrounding the structures, the land was as abandoned and neglected as the children who called these despondent huts home. The grass, neither fertilized nor irrigated, was burnt to straw and in some areas, weeds as tall as ready-to-harvest corn stalks sprouted. As we entered, I noted again that there were no windows. I guess, in a sense, it explained the terrible odor of mold and stale air.

When we crossed the threshold, we were greeted by another nun, an older woman dressed in a somber black habit, with a matching veil fastened to a white, starched, form-fitting cap that hugged her chin. A wooden cross fastened with ribbons sat firmly on her chest. Only her face and hands were exposed.

My memory is sometimes fuzzy, perhaps influenced by a strong desire to negate this atrociously painful period of my life. Therefore, I may not recall with unerring accuracy some of the more minute details.

The nun approached in silence except for the squeak of her leather shoes and the almost tuneful jangle of the black rosary beads dangling from her tri-knotted cord belt. Eventually, I was informed that the knots symbolized the vows of poverty, chastity and obedience that the religious take when they become nuns.

"Γειά σου, Avyrini," she whispered. Pointing to the hordes of youngsters wandering about, she continued, "As you can see, there are many children like you living here." Petite and slender, she had deep-set, dark eyes and an intense gaze that seemed to penetrate right through me. I felt as though she knew my every thought and feeling. When she spoke, her pale, olive skin assumed a flushed tint. What she lacked in stature she made up for with her intimidating demeanor.

Gazing around, I was floored by the thousands of rejected, abandoned children with whom I would share my days and nights. Was it possible that all these little and not-so-little girls had no one to love and care for them?

The children were separated according to age. Taking me by the hand, the nun led me to a large room filled with rows of wire cots. Placed on top of each was a straw mattress. The covers were long past their life expectancies. As a result, bits of straw had come through the tiny holes and ripped holes in the coarse material.

The walls, initially painted white, showed years of negligence. The constant traffic of children entering and leaving the room left them chipped, splintered and smudged. Some areas seemed as if they had been targeted with clumps of mud. Perhaps it was a game the children played. Toys were nonexistent; therefore, whatever was available was readily utilized by the children to create diversions.

"Ayvrini," the nun said, pointing to a cot at the far end of the room, "that's yours." Nodding my head, I walked over and sat down on the edge, nervously swinging my legs. It was not as bouncy as Uncle Evan and Aunt Cynara's bed, but it was certainly better than sleeping on the bare mud floor.

"Once you settle your belongings beneath the bed, we will visit you to make certain you don't have any problems that might affect the well-being of the other children," she told me dryly. "If everything is OK, you'll be able to go to school."

The mention of the word "school" excited me. Would I finally be taught how to read and write like the children my age in Ktismata? The thought was encouraging and left me with a feeling of hope.

Although there was neither running water nor electricity, I was accustomed to the discomfort of outdoor restrooms and the mortifying hardship of living in dire poverty. Nothing changed except for the fact that I had lots of other little girls my age to play with, talk to and share my days with.

My surroundings at Άγιοσ Έλενα, the Saint Elena Orphanage, were definitely unusual, and a far cry from my restricted space in the Ktismata shack. Furthermore, I was vaguely curious to see what life would be like in this new environment. It was almost a reason to live.

Visited by two other nuns dressed in a similar manner, I was stripped naked. Taller and heavier than the first woman, they also cut a daunting appearance. I was ordered to stand while they turned me in a full circle and looked me over. Gazing curiously at my deep scars, they ran their cold fingers along the raised marks, exchanging glances, never commenting or questioning how and why my body was so brutally disfigured.

"This child has head lice," the older nun announced, frowning. "Come take a look for yourself." The younger woman bent over and lifted a section of my hair to expose part of my scalp. "Oh, yes, she's infested. We'll have to take care of this right now."

"OK Avyrini," she said, "get dressed and come with us."

I was escorted to a large room filled with noisy children, all of who were laughing and chatting in unison. "Sit here, Avyrini," the nun said, pointing to a small, brown metal chair. "We have to take care of this lice problem before you can go to school. You do want to go to school, don't you?"

"Oh, yes," I blurted, eager to be like all the others and learn how to read and write.

One of the nuns grabbed a handful of my hair and before I question her action, she snipped it off. Quickly, she repeated the action, tugging several times before cutting. Lowering my eyes, I noticed with horror that long clumps of my thick tresses were strewn about the floor.

Gasping, I brought my hands to my head in a desperate attempt to grab on to some hair, perhaps to have the reassurance that I was not bald.

"Don't touch," the nun told me. "We're not done yet."

Not done yet? I shouted silently, warming from the rush of blood to my face. What else was there to do? They had cut off all my hair. Suddenly, my head was bent, pushed over a basin and drenched in icy cold water. I shuddered, feeling it drip into my ears. Then, as quickly as it was lowered, it was yanked upright.

What happened next caught me totally by surprise. Much to my embarrassment and displeasure, a hand, armed with a sharp, steel razor blade, passed over the entire surface of my head—once, twice, three times. The steel felt cold and I began to realize that my worst fear had become a reality: I had been shaved hairless.

Noticing my shiny, bald pate, some of the children began giggling, bringing their hands to their mouths to muffle the sounds. I felt another stream of warm blood rush through my chest, accelerating my heart beat.

"The problem is solved, Avyrini—the lice are gone. Now you can go to school!" the nun told me. I wondered if I was expected to demonstrate joy and or gratitude.

As the morning spilled into afternoon, I was given a briefing regarding the rules and regulations that governed life in the orphanage. The pre-dawn wake-up call was at 4:00 a.m. and bedtime was 10:00 p.m. Under no circumstances would there be any exceptions. The rules had to be obeyed.

That evening, after retiring to my assigned cot, I encountered my first experience of sleeping on a mattress in lieu of a hard floor. And although the sharp-edged pieces of straw often dug into my skin when I rolled over, it was undoubtedly a more comfortable alternative. For the first half hour, I scratched myself, sometimes even drawing blood, until exhaustion, in the role of savior, lured me into a deep sleep.

Attending school was all that I had imagined during the past eight years. I loved learning about different things and despite my almost four-year delay in getting stated, I was a top student, excelling in all subjects. In just a few short weeks, I had caught up with and surpassed most of my classmates. Excited to go further, I awakened every morning before the wake-up hour, unable to curtail my enthusiasm for acquiring new knowledge.

But apart from the fleeting exhilaration of school, life in the orphanage was filled with trials and tribulations. Even though I was not accustomed to nourishing meals, provisions were scare. There were too many unloved, abandoned children to care for, and accommodations were exaggeratedly inadequate.

Looking back, I often wonder how life would have been if generous caring, people like Oprah had been alive at the time. Had she been around and aware of the dire, almost inhumane conditions in which we lived, I'm more than certain that she would have intervened, bringing the issue into focus by drawing awareness to the tragic plight of these misfortunate children. Knowing her compassion for people with a vast plethora of needs and recognizing her willingness and ability to right the wrongs that are prevalent in society, I feel confident in believing that a "make a difference" crusade would have been waged, saving thousands of children from growing up not only deprived of material necessities, but emotionally and psychologically underprivileged—a condition resulting not only in a loss of identity but an unjust forfeiture of human dignity.

The innocent and the vulnerable need watchful eyes and the kindness and generosity of blessed individuals who are willing to give back. Sadly, there are too many demons preying on susceptible children who have no one to love them enough to cover their backs or defend their rights as human beings.

Although from time to time, the Americans donated cheese and other snacks like Snickers bars, sadly, the treats were not shared with the children. Instead, the provisions were divided and consumed by the nuns and the government officials who together ran the orphanage.

Given only the crumbs—tiny morsels of cheese and candy—we were nourished on a breakfast of powdered milk, into which slabs of stale bread were dunked to soften the texture. Many of the younger children were semi-toothless, having shed most of their milk teeth;

consequently, the hard-crusted days-old bread, baked by the elder girls, represented a hardship to chew. Many just left it untouched.

Lunch and dinner were meager rations, consisting of over-boiled rice, soggy potatoes and, when the season consented, a few vegetables from the orphanage garden. Bread was garnished with a spread of cold, greasy lard to prohibit it from sticking in our throats.

The nuns, on the other hand, suffered little deprivation. They dined on meat and fresh-baked bread, kneaded daily by the older girls.

Once I had a piece of American cheese between my teeth, I never forgot the sumptuous taste. One slice was divided in fours and each child received a quarter. The soft, smooth consistency of the cheese mixed with the salty tang that teased my tongue were indescribable. However, the enjoyment was so rare and short-lived, it never gained any momentum in my life.

One morning, about a year after my entry into the orphanage, I awakened with a terrible sore throat. It felt as if I had swallowed a glass of searing hot liquid that had scalded my entire esophagus. My nightgown was soaked in sweat, my hair was drenched and the palms of my hands were moist and clammy. Beads of perspiration trickled down my forehead, meandering into my ears.

Listless and weakened, I was unable to lift my head from the mattress. I called out for assistance. The two attending nuns rushed over to my cot. One held my mouth open while the other pushed my tongue down with a makeshift tongue depressor she extracted from a pocket hidden in one of the folds of her habit. I gagged several times, turning my head to avoid reinsertion of the depressor.

"Be still, Avyrini," the nun whispered. "We have to find out what's troubling you... I see the problem," she said, rather sure of the layman's diagnosis she was about to make. "Avyrini has severe tonsillitis. I can see that the right tonsil is inflamed and oozing pus. She'll have to have a tonsillectomy. Get her up and seat her in that chair," she ordered, pointing to a dilapidated relic leaning up against the wall.

I was eased out of bed and placed in the designated seat. Both my hands were fastened to the arms of the chair with long pieces of cord, wrapped several times around my wrists. A third piece was strung around my waist, firmly anchoring me to the back of the chair.

Terrifying, violent scenes of Aunt Cynara's lashings and hangings flashed before my eyes. In a split second, I relived all the horror and anguish of my life in Ktismata. However, too weak and agonized to protest, I submitted.

"Open your mouth Avyrini," the petite nun commanded with the assurance of a surgical nurse boasting decades of experience.

I obeyed, and a flashlight was beamed down my throat. Before I realized what was happening, she grabbed my lower lip and tugged my mouth open wider. Inserting her hand, she injected me with Novocain on the right side. "We'll wait a few minutes," she murmured, "until the area becomes fully desensitized—then we'll remove the tonsils."

My heart was racing. Understanding my fear, the self-proclaimed surgeon-nun responded, touching my shoulder. "Don't worry, you won't feel anything. That's why we gave you the injection."

Somewhat reassured, I took a deep breath. The Novocain had calmed the burning in my throat. It was something to be grateful for, though it was a short-lived reprieve.

Suddenly, I felt an excruciating pain, more gripping and intense than the electrical power running through my body the day I was electrocuted on the roof of my neighbor's shack. It seemed as if my entire gullet had been ripped out. Cringing, I shouted out in pain: "Stop—you're hurting me!"

After mistakenly administering the anesthetic exclusively to the right side, the nun had sliced through my left tonsil. It was resistant, and she tugged at it violently, with all her strength. I was in agony. I felt a steady drip of thick, warm blood slide down my throat. Some of it spilled out through the corners of my mouth. I gagged several times, gasping for air.

"Untie her," the nun shouted. "Hurry, turn her upside down before she chokes to death." I was unfastened and somersaulted until my head pointed to the floor. The nun shook me as hard as her physical strength consented.

"Spit it out. Cough—keep coughing! Spit out the tonsils, Avyrini," the "full medical staff" shrieked in chorus.

I coughed and choked for several minutes as bits of bloody tonsils came up in my mouth. "It hurts," I cried, as the pain intensified every time I gagged. "God, please help me" I prayed. "God, where are you?"

I coughed; several pieces of my severed tonsils bounced along my tongue and dropped out. I lost consciousness. God heard my prayer once again during a moment of anguish and took away my senses. I had a momentary respite from my torture. By the time I regained consciousness, I was lying on my straw mattress with a cold, wet rag tied around my throat. Presumably, this remedy would lighten the pain. It didn't. But I survived, and as the days passed, the burning and throbbing began to gradually subside. Soon, I was able to take in nourishment with little if any difficulty.

Although my follow-up treatment involved a year-long series of painful penicillin injections which left me with scars on my arms and thighs, I had the confirmation that God was with me. Once again, He was there, giving me hope in my misery and torment. Maybe He really did listen—if I cried out loud enough! Perhaps He cared about me when no one else seemed to. The seeds of my faith, planted in Ktismata, were beginning to sprout the tiniest of buds.

SEVENTH EPISODE

"Death is no more than passing from one room into another. But there's a difference for me, you know. Because in that other room I shall be able to see."

—Helen Keller

Life at Άγιοσ Ἑλενα orphanage continued to be a rigorous test of endurance and a repeated assessment of my blossoming faith in a superior power. Imploring the assistance of the Lord in desperate moments, I continued to discover that He was there for me. Still too young to understand the why behind my life of deprivation and suffering, I tried to focus my energy on school and perfecting my skills as a seamstress in spite of the often exaggerated and distracting pandemonium in my daily environment.

My favorite part of the day was sitting in front of my teacher, listening to whatever she had to say. Every word I heard was mesmerizing; every story she told was fascinating. It made no difference what subject she was teaching or what she was discussing—I loved it all.

I was growing up and at ten years old, I was beginning to grasp the events and circumstances of my surroundings in a more comprehensive manner, including some of the concealed political innuendos the older girls often whispered about.

No longer Aunt Cynara's scullery servant, I did not have to slave to keep her ramshackle shed orderly. And no longer responsible for Uncle Evan's needs, I was freed from gratifying his perverted whims and keeping him in clean clothes. But best of all, I was liberated from my aunt's severe whippings and the endless hours tethered to a table whenever, according to her warped judgment, I was wayward.

Instead, I was now thrust into a new world, a world that amply filled the vacancies left behind from the shattered old one. However, it was filled with what I had so hoped to leave behind—additional agony and torment.

Hardships were numerous, including fetching water from the river, laundering my own clothes, keeping silent during school hours as well as the strenuous exercise regime required and enforced with military precision. Nourishment was pitiable, especially since growing girls must meet stringent dietary requirements to develop into healthy teens and adults. However, undoubtedly, this was not a priority.

Muffled comments spoke of a government-run orphanage in which the politics of the day was centered on the accumulation of dietary/personal provisions and monetary donations. Yet in lieu of applying the benefactors' generosity to improve the children's lives, fingers pointed toward the government officials and nuns who were alleged to have horded the bounty for their own personal gratification, leaving mere crumbs for the disadvantaged orphans.

Instead of a guard dog government protecting the welfare of its most vulnerable citizens, it fed them to the lions. Other hushed phrases insinuated the existence of a child-trafficking ring in which children were sometimes entrusted to the orphanage by parents reduced to dire poverty and eventually, without parental consent, given up for adoption for a specified fee. It was a business with human lives marketed as merchandise.

Not only did these children face the atrocious rigors of life in an abusive institution, but they were traded for bounty to swell the pockets of third-party individuals. In a sense, it made me think of how Jesus was first tortured, His life extinguished on the σταυρό, then, as if crucifixion on the cross were not sufficiently humiliating, He was robbed of His possessions. As it said in Matthew 27:35, "And after they had crucified him, they divided his garments, casting lots." This was human dignity compromised for egotistical gain.

Therefore, despite the generosity of kind sponsors, in particular the Americans, the nuns continued to rear the children with table scraps and beggars' rags.

I tried to concentrate on my studies and sewing projects, which I so enjoyed. It gave me an outlet for my stifled resourcefulness and encouraged me to express my creativity. I was awarded the title "best seamstress in the class," and my hand-embroidered creations were repeatedly offered to European royals. In the late '50s, my embroidery was sent to Paul I, king of the Hellenes, and his consort, Queen Frederika.

Healthcare was practically nonexistent for most of the children, except when a serious illness threatened the life of one of the girls. However, the "adoptable" children were given regular check-ups, paid for by the interested families. If a favorable-to-the-orphanage exchange of money was involved, the system turned gracious and obliging as quickly as the rainbow makes its colorful debut after a tropical storm.

Following a year of painful penicillin injections three times daily, I was declared healed from the nasty infection resulting from the back-room tonsillectomy performed in a non-sterile environment. I was happy not to have to deal with the painful needle punctures and annoying burning afterwards.

Convinced that my survival and recovery were a blessing from God, I thanked Him daily during the early morning hour in which we were obliged to pray on bent knees in the pewless chapel. Tired from the pre-dawn wake-up, we veiled our heads, silenced our thoughts and tried to keep upright on the dark stained, carved oak prie dieu kneelers facing the altar.

A mysterious aura of serenity sprang from the poignant quietude and the striking image of the troubled girls in deep reflection. Parted lips, in adoration, mimicked fervent prayers, tearful implorations and desperate supplications for mercy. It was a testament of faith—a faith that delicately cradled the promise of hope. It was all we had.

Somehow, finding myself on my knees in the chapel created a consoling, albeit flimsy, sense of escape. For sixty minutes a day, I felt as if I were removed from my awful circumstances and granted amnesty. I never really knew if I emanated holiness or a likeness to God during those moments.

Chapel represented a time to think and reflect and a time to dialogue openly, heart to heart with God. There was no one else who cared enough to listen to my thoughts and feelings—no one who worried about my today and or if I would even have a tomorrow. Therefore, in God, I discovered the mother and father I was denied. Consequently, I always found comfort in addressing my feelings to the Divine Creator. I was unconditionally receptive to the presence of God in my life. He was my security.

Although the chapel was a peaceful refuge from the grueling routine and a momentary escape into my own reflections, the exaggerated groupings of lit candles rendered the air stifling. From where I knelt, I could see the brown, braided wicks curl as the bright yellow flames melted the beeswax to liquid. Eventually, it would drip down the long, slender, white pillar, forming thick clumps of rehardened wax.

Sometimes, the smell was so pungent. Trapped in the dark, poorly ventilated chapel, it was challenging to catch my breath. I remember feeling light-headed, a strange feeling that characteristically culminated in a moment-saving fainting spell.

Among the girls, I singled out one in particular with whom I built a friendly, almost sisterly relationship. Alexis was a small, slender girl of unknown identity and age. Having neither parents nor relatives willing to care for her, she had been wrapped in a white linen cloth, packed in a straw basket and entrusted to the nuns at the orphanage.

We became acquainted soon after my arrival. Following a medical visit, the nuns had approximated her age to be in the same range as mine. Alexis had the darkest eyes. Set deep beneath her smooth, olive forehead they seldom gleamed, not even during the odd moments in which she would laugh. Her gaze was retiring, almost detached, and rarely focused on anything for longer than a few seconds. And when she spoke, I noticed she had a sight lisp, which actually made her more endearing.

Frail and withdrawn, Alexis seemed to feel comfortable only in my company. During the very few and far between periods of recreation wedged between chapel, eight or nine hours of school, and late-evening sewing stints in the sweatshops, I often engaged her in a game of hop-scotch, sometimes inviting a couple of other girls to join us. It was a way to unwind from the grueling schedule and the terrible, exasperating sweatshop conditions.

Since the Quonset storage huts were not wired for electricity, we had to use kerosene lamps or flashlights to save ourselves from the blackness, leaving each girl a solitary figure in a heavily populated room. Obviously, there were no bed time stories and very limited reading in bed before "flashlights out" signaled the end of day.

In school, Alexis and I always sat side by side. I think she found a bit of the constancy and stability she craved in my friendship. Having her beside me increased my pursuit of knowledge. In addition, I felt reassured that I could always talk to her about the different lessons learned.

Meanwhile, one of the lay teachers had developed a special fondness for me, shinning some much-welcomed attention in my direction. Of course, emotionally impoverished as I was, I thrived on her doting interest. It was new. It was different. And it felt so good to realize that someone could possibly like me!

"Oh, please, can I go home with you?" I'd beg, tugging on her skirt at day's end, after she expressed her approval for my work. Patting my head, she would just smile and brush off my question with a sigh, knowing full well such luxuries were prohibited. Afterwards, I would go to the kitchen and peel dozens of potatoes until my hands felt numb and my arms ached.

From time to time, childless Americans toured Saint Elena in search of a little girl to enrich their lives. During these "shopping sprees," the nuns would line up the children, tallest first, like a display of articles at a trade fair. Since I was petite of stature notwithstanding my years, I was always mandated to the far rear of the line, and thus passed up by the couples who had made their selection long before scrutinizing the entire roster of candidates. Perhaps they felt that the best "merchandise" was presented upfront. However, the strategy comprised pushing the older children first, as they were more difficult to adopt.

"I'm here! Hey, I'm here, come get me," I would shout from the back of the line, jumping up and down and waving my arms wildly above my head while breaking ranks to gain attention.

"Be quiet, Avyrini," one of the nuns would whisper, shoving me back in line. "Just keep still."

"But I want to go to America," I would shriek, right before receiving a slap across the face, meant to suffocate my energy.

I would quiet down, giggling at the strange way in which the American men dressed, with their loose-fitting, untucked, Hawaiian motif, colorful plaid and striped shirts, white buck shoes that made their feet look humongous, and the crisscross-patterned sport coats that seemed a size too large.

Standing beside them, often dabbing their eyes with embroidered linen handkerchiefs, stood their emotional wives, in pastel, fitted-bodice dresses and bold circle skirts so tightly cinched at the waist, they appeared to risk being severed in half.

Some of the younger, more avant-garde ladies were in snug pedal pushers à la Audrey Hepburn, apparently unafraid to appear a bit audacious in a foreign country. It was such a stark contrast to the stern-faced nuns in their austere habits, and the few lay women who patronized the orphanage dressed in somber, conservative suits.

After the Americans left, I would lower my head and break into sobs, envying the lucky children who were escaping the pain and anguish of life within the bleak orphanage walls—girls who now had parents to love them, comfort them and cover their tiny faces with kisses.

Many nights, before drifting off to sleep, I would try to imagine what a hug would feel like. I would visualize a smiling American woman in a fancy pink or yellow dress, beckoning me to come toward her. Eager for love, I would oblige and when I arrived, she would bend over and cuddle me in her arms ever so tightly, squeezing the breath out of me. I imagined feeling warm and safe and above all, protected. Was this what the happy, laughing children of Ioannina had experienced every day?

The following morning, while kneeling in the chapel, I would lift my head and gaze toward the heavens. "God, please" I would pray, "I want to go to America. Please, let me be next. Please, let one of the funny-dressed Americans pick me. God, I don't care what you do with me but please, just let me go to America. I don't want to suffer anymore. No more penance—please, God, hear my prayer."

One afternoon, during a rare recreation break, I was playing tag with Alexis and a couple of other girls in the yard surrounding the orphanage. It was late spring and a teasing breeze lifted our dresses, mussed our hair and dried off the beads of sweat running down our cheeks as we ran about with extended arms, trying to tap each other on the shoulder.

Our girlish giggles harmonized with the chip and chirp vocalizations of the yellow and white wagtails circling the playing field. Once in a while, the echo of several wing flaps enhanced the sounds of spring.

Suddenly, Alexis stopped, bent her head and after several dry heaves, vomited. Choking and turning a deep crimson, she fell to the ground.

"Alexis, what's wrong?" I questioned, grabbing her arm. Silence was her response.

Several seconds later, her body started to twitch. She seemed to have lost control of her limbs as spindly arms and legs broke into fits of trembling. Alexis was convulsing, frenziedly twisting her head while frantically slamming her arms on the cement path in wide, semi-circular motions. Although her lips were quivering, no sounds came forth. Terrified, I leaned forward.

"Don't touch her, Avyrini," a nervous voice commanded. I paused and stepped back, noticing that the flesh around her elbows had been sliced open and was bleeding.

My mind wandered to Ioannina and the ghastly experience with the electrical wires on the neighbor's roof. Reliving the excruciatingly painful moment in which the current had mercilessly invaded my body, I broke into a cold sweat. For a moment, I trembled like Alexis. "But there are no wires here," I whispered to myself. "What's happening to Alexis?

"Alexis, are you OK?" I insisted, looking into her glaring eyes. Two nuns who were monitoring the children rushed over. Lifting the unconscious girl, they carried her into one of the Quonset storage huts. Following in their tracks, careful not to step on the bright red splotches of my best friend's blood, I was abruptly halted. "Stay outside, Avyrini, we will take care of Alexis."

There was no news about Alexis—no mention of her name or her medical condition—for two days. "How is Alexis?" I asked one of the nuns before retiring one evening. "Is she in the hospital? I miss her. Will she be back soon?"

"Avyrini, we are taking good care of her—just pray for Alexis."

On the fourth day, the Mother Superior of the orphanage, grim-faced and somber, summoned the girls to the backyard. In single file, we obeyed, eyes lowered and in silence. Two of the younger nuns were digging a large hole in an isolated area under a century-old oak tree. It was a warm day, but despite the mild season, I felt a cold chill run down my spine. Although it was several hours after sunrise, nature seemed still asleep. No twittering echoes and no overhead vigilant flights met our arrival.

"Gather around, girls," the Mother Superior whispered, "and be quiet." She nervously cleared her throat several times. "This is a very sad day," she continued. "Alexis has gone home to God. We gave her medicine and did all we could for her, but God called her. She had a peaceful death—just closed her eyes and left us."

I was devastated. "Alexis is dead," I whispered. "How can that be? She is just ten years old." I always knew that only old people died. That's how it was in Ioannina. But Alexis was a child!

Tears rolled down my cheeks and as much as I tried to muffle my sobs, they fought a winning battle for freedom, bursting forth in convulsive eruptions. Why didn't the nuns bring Alexis to the hospital? I questioned over and over again in my mind.

We were ordered to form a large circle around the newly excavated opening in the ground, leaving a three-foot space between the first and last girl. Two nuns stood on either side like guards.

"Bow your heads, girls," the older nun said. "Alexis will be out shortly." Obediently, I lowered my head, not even daring to imagine what was going to happen. Weighty footsteps and heavy breathing broke my thoughts. Two nuns neared the area, dragging a black, makeshift cloth sack, on the surface of which was ornately embroidered, in braided violet and white threads, a large cross.

"Θεοτόκε Παρθένε, χαίρε κεχαριτωμένη Μαρία... Mother of God and Virgin, hail, Mary," they chanted, encouraging us to join them in prayer. Realizing that Alexis' remains were in the bag, I chanted louder, fighting the nausea rising within. My heart was broken over the loss of my one and dearest friend.

The Mother Superior said a few words about Alexis and reassured us that she was at peace in heaven.

"Alexis has gone to her final resting place. She will suffer pain no longer. She has been absolved from her sins and is enjoying eternal happiness with God."

Everyone was in tears. After the final eulogy, two nuns rolled the black sack into the hollowed-out ground. Alexis reached her earthly destination with one quick, echoless thud and settled into the serenity of quietude.

"Girls," the Mother Superior said, "no one is to talk about Alexis ever again. Is that clear?" We nodded our heads in agreement.

"There will be neither mention of her name nor any discussion regarding what happened to her. We will keep this incident a secret. God called her and she obeyed. One day, God will summon each one of us and we will heed His call, one at a time. No one is exempt from death. Now we will pray for her departed soul."

Soil was pushed on top of Alexis and I watched as the black sack sank beneath the earth. "Goodbye, Alexis," I sobbed, burying my face in my hands. "I'm going to miss you.

That evening, I cried myself to sleep. I had lived through the experience of death—but God had given me a beautiful gift in her friendship.

Drifting off to sleep, I dreamt about Alexis. Dressed in blue, she was smiling. Amazingly, her deep-set eyes glowed with all the happiness that had been missing in her life until now.

I wanted to believe that God had a blessing for me also—a different blessing. And I hoped that one day, when He thought the time was right, He would give it to me. I just had to be patient! But patience was a lot to ask when the suffering was so intense.

EIGHTH EPISODE

"A wretched soul, bruis'd with adversity, We bid be quiet when we hear it cry; But were we burden'd with like weight of pain, As much, or more, we should ourselves complain."

—William Shakespeare

Crushed by a suffocating loneliness after Alexis' passing, I had a challenging time readjusting to the austere orphanage regime. Life seemed despondent, a thorny, almost pathless journey without even the briefest recess or detour.

Alexis' mislaid presence had a striking impact on my state of mind. But as a visionary with a far-sighted focus, I was reluctant to give up on my dream. Crawling into my own world, I never abandoned the hope that perhaps one day, a nice, American couple would take a liking to me and adopt me.

I continued to entertain myself with inventive apparitions, forcing them to fill the bitter hollowness within with ripples of tenderness. My vision opened with a colorfully dressed couple smiling, taking me by the hand and leading me through the big, rusted door of the Quonset storage hut while whispering endearing phrases in my ears.

"Avyrini, everything is going to be fine. We are taking you to America with us. We love you."

In my dream, I never said goodbye; I never looked back, and I never moved my gaze away from my hands, each of which were firmly entwined in the reassuring grip of my new parents.

This was how I spent my free moments when I wasn't studying hard or perfecting my sewing techniques. The daydreams were like μάννα, like manna in the desert, keeping me moving forward. It was the hand of God hailing down life-sustaining sustenance as he did for Moses and the famished Israelites.

Reality, however, was stamped on the back side of the coin. Left undernourished and hungry, together with two accomplices, I would slip under the broken and discolored wire fence that separated the orphanage from a private chicken farm. Once on forbidden territory, I would authorize the girls to catch the strutting birds, demonstrating how it should be done. I pointed to my culprit, pounced, grabbed her around the belly and set her down between my legs.

"Let's get the eggs," I said, giggling. "They will be so good to eat—a lot better than the cold potatoes, dried rice and stale bead we get every day."

"How do we do that?" one of the younger girls asked.

"Just watch," I chirped, imagining the soft smoothness of the delicious egg in my mouth.

In silence, the girls stood at attention as I carried the chicken back to the orphanage. The poor bird was terrified. She tried to flap her wings and take flight, losing her feathers. During the intermission of my sneezing cycle, I squeezed the chicken. Out popped a warm, white, oval shell, precociously, before nature dictated the chicken was ready to lay eggs.

We continued to isolate our prey, catch them and compress their round middles until the eggs were expelled. Afterwards, the unfortunate chickens were returned to the farm where, hours later, they were found dead after having hemorrhaged from severe internal injuries.

Eventually, unsatisfied with just the luxurious, fresh-egg breakfast we enjoyed from time to time, I wanted to feast on the chicken. I realized this objective was a bit more challenging to attain, but I was not one to shy away from an obstacle.

Innovative and creative by nature, I devised a method I was eager to test. Gathering a couple of slender twigs, I built a sling shot. Armed, I selected my quarry, inserted a stone into the rubber band, aimed, pulled and let loose. The elastic snapped, the stone took flight, and in an exhilarating swoosh, I had my chicken.

Once in my possession, the helpless bird was strangled, boiled and plucked smooth. Savoring the delicacy in my mind, I impatiently waited until the wrinkled carcass cooled down.

Reaching in with the cold-blooded determination of a surgeon, I dug into the belly, grabbing and pulling out whatever I could feel until I extracted all the internal organs. Upon completion of my surgical procedure, I roasted the meaty flesh and offered my accomplices a delicious, hearty meal.

The tender, succulent chicken was a memorable gourmet experience. Moist and tender, every chew brought a mouthful of delirious pleasure.

"If the nuns can dine on this scrumptious chicken," I asked aloud, "why are we given menu selections of rice, potatoes and days-old, hard bread?" Although at the time, I was incapable of finding responses to the multitudes of questions brimming over in my mind, I was old enough to conclude that something was very wrong. We were growing girls—children—nourished like cattle too old for slaughter.

Some of us were reaching puberty and offered little if any explanations, instruction or guidance. We were terrified of the strange, often mysterious changes and evolutions our bodies were going through.

Handed old sheets, were told to tear them in strips and use to take care of our monthly problems. An indisputably dysfunctional remedy, the home-made solution resulted in devastating, unsanitary consequences.

Difficult as it was, I tried to make the best of what I was given and find a bit of pleasure in other aspects of life—like my quest for knowledge.

Committed to both academic and sweatshop pursuits, in just a short time I had mastered the knots and loops of shuttle, needle and crotatting, producing beautiful lace collars, doilies and numerous other sought-after items.

However, since I had no one to applaud me and no one with whom I could share my joy, my accomplishments were of little merit. Never offering a word of praise, the nuns repeatedly evaluated me as a child of deficient value. Furthermore, emulating Aunt Cynara's punitive disciplinary philosophy, they believed that physical violence was the perfect solution for childhood waywardness and noncompliance. Consequently, unafraid to badger me with slaps and swats, I was often left hurting and in misery.

One afternoon, urgently seeking an escape, I climbed the spreading, old oak under which Alexis was buried. Hundreds of dried-up acorns rejected by the squirrels were scattered over the unmarked gravesite. Gently teasing the scaly, capped nuts with my pointed toes, I bungled their once-unique design as I shuffled over to the tree, careful not to upset the thin blades of grass beginning to cover Alexis' remains.

On the rare occasions in which I stole some moments just to be at leisure and catch up with my thoughts, I sought refuge amid the copious late-spring bloom of green foliage.

During the late autumn and winter months, the cooling temperatures turned the leaves crisp and brittle before zapping their energy, compelling them to desert the huge oak branches Therefore, I left the old tree alone for the duration of the chill and frost.

However, once the vibrant Hellas awakened, creating a synthesis of pinks, reds and apricots, and once the purple herons broke the winter stillness with their early-morning song, I befriended the big oak. In return, it gave me an opportunity to be alone with my thoughts, offering me a sanctuary away from public view.

Once snuggled securely between its massive arms, I found comfort in the feeling of security the old tree presented. In addition, I discovered a measure of solace in my irresponsible thought that I could actually become invisible to the nuns and girls in the orphanage.

Wheedling my imagination to suppose for a few fleeting moments that I would not have to return to life within the seedy walls of the Quonset storage hut, I fantasized about a world in which everyone at Saint Elena would just forget about Avyrini. Maybe God would just lift her up and carry her far away, to another life. I knew He could do it if He wanted. After all, He was invincible—"παντοδύναμοσ," the nuns would say, gazing toward the heavens—"God is omnipotent!"

In reality, I was swaddling myself in childish desires, overindulging almost daily in wishful thinking. But at dusk, when heads were counted and mine was discovered missing, one of the nuns marched directly to the tree. Her long, black robe swelled in the breeze, giving her a comical appearance that clashed with the visible signs of her anger.

Standing on the tips of her toes, she reached up and tried to grab me by the legs. Repeatedly falling short of her target, she changed her strategy. Jumping, she encircled my ankle with both hands, tugging with all her might until I was forced to relinquish my grasp. Letting go of the branch, I tumbled down.

"Avyrini," the nun growled, preparing her open hand to slam my face, "what are you dong out here all alone in the darkness? Why aren't you inside with the other children?"

Far too irritated to wait for a response, she continued, "You missed dinner and you missed sweatshop. We'll have to punish you severely for this misdeed. You know you have been defiant, and you know what happens to girls who are bad."

Pulling me by the ear, she dragged me inside. The other girls were preparing for the evening's rest, speaking softly among themselves, sharing the day's events.

"May I have you attention, girls," the nun said, clapping her hands to hush the room. The somber tone of her voice betrayed her annoyance.

"Please be silent a moment." After recounting my evil deed and successfully humiliating me with her offensive parlance, she delivered a slap to my right cheek in full audience view.

Neither flinching nor demonstrating alarm, I turned the other cheek, quietly reciting the words from the Sermon on the Mount, which the nuns were so fond of quoting: "But I say to you not to resist the evildoer; on the contrary, if someone strike thee on the right cheek, turn to him the other."

Accepting my Christian invitation, the disciplinary religious woman obliged, backhanding me across the other cheek. It stung. Fighting both the swell of tears and the urge to rub my cold palm across my burning face in her presence, I lowered my head.

"I'm not finished with you," she hissed. "Girls, Avyrini will not be sleeping here for a while. We all know what happens to naughty children. Avyrini misbehaved and must be held accountable."

Turning on her heels, she grabbed me by the arm. "Come along with me," she said, propelling me toward the exit.

We walked over to a rusted door. The nun pulled it open, and with a violent thrust, shoved me into a tiny, gloomy area.

"You have three days to think about the awful thing you did," she shouted, slamming the door. "You have seventy-two hours to repent. Maybe this will teach you to be obedient."

Locked in the dark, humid closet, I was denied nourishment and water for several days. The cubicle was severely restricted, and at twelve years of age, I was beginning to near adult height. Consequently, my legs suffered agonizing cramps from the crouched position I was forced to assume and maintain. Whenever I attempted to stretch, I felt a mounting stiffness in the curve of my back. Within a few short hours, I was in unbearable pain.

Scared, hungry and thirsty, I was free to catch neither a breath of fresh air nor a glint of daylight. Worst of all, I was obliged to satisfy my needs using a tiny pail with neither cover nor deodorizer. The other option was to soil myself. Either way, I had to remain in the enclosure for the duration of my closet sentence.

Although it was pitch black, strange sounds confirmed I was not alone. It was common knowledge that predatory spiders were busy spinning webs as other unidentifiable insects crawled along the mud floor and up the walls. I had seen them many times before but had always distanced myself. Now I was forced to share my living quarters and accept these creepy insects as roommates.

Sleepless and too exasperated to even cry, I questioned the Golden Rule that the nuns preached to us daily: "Therefore all that you wish men to do to you, even so do you also to them; for this is the Law and the Prophets."

I wondered if they really thought it was just and in keeping with the Lord's wishes to enclose vulnerable children in a dismal cell without the basic necessities of life. Could they possible believe this type of tortuous behavior would be divinely sanctioned?

In the silence of my solitary confinement, I whispered barely loud enough for just God and me to hear: "These holy women, these self-proclaimed brides of Christ hiding behind the holiness their wimples proclaimed, certainly don't practice what they preach."

The echo of heavy footsteps approaching and retreating with the same rapid pace interrupted my reflection, sending me on a hiatus of bogus hopes and mammoth disappointments. My pulse accelerated and for one brief instant, I actually believed they would check in on me, maybe bring me a glass of water or a piece of stale bread, perhaps even let me stretch my legs or take a restroom break. I was fantasizing again—never once did they open the door to see if I was still breathing, or having problems adjusting to the brutal conditions to which I was subjected.

At the conclusion of the seventy-two hour sentence, the door was dragged open. It screeched on its rusted hinges like a mouse caught in a trap. I was ordered to step out.

"Avyrini," the religious woman shrieked, slapping me across the face, "what a disgusting mess you made in there. The stench is absolutely sickening!" I had no idea how I could have done things differently, so as not to warrant her ire and the physical violence that expressed it.

Accustomed to total darkness, I blinked several times and then shut my eyes, hoping to eliminate the shock of the initial glare.

"Stop that,' the nun shouted, shaking me. "Keep your eyes open or you'll go back in for another three days. Is that what you want?"

I shook my head in response. "What did I do that was so awful?" I mistakenly inquired. "Why did I get such a terrible punishment?"

"Avyrini," she said, pausing to take a deep breath, "we told you over and over, but you just don't seem to understand. God does not love you! Why? Because you were born out of wedlock! You have been beaten and punished and you will continue to be chastised because you are a wicked child. This is why you will always be destined to suffer. It is your lot in life—your penance. You must make amends for your mother's grave sin. She enjoyed immoral pleasures without any concern or responsibility. Avyrini, your mother offended God! Do you know how serious it is to offend God? She did not marry your father and for this misdeed, you have to pay the consequences. You are illegitimate. You are not like other children who have mothers and fathers to love and care for them. This is why you are here in the orphanage. Nobody wants you, Avyrini. People don't love or respect children like you—you just don't deserve it. You are the result of sin. And God will continue to punish you."

I listened, shocked, unable to bear the crushing pain within. It felt as if I had been trampled on by a heard of irrepressible animals. The harder I struggled to push them away, the quicker and more strongly they returned.

My heart thumped. I couldn't catch my breath. A huge knot formed in the rear of my throat. I coughed repeatedly, trying to dislodge the annoying object. It felt as if the fragments of severed tonsils were still trapped in my throat, gagging me. It didn't work. I swallowed long and hard, repeatedly, to force the knot down—but it returned bigger and more durable.

A current of hot air flushed through my cheeks. Suddenly, I felt a spray of water trickle down my forehead and neck. An insufferable heaviness pressed down on my chest, suffocating my breath. It was all-encompassing. I was powerless against the warfare these overpowering demons were waging.

But if God made me, I questioned in my mind, why doesn't He love me like He loves the other children? And if He doesn't care about me, will He listen when I pray? Can I still ask Him for help? I asked question after question, always fearful of the answers.

A strong feeling of nausea swelled in the pit of my stomach. "God, please help me," I whispered. "Help me, God!"

The room spun around. The floor trembled. Colors blurred. Faces took on a distorted, almost scary look. Words became incomprehensible sounds. I wanted to run but my legs felt as if they were set in cement. Right before I hit the floor, unconscious, I screamed in silence, God even if you hate me, make this agony go away.

God answered my prayer by separating me from my senses in a moment of excruciating duress. My thoughts were quieted and my feelings numbed. When I came to, the nuns were standing over me, fanning my face. "Avyrini," one said, "you passed out. Here, drink this glass of milk." I was given a cup of lukewarm milk into which had been drowned the usual crust of stale bead.

There was never any medical intervention; therefore, I was not visited by a physician. The religious ladies were "doctors" and "nurses" attending to the ills that inflicted the majority of girls. Only the "adoptable" children received any medical care since they put currency into the hands of the orphanage officials.

The cruel words I heard that day never left my consciousness. Instead, they rolled around, gathering momentum until they became a part of my every waking moment, tormenting me with distressing thoughts. There was neither respite nor refuge. They would neither stop nor go away.

I continued studying and sewing and although I was progressing admirably, I just couldn't feel proud of my accomplishments, knowing that God hated me and was angry at me for being an illegitimate child.

The despondent feelings swelled and intensified. Unable to deal with the incessant agony, I longed for a bit of inner peace. I just wanted the painful thoughts and feelings to disappear. I longed to be happy and I yearned to leave the orphanage. However, it was not yet in God's plan.

My day-to-day chores were performed almost mechanically. Often, I daydreamed about Alexis, envying her death and special new life in a peaceful world.

"Alexis," I said one morning while filling the bucket with water before mopping the floor, "I want to be where you are. I want to be with you and God."

The girls were responsible for washing the chapel floor. We were directed to walk down to the river, fill three-quarters of the bucket with water and add several cupfuls of Clorox. The bleach would get rid of the nasty stains. I hated the smell of Clorox, and it always burned my nose and throat, but I knew I had to obey or face the wrath of the religious women.

"Be careful," a nun cautioned. "Don't get it in your mouth or eyes—it's poison."

Returning to the Quonset storage hut, I placed the pail on the ground and walked over to the dispensary to get the Clorox. Anticipating my inability to reach the detergent cabinet, I dragged over a two-step stool.

The harsh chemicals and toxic cleaning products were placed at a height to prohibit the small children from gaining easy access to the potentially harmful substances.

Still traumatized by my imprisonment in the closet and the nun's psychologically injurious tirade, I lost the will and ability to love myself. It was more than evident that I was of no value—a child unworthy of another person's love and affections. Even God disliked me.

At twelve years old, I questioned why I was alive. The days blurred into a mass of time—minutes, hours and weeks of interior darkness. I lay in bed, writhing in destructive thoughts, scared of my own feelings. I shivered even in the middle of summer, when the sun was at its brightest, never once basking in the warmth it offered, asking nothing in return.

My appearance and bearing changed. My shoulders hunched in deep mourning for lost expectations. Wicked as I was, how could I possible expect any happiness from life? The glow in my eyes dimmed. My face no longer played gracious hostess to a child's sweet smile.

"God hates you, Avyrini" churned in my thoughts, preying on my serenity like a famished animal fighting for survival. Broken in spirit, I realized that without the help and solidarity of a loving God, life was hopeless. I lifted the Clorox bottle to my lips and without even a prayer, drank a big swig of the putrid liquid, clumsily spilling it down the front of my dress.

My throat and esophagus burned. It seemed as if I had satiated my hunger with a repast of fire. The room spun. My stomach flipped, flushing out all the unwanted contents along with my lunch.

Obliged to eliminate all the evidence of my criminal attempt or face another tortuous round of punishment, I scrubbed the area clean, removing all traces of my sin. In tears, I realized that death was not in God's plan for me—at least not at that precise moment in time.

According to Billy Graham, "The angels minister to God's servants in time of hardship and danger." Saved both from destroying my life and getting caught, I drifted off to sleep with the name of God settled snuggly on my lips.

NINTH EPISODE

"I've learned that no matter what happens, or how bad it seems today, life does go on, and it will be better tomorrow."

—Maya Angelou

"Gather your belongings, girls," the somber-faced nun ordered, "and be ready to leave in ten minutes. Hurry and don't waste time with idle chatter."

"Leave?" I repeated. "where are we going?" Could God have answered my prayers? Was I going to America with a funny-dressed mom and dad?

Although the answers would soon arrive, the response was certainly not what I had hoped or prayed for.

"No talking. Just pack up and form a line in front of the door," she answered rudely. I dropped to my knees, reached under my bed and pulled out the few articles of clothing I counted as my possessions. Blowing off the dust, I reached under once again, sweeping my hand up and down, searching for my diary. When my fingers hit against its cover, I tugged, dragging the notebook across the mud floor until it was in front of me.

One more trip under brought out the scratched and worn suitcase Aunt Cynara had packed a few years earlier when I'd left Ioannina. Clicking open the bag, I slipped in my few garments, a couple pairs of scuffed shoes and the dusty diary.

"You'll have breakfast first," the nun announced once we were standing in line, "then you'll be leaving the orphanage."

"It's true," I whispered to the girl standing beside me. "We're going to America."

"Be quite, Avyrini," the religious woman blurted. "And pay attention to what I am saying. There are too many children here. We are overcrowded and can no longer accommodate you. You will be going to another place."

I was dazzled by the words "leaving the orphanage," though not fully capable of understanding exactly what was happening. In silence, I consumed my last glass of warm milk and stale bread, powerless to rein in my excitement. Children talked, children giggled, children questioned: Where were these lucky girls with their bags packed going?

When the time of departure arrived, some of the girls lowered their heads to hide their tears. Was it sadness over our leaving the orphanage or the envy associated with the idea that perhaps we were destined for a better life? Unable to make the distinction, I let the thought evaporate.

Afterwards, we were escorted outside, where several buses were waiting to take us on our journey. Usually parsimonious with their displays of affection, the nuns smiled and gave each girl a quick, clumsy hug.

"Goodbye Avyrini," they whispered almost in chorus as I passed through their receiving line. At one point, a hand brushed against mine. Quickly, it was withdrawn as if any nonpunitive contact was a grave sin. This behavioral duplicity always confused me. I questioned why the nuns didn't seem to suffer any pangs of conscience when they touched us inappropriately for their own selfish motives, a practice that occurred more than sporadically.

The driver, a kind-looking gentleman with overscaled glasses and a dark hat, rescued me from the awkward moment, helping me up the steps. Last to come onboard was one of the lay teachers, whose mission it was to chaperone us on the ride. A middle-aged woman with grey hair who apparently shunned cosmetics, she was rather heavy-set. Blatantly inelegant, she was dressed in black oxfords and a dowdy, ill-fitting, print dress that enhanced her matronly silhouette. However, knowledgeable and adept at sharing fascinating facts in an attention-captivating manner, I always looked forward to her lectures in class.

When everyone was safely on the bus, the driver slid behind the wheel, backed up and with a chortle, reversed the vehicle and moved away. Gazing out the window, I watched the three nuns slowly diminish in size. Their flowing habits seemed like dark clouds passing along the horizon. It was a goodbye without tears, a farewell powerful enough to foster my hopes for a better life—at least in that precise moment.

My heart felt surprisingly light once Saint Elena faded from view and took its place in my memory. Breathing a sigh of relief, I indulged in a brief instant of serenity before an all-too-impending anxiety of the unknown took precedence.

Requiring neither an accompanying event nor the certainty that my gut feeling was authentic, my mood became less optimistic. Butterflies danced in my stomach—not Ravel's exhilarating Boléro, but an ungainly boogie of indiscernible rhythm. Although I was happy to banish the orphanage to my yesterday, a suddenly unwelcome gut feeling told me I was not en route to America with a mom and dad.

The bus ride was short and bumpy and finally, the driver stopped short in front of the train station. There were so many people outside, both adults and children—people laughing, people crying, people kissing and hugging. Some were speaking; others were silent. A few looked sad and many were nervously lighting cigarettes, dropping the burnt matchsticks on the ground. Imagining the nose-tickling scent of sulfur, I sneezed even before the little matchstick heads ignited.

But the children looked so happy, skipping and hopping about on one leg as youngsters often like to do. One little boy, impeccably dressed in a navy short-pants suit, blue, knee-high socks, black leather oxfords, a white shirt and a red-striped, clip-on tie was running in circles around a smiling woman who most probably was his mother. His frenetic antics caused him to drop his navy cap several times. Gracefully, his mother bent over, retrieved it, dusted it over with her gloved hand and set it back on his dark brown curls, each time affectionately planting a quick peck on his flushed cheek.

I had never before seen a train so close up, and its huge proportions caught my attention. I turned my head in all directions to get a better view. Pulled by the arm, I followed the teacher, trying to keep pace with her hurried stride.

We climbed up a few steps as the conductor tipped his hat in greeting, cautioning us to be careful. Once onboard the train, we were led down a long, narrow corridor until we came to an area filled with seats. Passengers of various sizes and body shapes were settling themselves. Several accompanied by children were trying to coax the little ones into unwinding by quieting their chatter. As we made our way to the seats, an attendant in a black cap gestured toward a vacant row. I noticed that one place was unavailable.

A dour woman rose from the one occupied seat. Her dark brown hair was heavily laced with silver strands. Cut short, it was tightly curled and modestly contained under a flat, semi-veiled, black pillbox hat. Grabbing my hand, the teacher dragged me in front of her feet, positioning me directly in the woman's view.

Her slim red lips broadened into an indistinct smile that faded with the same speed with which it appeared. She wore a drab, green, hourglass blazer with the vaguest hint of a peplum and a mid-calf, pencil-thin, matching skirt. It was an austere suit, an ensemble that gave her a pronounced aura of inclemency. On her left lapel, a brooch designed with a configuration of acorns and reddish-brown autumn leaves accented the outfit.

The train ride seemed endless. We were sandwiched in like an overpopulated can of sardines. With chain smokers having nothing to focus on but lighting one cigarette after another, the air was foul and clouded, making it impossible to clearly distinguish my own feet.

About an hour into the trip, the stern-looking lady opened her handbag, retrieved a small, gold-framed mirror, pulled out a matching lipstick tube and, squinting, perhaps to get a better view, re-outlined her lips, filling in the narrow space with the deep crimson color. This signaled we were nearing our destination.

Satisfied with her appearance, she dropped her lipstick back into her handbag along with the mirror, ceasing the moment I turned toward her.

Where are we?" I asked, eager to unravel the riddle in my mind.

"We are in Θεσσαλονίκη—Saloniki," she responded.

"Why are we in Saloniki?" I persisted, hungry for more answers. "What are we doing here?"

"Avyrini, you are going to live in a monastery in the mountains," she said, visibly irritated by my round of questioning. Surprised by her response, I didn't know how to react. Was this a God-sent reprieve from Saint Elena? Would life be better here in the mountains?

A quick, jolting stop cut short my thoughts. Stepping off the train, I was welcomed by a teasing breeze that wrecked havoc with my hair. Capriciously, it brought all the aromas of the city with it. The scent was vaguely fresh, probably from the mountains. However, its mischievous nature left me giggling while I watched the somber lady slam her hand on her head to save her hat from flying off. The threat of her possibly losing her regimental look thrilled me.

A car was waiting for us just several yards from the station. Puffing on a cigarette, the driver was nervously tapping his foot. A dark, wrinkled suit that looked as if it had been borrowed from a gentleman at least two sizes larger spoke of an inelegant personality. Under the early morning sun, his bald pate gleamed like a full moon recklessly adrift in a cloudless sky. In the eyes of a twelve-year-old, he had an indisputably comical appearance.

Politely, he bowed to acknowledge our presence, opened the door and gestured for us to enter. His silver-streaked moustache curled at the ends when he smiled. Entering, I slid along the smooth leather seat to the opposite end of the car, clearing the path for the lady. As soon as she was settled in, he closed the door, walked to the driver's seat and assumed command of the vehicle.

The drive up the mountain path to the orphanage took about twenty-five minutes. Despite the open windows and the strong wind, the odor of tobacco persisted. A familiar scent in post-war Greece, it never ceased to disturb me.

Although hungry, thirsty and tired, I refused any happy expectations. There were just so many unanswered questions and a deep, stomach-wrenching fear of the bleak unknown into which I was thrown.

When the driver shut off the ignition, I realized that we had arrived. Excited about my new home, I turned my head back and forth in sweeping, 180-degree waves, eager to take it all in.

The monastery was quaint and demonstrated no resemblance to the Quonset storage huts at Saint Elena. The soft chirping of birds produced an almost welcoming aura. The surrounding verdant grounds were a strong contrast to the brown, seared lawn and unkempt garden under the nuns' patronage in Ioannina.

The minute we arrived, an elderly, rail-thin man appeared in the doorway. It almost seemed as if he had been standing guard in anticipation. Dressed in a long, brown, hooded robe fastened at the waist with an off-colored, white, triple-knotted cord, his bare feet were pressed into well-worn, grazed leather sandals in a color that was in perfect harmony with his garment. He had glowing eyes set deep within arches of bold wrinkles and a smile somewhat concealed behind an unruly mass of facial hair.

Bowing, he extended his right hand to the lady. I noticed how gnarled and knobby his fingers were. Heads bent, they exchanged several whispered words before she turned on her heels. Without eye contact or a greeting, she walked over to the car, got in and was whisked away.

Left in a strange place with a group of monks and a few other girls, I was almost afraid to think or form any opinion about my new circumstances. However, although apprehensive about the unknown, I felt an aura of stillness when in the company of these introspective individuals. It was a conspicuous contrast to the past, where the most atrocious memories of my life had been designed.

Inviting us into the monastery, the pious gentlemen were frugal with their soft-spoken words, unlike their female counterparts at Saint Elena. Prayer and silent meditation seemed to epitomize their lifestyle.

A frail, hunchbacked monk of small stature, with a glint in his sky-blue eyes, escorted us to our living quarters. Pointing a curved index finger, he indicated the bed in which I would rest my weary bones after a long study-work day. Leaning over to touch the beddings, I noticed the softness. I sat down on the edge of the bed. The suppleness was a major contrast to the abrasive, irritating, straw bedding in the orphanage. Surprisingly, my new resting place had a narrow, wool-filled mattress. Curious, I was eager to have the day end so I could give it a try.

As I settled my belongings, I noticed that the monks were parading up and down the hall, reading from old books. Their shuffling footsteps echoed in the quiet. From time to time a cough, a sigh or a slight grunt would harmonize with the dragging of leather soles across the marble floor.

Kind and gentle, they ate sparingly, each consuming the rations of a toddler. My main staples were no longer cold potatoes, dried, boiled rice that never ceased to solicit a gag reflex, and lukewarm milk with a slab of stale bread. Instead, I was able to nourish myself with Κοτόπουλο με πιλάφι, chicken with rice, Σπουπιές με σπανάκι, cuttlefish with spinach, Φασόλια σαλάτα, an off-season, Lenten bean salad, and some home-grown garden vegetables. In addition, the tiny chunk of Χωριάτικο ψωμί—Farmer's bread—that I got was fresh-baked daily. Once a week, usually on Fridays, we received a narrow piece of φέτα—Feta cheese. This palate-pleasing mountain specialty was produced from a blend of cow's and goat's milk, aged until the taste and texture were perfect.

The culinary variations were unlike what I had experienced in the arc of my short lifetime, and I began to look forward to and enjoy midday and evening meals. It was a new experience and I wondered why I'd had to wait so long to experience a pleasure at the table. Of course, there was the pancake breakfast Aunt Cynara had prepared—but that feast had carried the memory of unbearable anguish.

With a pacified if not full stomach, I retired in the evenings. Although my bed was comfortable in comparison to what I had been obliged to sprawl on in the past, the monks' almost regimental pacing, in addition to the scuffling echoes of their uneasy way of life, often left me wakeful.

Sometimes, the unexpected break of the monastery's usual stillness unsettled me. I couldn't understand why these shy, reclusive, holy men walked incessantly either with their heads buried in books or with indecipherable words slipping from their lips. And in the early hours of the morning, when even the drop of a feather bred an echo, it was downright eerie.

However, despite the peculiar nighttime occurrences, the monks were wonderful mentors. Neither elevating their voices nor resorting to abusive physical violence as disciplinary measures, they proved to be interesting and effective teachers in school.

One afternoon, at the conclusion of my last class, when the standard daily greeting—"Ο Θεός να σε ευλογεί," "God bless you"—was pronounced, the pious man cleared his throat.

"Girls," he began in a raspy voice, "today, after school, you will be going on a little trip. Prepare yourselves to leave the monastery for a few hours."

"Where are we going?" I asked, fascinated by the anticipation of a change in our itinerary.

"You will be going down into the city to begin a work-study program at a hospital in Thessaloniki, where you will be enrolled in the nursing course."

Unable to fully comprehend the significance of this new twist in my life, I considered it another adventure. Gathering my books, I headed back to my sleeping quarters to prepare myself for the trip to the hospital.

Situated on a mountain hill, the monastery was accessible by auto, donkey or the basket vehicle. In view of the fact that the monks did not have a car and given that transportation on the derrière of a donkey took several hours, another means of transportation had to be utilized.

Creative in a resourceful way, the pious men had resolved the commute dilemma by weaving a large, straw basket, roomy enough to accommodate three thirteen-year-old girls. Each side had been perforated, resulting in two circular holes, large enough to insert and knot a tightly braided, thick cord.

The monks invited three girls at a time to climb into the basket. Once we were seated with our knees pulled up to our chins and our arms snugly entwined around our legs, we were slowly lowered down the mountain side.

Too young to imagine any precarious scenarios possibly involving the cord snapping or the basket swaying and tipping over, we giggled, enjoying the amusement-park-like thrill. When we reached the ground, we waited while the basket was lifted and the next round of passengers landed. As soon as everyone arrived, we headed to the hospital. The pious men had given explicit instructions; consequently, we were able to reach the hospital with little difficulty.

Once at the hospital, I was immediately introduced to a stern, antiseptic woman of portly proportions, dressed in stark white from head to toes.

"Avyrini, you are going to be a nurse," she said, meeting my glance with a pair of ice blue eyes. "You will have study time and lectures, and you will be taking care of the sick."

After the brief introduction, I was assigned specific chores, which immediately left me unmotivated to pursue a nursing career. However, I had no choice but to abide by the rules.

Following classes at the monastery, the hours of my late afternoons and early evenings were filled with administering bed pans, changing soiled sheets, flipping immobile patients to prevent or alleviate the pain of irritating bedsores, and cleaning the rooms. It was exhausting, but determined to learn and move on, I worked and studied diligently.

Several months later, I was summoned by the sterile-looking head nurse with the soul-piercing glance.

"Avyrini," she snapped, never switching her gaze from mine. "You are being transferred to the maternity ward."

Not quite sure if this was a good or a larger evil, I took the news unemotionally, nodding my head to confirm that I had understood her order. Never one to shy away from a challenge even as a child, I inhaled a deep breath and walked over to maternity, questioning if in effect, this would be a lamentable or a welcomed change.

Never did I imagine just how traumatic this new experience would be. But demonstrating neither fear nor disagreement, I presented myself in the maternity ward, ready to carry out any instructions given. Immediately, I was sent to the delivery room.

"Avyrini," the attending nurse whispered, pointing to a woman in obvious discomfort, "you will help prepare this girl for the birthing process. Eventually, the physician and nuns will take over." Again I nodded my consent, even if in lieu of being asked, I was put in front of an already-made decision.

The pregnant girl, in her early twenties, confirmed with her scowl that she was in agony, and reasonably scared by what was happening to her. I learned that this was her first child; therefore, like me, she did not have the vaguest idea what to expect. Apprehensive in these unusual surroundings, and totally ignorant of the facts of life, I was unprepared to be a witness to the birth of a baby.

"Her contractions are coming every twenty minutes," said the nurse, who was also a nun, shattering my thoughts. "I don't think it will be too much longer." Observing the religious woman take command swished me back to my horrendous tonsillectomy at Saint Elena. Quivering despite the elevated room temperature, I prayed that the woman giving birth would not have to endure the atrocious torture I did.

The nun lifted the young girl's hospital gown and anchored each foot in an elevated stirrup. A swelling scream rang through the room and kept increasing in volume and frequency. My stomach tightened. My legs froze. The room seemed to have been hit by a monumental tidal wave.

Violet-faced and sobbing, the mother-to-be waved her arms in shaking fits, frantically twisting her head from side to side. I could see she was in misery. However, roused to curiosity, I did not understand why her gown was pulled practically over her head, exposing her private parts.

Inquisitiveness was like a magnet, even if I struggled to disengage it. The more I tried to pull away, the stronger grew my attraction to find out what was going to occur next.

"Stop that howling," the nun bellowed. Her narrow, almost non-existent lips withdrew from her protruding front teeth, giving her the ferocious look of a rabid dog.

"You had fun, didn't you," she snarled, intending to overpower the girl's shouts. "You enjoyed yourself, no? Well now you are going to pay for it!"

Even before finishing the sentence, she slammed the back of her hand across the flushed cheek of the young mother-to-be.

"Be quiet. Stop fussing like a child and let's get this over with—you are not the only one giving birth today."

My eyes traveled from the poor girl's face to her swollen stomach. Certain the doctor would slice through her to take out the baby, I was totally unprepared to learn differently.

"I see the head—I see the baby's head," one of the attending nurses screeched.

"Call the doctor. Hurry, I think she's ready," the nun replied.

Several minutes later, a tall, stocky, middle-aged man stepped into the room. His bushy, graying eyebrows were partially hidden behind round, tortoiseshell glasses, far too small for his rather full face.

"How far is she dilated?" he asked.

"She's ready," the nurse responded. Frozen in my own body, I watched in shock as the infant's head gradually emerged from the woman.

"Push," the doctor ordered. "We're almost there."

Suddenly, the baby seemed to glide out, right into the doctor's hands.

"It's a boy," he said, holding up the tiny, new creature seconds before giving him a slight tap on the back, awakening his screams.

Disturbed neither by the blistering cries of mother and son nor the bloody mess, I was awed by the beautiful miracle of life I had just witnessed. Unable to control my own tears, I buried my face in my hands and cried. Still a child, I had been a spectator at the birth of a baby. The exhilaration kept my pulse racing throughout the day. I had seen the beginning of life.

Shortly thereafter, I received a new assignment. No longer stationed in the maternity ward, I was transferred to the morgue in the lower level of the hospital. My new job as a diener entailed cleaning the corpses and administering enemas. Besides the sheer morbidity of spending time in a room populated by lifeless people, the stench of decaying flesh together with stagnant waste materials was beyond nauseating. Even the pungent aroma of the formaldehyde and ethanol embalming concoction did little to camouflage the smell.

Halting my own breathing to have a respite from the dry heaves, I felt light-headed and woozy on my feet. Holding on to the gurney to catch my fall, I noticed that the corpse was identified by a toe tag fastened to his big toe with a piece of twine.

Gathering my wits, I started sponging the face of this new arrival. Suddenly, his arm jerked, hitting me in the stomach. "He's alive! He's alive!" I shouted, running hysterically from the morgue. "His arm moved—he's not dead!"

Presenting the princess of Greece (now the queen of Spain) with a skirt I made for her.

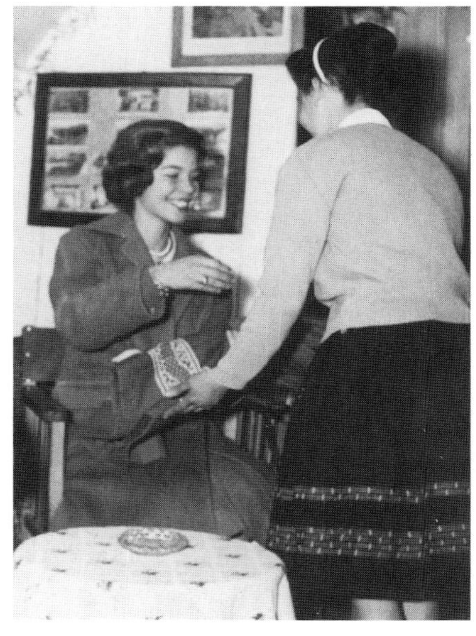

The princess' brother Constantinos, giving a military salute.

Me as a young girl in Greece.

In my wedding dress.

THE UNITED STATES OF AMERICA

No. 11437299

CERTIFICATE OF NATURALIZATION

Petition No. 02760 · ORIGINAL · Alien Registration No. A18 972 387

Personal description of holder as of date of naturalization: Date of birth May 27, 1947 ; sex Female ; complexion Dark ; color of eyes Brown ; color of hair Black ; height 5 feet 3 inches; weight 125 pounds; visible distinctive marks None

Marital status Married ; Country of former nationality Greece

I certify that the description above given is true, and that the photograph affixed hereto is a likeness of me.

Angela Rosemary Mattox
(Complete and true signature of holder)

United States of America
Southern District of Illinois } ss:

Be it known, that at a term of the United States District Court of the Southern District of Illinois held pursuant to law at East St. Louis, Illinois on June 1, 1983 the Court having found that Angela Rosemary Mattox then residing at 34 St. Gregory, Cahokia, Illinois 62240 intends to reside permanently in the United States (when so required by the Naturalization Laws of the United States), had in all other respects complied with the applicable provisions of such naturalization laws, and was entitled to be admitted to citizenship, thereupon ordered that such person be and (s)he was admitted as a citizen of the United States of America.

In testimony whereof the seal of the court is hereunto affixed this 1st day of June in the year of our Lord nineteen hundred and Eighty-three

Seal

A. MARVIN HELART
Clerk of the U. S. District Court.
By [signature] Deputy Clerk.

IT IS PUNISHABLE BY U. S. LAW TO COPY, PRINT OR PHOTOGRAPH THIS CERTIFICATE.

DEPARTMENT OF JUSTICE

My certificate of naturalization, obtained on June 1, 1983.

This photo was taken during the seventeen years I suffered with bulimia. I was close to death, weighing only 69 pounds.

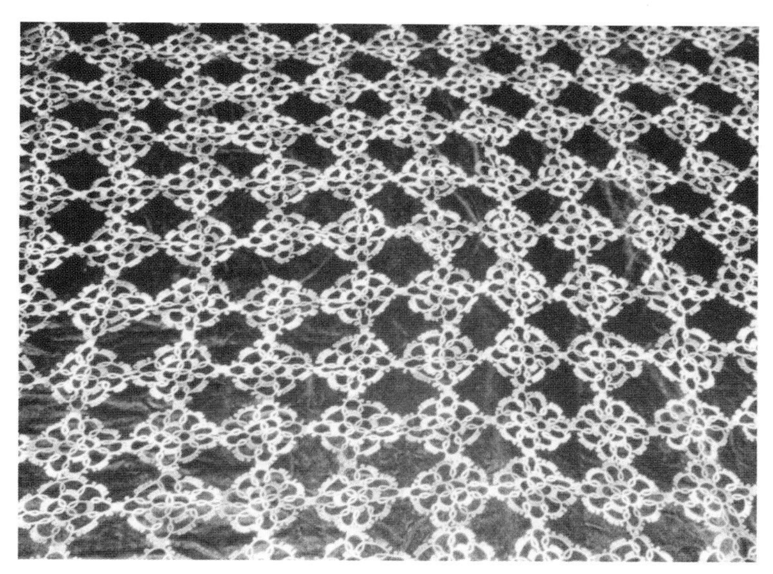

Tatting bedspread—twelve months of work.

Appliqué.

The appliqué seen here on denim once
addorned a pair of jeans.

Appliqué animals.

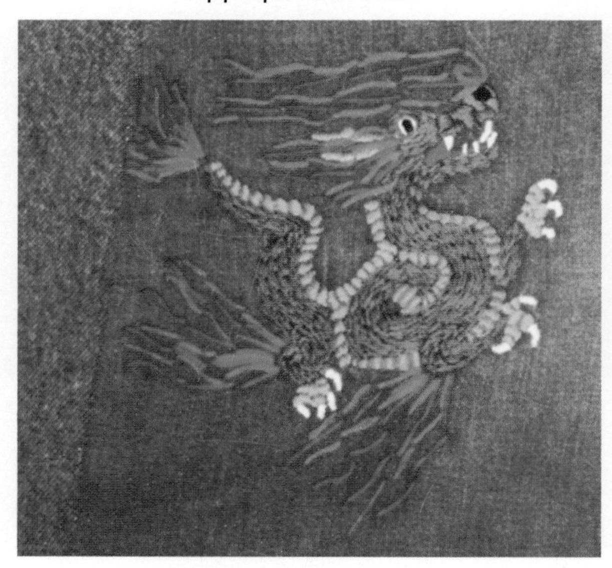

Appliqué dove and fish.

A cross-stitched tablecloth.

Appliqué dragon.

Where I make the magic happen.

There's no business like Sno-Bizness.

My rowdy panic brought the pathologist running.

"Calm down, Avyrini," he said, chuckling. "This happens sometimes to dead people. During rigor mortis, muscles contract—that's all it is. The man has passed on." He took me by the arm and brought me over to the corpse.

"See?" he said, placing my hand on his jugular. "He has no pulse."

Although I was convinced the pathologist was telling the truth, I suffered quite a few restless, wide-eyed nights, alternating with harrowing nightmares in which I envisioned myself awakening in a grave, alive and unable to get out of a sealed, brass coffin.

The following afternoon, once the corpse was cleansed and ready for the pathologist, I was expected to remain while he dissected the body, exposing all the organs, bones, muscles and tendons.

Thankfully, my stay in Saloniki was of short duration. Although the pious men were gracious souls, I detested working in the hospital. It was an awful ordeal that clearly confirmed that nursing was not my calling.

Summoned by the monks one evening after dinner, we were again instructed to pack our belongings and be ready to depart in the morning once prayers were said and breakfast consumed.

Excited by the prospect of yet another journey, I questioned if I dared hope God was answering my prayer. "Am I finally going to America?" I whispered.

The thrill of the new and unknown, away from the distressing and despondent certainties of my life, together with the wide gamut of uncensored suppositions a thirteen-year-old imagination could devise, left me sleepless, though eager to catch the radiance of the next sunrise. I folded my arms across my breast, exchanged a few words with God, and awaited daybreak.

TENTH EPISODE

"I have come to realize more and more that the greatest disease and the greatest suffering is to be unwanted, unloved, uncared for, to be shunned by everybody, to be just nobody [to no one]."

—Mother Teresa

It was 1960—twenty years after the start of the Ελληνοϊταλικός Πόλεμος Ellēnoïtalikós Pólemos, the Greco-Italian War, when an attempt to thwart the Italian invasion resulted in the successful ousting of Mussolini's Fascist regime from Greek territory.

It was also fifteen years after the end of World War II. However, despite the passage of time, disfiguring battle scars, most of which were striking, structural wounds, were still very much a part of Greek life.

At almost fourteen years of age, I was sufficiently mature to identify and understand the ravages of this world conflict. I was also aware of the insecurity emanated from a country engaged in a long-term struggle to regain a certain political, economic and social serenity as well as well-being.

Uncertainty was not exclusively a national issue. Instead, its far-reaching tentacles groped around my life, settling me once again on tremulous ground. Leaving the familiar for the unfamiliar, I was on the road toward my next adventure, accompanied by several other nomadic, seemingly misplaced young teens without roots.

With neither the aura of a venturesome expedition nor the pulse-racing romance of an exotic destination, I boarded the train for yet another unknown. It was comparable to being part of the American Orphan Train Movement, except I was not en route to a host family, as were the hundreds of thousands of abandoned children who had been accepted for adoption.

The quick, chugging locomotion seemed to tousle my thoughts.

Where was I going this time? Would I be happy? Would hardships and pain be no longer a part of my days?

The train passed through a couple of foreboding underpasses. Before the swishing was quieted and the vehicle came to a thundering halt, it sliced through large expanses of uncultivated land reflecting the barren aspect of a dormant nature. Anticipating the uncomfortable volume of the by-now-familiar air horn blast, I pressed my palms across my ears to stifle the uproar.

Jostled one last time by an abrupt movement, I gazed out the window, curious to learn my destination. A huge, off-white, octagonal sign with chipped, rusted edges and discolored, black lettering announced that I was at Καβάλα Station.

Kavala was a seaport town in northern Greece, situated across from the Island of Thasos. Not too distant from Turkey, its unique, old houses, Byzantine fortress and quaint hotels made it quite a striking contrast from the rural Ioannina where I had spent the earlier years of my life.

It felt good to be on my feet and out in the open air after being enclosed in a restricted area with chain-smoking passengers. I took several deep, invigorating breaths just as several government officials associated with the orphanage pulled up in dark cars. The vehicles were covered with a thin film of brine, a combination of heavy winds and sea air.

We were asked to divide up into threes. Each trio slid, one by one, into the back seat of an auto.

"Good morning, girls," the young, clean-cut driver, chirped as he climbed in and put the car in motion. Elegant in his double-breasted, brown suit, he had a warm, charming smile.

"We should be at the orphanage in about forty minutes," he said reassuringly. "I'm sure you'll be happy to be settled in."

Another orphanage, I thought to myself, feeling somewhat queasy. I felt anything but eager to be "settled in" at another institution. "I guess it's not yet time to go to America," I whispered softly. "God, please don't let anything bad happen to me. I'm supposed to have faith—but when will you relieve me of this pain?"

"We've arrived," the young government official announced, shutting off the ignition as well as the flow of my thoughts. Stepping from the car, I felt a weight in my chest. At first, it was minimal, almost tolerable, until, left untamed, it lingered and expanded, leaving me short of breath.

A rather common occurrence, I learned to diagnosis it not as a physical malady but as the emotional penalty for anxiety.

Cautiously breathing in spurts, scared of crumbling in a swoon, I walked a few paces away from the car. A quick look around told me that the shabby buildings were in need of painting and restoration. Many of the windows were cracked or shattered. In some rooms, yellowed newspapers had been taped over the broken glass to defend against the elements.

Unbroken windows poorly dressed with discolored shades and mold-encrusted curtains were mucky to the eye. Fingerprints, like intricate designs embroidered on a quilt, were visible when the sun reflected on the pane. The general impression was one of neglect, disregard and exaggerated indifference.

A young, brashly dressed woman of abundant proportions met us at the door, accompanied by two middle-aged nuns whose austere, black habits were softened by the brightness of their starched, white wimples.

"Come with me," the young woman mumbled through full, pouting, crimson lips. "I'll show you where to put your things." Trailing behind her, we walked down a long, dim corridor. The stone floor seemed cold and unassuming. Along the perimeters were the bloodied carcasses of several deceased roaches. It was difficult to discern how they had met their death, but that was terribly unimportant.

A stride slowed by excess weight forced me to readjust my own pace to keep respectfully behind the young woman. At the open door, she stepped aside. Motioning with her left hand, she beckoned us to enter.

My new living quarters were larger and a bit more spacious than at Saint Elena and the monastery, but the familiar smell of mold intermingled with body odor remained status quo.

It was an old, familiar scenario. Nothing had changed except a tiny panorama of the surroundings. We now had windows, though they were stained and flawed.

Life followed a similar regimental pattern for the next few years. A pre-dawn wake-up, prayers, a breakfast of spare rations, school, the hospital and late-night hours in the sweatshops were part of the routine.

Behavioral issues were resolved with physical violence and periods of twenty-four to seventy-two hours of solitary closet confinement in which neither food nor water were offered.

I prayed longer and harder, imploring God on bent knees for a reprieve. Every morning, as my eyes opened on a new beginning, I begged, and every evening, as I shut them on the pain and sorrow, I pleaded for clemency—for an end to the torment. However, I continued to hear only silence amid the internal uproar. There had to be a reason for the Divine Silence, even if I was not apparently smart enough to get it.

The icy emptiness sent chills scurrying up and down my back. My mother had deserted me; Aunt Cynara and Uncle Evan had discarded me; the nuns at Saint Elena had rejected me; the Monks had sent me away. But worst of all, God didn't listen to my desperate pleas. Perhaps the nuns were right—maybe God really didn't love me because I was illegitimate. Could this really be the reason for all my misery and loneliness?

Holding on to my dream of going to America gave me the sustenance I needed to survive and continue. Grinding my teeth, I did my best to commit to assisting the sick recover in the hospital in Kavala, absolutely certain that nursing was not my life's vocation. Hopeful of finding a better life one day, I moved forward.

Once in a while, talent scouts patrolled the orphanage on a quest for interesting girls with acting potential and expressive facial features. Unbeknown to me, I was considered "theatre material." How and why still remains a mystery, though I often wondered if perhaps it was God answering my prayers for a truce.

Whisked off to Roma, Italy, with a few other lucky girls and several nuns, I spent months rehearsing and performing at the Colosseo. Standing inside the open, circular coliseum, my mind created exciting scenarios of bloodthirsty gladiators dressed to the hilt in their eye-blinding armor and fancy helmets.

In my imagination, totally unhampered by the weight of their breastplates, I allowed them to pillage riches and transpose humans to mounds of inanimate carnage in front of jeweled emperors applauding in sync with ear-piercing shouts of "bravo, bravo!"

It was a most welcomed interlude in the life of a young teen destined to crawl around in a hornet's nest, barred from anything less than the insufferable. My fantasy molded dreams not so much focused on ancient Roman soldiers, but on intricately woven reveries of crossing the limpid Mediterranean and Atlantic waters to reach America.

Upon completion of the theatrical tour, we returned to Kavala and the penitential orphanage life. I was back in the hospital, pursuing nursing studies, cleaning and dressing wounds, giving and removing bedpans. An exceptional student, I excelled in all subjects, even if my heart was not in it.

However, my talents did not pass unnoticed. "Avyrini," my teacher said one afternoon, "you are one of our best nurses' aids. We are going to take you to Switzerland to study and work. You can earn a nursing degree and you'll be able to leave the orphanage. The time has come, and you'll certainly be happier."

Unable to fully process what was being proposed, I nodded my head in agreement, trying to sort through the confusion. I had to understand the significance of what I had just been told. Struggling to determine the whys behind my turbulent existence and the presence of such evil in my life, I was bombarded with an intimidating muddle of ricocheting inquiries.

Mulling over the teacher's words, I realized that I had an opportunity to leave Greece and the orphanage—perhaps forever. Although Switzerland was not America, it was certainly a more attractive alternative to the εφιάλτησ, the nightmare, I was currently living.

"This must be the hand of God," I whispered. "Maybe I'm finally being redeemed. How much longer will I have to pay for my mother's sin?"

What I failed to realize was that the decision was made by the Greek government, in collaboration with the royal family and the nuns who ran the orphanage. Later, I learned that there was an alleged monetary exchange attached to this transfer.

As orphans, we existed within fuzzy boundaries—institutional children without personal documentation or identification. Although there were neither recorded medical histories nor official birth certificates, the Swiss hospital representative was not deterred from moving the project along.

Consequently, several weeks later, hours before the first brightness of dawn exploded, I was awakened along with a group of about 200 girls. To the familiar "pack your belongings and be ready to leave," we responded with the same meticulousness and speed as a military corps receiving an order from their highest-ranking officer.

At sixteen years of age, with a few worthless possessions, a surplus of demoralizing memories and not even one solitary tear, I boarded a train for Switzerland. Lowering the curtain on my native Greece, I bowed away without once pausing to peer over my shoulder for a last farewell.

Two forty-something Swiss hospital representatives accompanied my group of about fifty girls. Tall and blonde, their slender hips fit snugly into narrow, navy, tubular skirts. Smooth, velvety complexions were enhanced with just the vaguest trace of make-up.

Although I had studied some French, the mixture of French and German they spoke was often difficult to understand. Once in a while, they would interject a word or two in Greek or English. Oddly, we were able to communicate, depending heavily on facial expressions and creative hand gestures.

The train was overcrowded, the air hot and stale, and the echo of multiple simultaneous conversations created an incomprehensible, irritating buzz. Food was served in spare rations and there wasn't much to drink except tiny glasses of water.

"The trip will be long, girls," one of the representatives said, "but midway, we will be stopping in Skopje, Yugoslavia."

Although it was encouraging to look ahead to a destination, I was a bit overwhelmed by the idea of being in a Communist country. In school, the nuns had emphasized the perilous nature of a political system despised and boycotted by God.

"Communism is an evil," they would say, slamming their fists on the blackboard. "It's a terribly wicked force to reckon with."

As the train pulled into the station, I imagined being forcefully removed and held prisoner. Spotting the soldiers with their rifles slung over their shoulders flushed a wave of terror through me. Without thinking, I cranked open the window.

"I'm not going with the Communists," I blurted. "I'm not getting off the train and I'm not staying with anyone who is a Communist!"

Hearing my verbal rampage, one of the soldiers grabbed his rifle. Ready for trouble, he stood, staring straight ahead not daring to blink.

"Avyrini, taisez-vous—be quiet," the Swiss woman shouted, upset by my unexpected outburst. "If you don't shut your mouth, they'll kill you." With a brusque arm sweep, she shoved me down into my seat. Her few alarming words stilled my tongue.

Luckily, the soldier noticed my young age, apparently equating it to a lack of common sense and perhaps even ignorance. Considering me just a foolish girl, he recognized the nonthreatening nature of my outrageous behavior. Replacing his rifle, the soldier took a few steps back and withdrew from his post. His colleagues followed suit.

After the military men departed, we continued the journey. A month after the summer solstice, the heat was excruciating. Crammed into hard, unaccommodating seats, tired, hungry, thirsty and in dire need of a bath, I prayed we would soon reach our destination.

Distracted by my intense dialogue with God, I was suddenly jolted forward and then slammed back into my seat. The pain was quick, sharp, but fortunately not lingering as the train came to an abrupt halt. Echoes of shattering glass, screaming adults and sobbing women and children immediately silenced the passengers. Gazing out the window, I noticed multitudes of people scrambling about, covered in soot. Some were barefoot, others shirtless.

Several men with open forehead and arm wounds were carrying hysterical children in their arms. Women, their clothing torn and soiled, lay prostrate on the ground, wailing.

"Oh my God, what's happening?" I screeched, covering my mouth with my hands.

"Hurry, girls," a uniformed man shouted. His face and jacket, covered with thick, black dust, gave him the appearance of a chimney sweep who had climbed endless crow-stepped gables to clean the smokestacks.

"Leave your things behind and get off the train right now! Don't waste any time." His hat was missing, putting in full view the gash on his head, about six inches above his right temple. Through his short, cropped hair, I could see the trickle of bright red blood.

We were in the Socijalistička Federativna Republika Jugoslavija, the SFR of Yugoslavia. It was July 26, 1963, approximately 5:30 a.m.—just thirteen minutes after the Skopje earthquake had destroyed the beautiful panorama of Mother Teresa's birthplace, crushing more than a thousand lives and leaving a homeless toll of over 100,000 people.

Despite its massive proportions, the train shook, spilling people into the aisle. Trembling from fright, I leaped from the coach. What unraveled before me was far more chilling and gruesome than the most devastating nightmare I had ever experienced.

Cloudy and murky, the air was filled with huge, pelting chunks of mortar and brick, sharp-edged slices of broken glass, heavy scraps of metal and endless particles of various unidentifiable substances, probably remnants of destroyed personal furnishings.

The earth vibrated from the aftermath of seismic waves. Around me, the ground continued to rupture. Buildings toppled like overstacked mounds of dominoes, leaving the interiors of homes exposed and unprotected by exterior walls.

Panic-stricken, I froze in my tracks just long enough to see a man literally sucked into a huge crater. The path he was treading along tore wide open. Two little children, not more than six or seven, trailed their Dad to a tragic end, swallowed by a force too powerful to fight.

The odor of chemicals was noxious. My throat burned. My eyes stung. A strong nausea whirled in my stomach. Losing control of my bladder, I soiled myself. Dizzy and light-headed, I was certain I would collapse. Just seconds before the earth trembled one more time, I threw myself down on the rubble, cutting my knee and elbow. Accustomed to the frequent spurt of my own blood, I ignored the wounds, too scared to worry about a bleeding cut.

Conflicts, challenges and atrocious physical pain were sadly an acceptable part of my life. In fact, the repeated encounters with adversity had taught me that with faith and perseverance, I could not only endure but hope. Nevertheless, an earthquake was far too overwhelming. Catastrophic, this fuming eruption of nature involved the ultimate destiny: death.

Powerless, I could only pray and ask God to help me through the confusion and terror. Was it my time? Was God calling me? Was this the answer to my repeated pleas for an acquittal from the disheartening events of my life?

I knew that one day, God would come to my rescue, although the when and how remained shrouded in mystery. Undoubtedly, this required divine intervention. God alone would script the final scene.

When the tantrum subsided and the earth settled, the soldiers took control of the stranded individuals. Dazed and in shock, we were directionless—lost souls on a battlefield fighting an unknown enemy, certain only that we had survived.

Working to calm the chaos, the soldiers gathered us together. "No one is going anywhere today," a young man repeated in several languages. "The railroad tracks have been totally demolished by the earthquake and any road travel is risky. You will all have comfortable accommodations until it is advisable to resume your journey."

Kind and courteous, the young military Slavs helped us board their sturdy, BOV-armored carriers. Looking like tanks, these massive personnel transport vehicles accommodated eight passengers. Driven to a safe haven distant from the earthquake center, we were treated rather chivalrously, and offered food and shelter and first aid for our wounds until the emergency disaster warning was lifted.

I enjoyed the doting attention together with the gallantry exhibited by the Jugoslovanska Armada—the Yugoslavian army. It was so new and different, I didn't know how to graciously accept it. Accustomed to a demeaning, despondent lifestyle of deprivation and sadistic hardships, I had never before experienced any gentleness or cordiality. Initially, I felt embarrassed, until I realized that for the first time in my life, I was being treated like a respectable young woman.

It was now more than apparent that my life as an emotionally, physically and intellectually insolvent child, an orphan at the mercy of the Greek government and the religious women, was over. But would I ever be able to pick up the pieces from my own childhood earthquake and rebuild a new life? Would I be capable of burying the λίγοσ μπάσταρδοσ, the "little bastard" label that was the core of my identity, the who and what I had been for sixteen years? Or would there be more seismic waves in my life before, on bent knees, I could thank God for prayers answered and blessings received?

Resuming my journey to Switzerland, I couldn't help the urge to question further, "What now?" Although it was too soon for answers, the time was right for hope.

> *"Skopje is not a film, not a thriller where we guess the chief event. It is a concentration of man's struggle for freedom, with a result which inspires further struggles and no acceptance of defeat."*
>
> —Jean-Paul Sartre

PART II

πάλη
Struggle

ELEVENTH EPISODE

> *"We shall not flag or fail. We shall go on to the end... We shall fight on the beaches, we shall fight on the landing grounds, we shall fight in the fields and in the streets, we shall fight in the hills; we shall never surrender."*
>
> —Winston Churchill

Another violent tempest had rumbled my spirit like an extraterrestrial furor for which I had no reasonable explanation. One moment, children were giggling, filled with hope and expectations for a promising tomorrow, their eyes aglow with the excitement of anticipation, and a split second later, they were snatched from life, dragged into the bowels of the earth, their eyes forever thrust into the darkness of finality.

Before then, it was unimaginable. Then, suddenly I was forced to come to terms with the unbending nature of the human condition—with mortality. It was a haunting impact, especially for a teenager.

Perhaps it was a blessing not to understand every circumstance and event of life at sixteen. Maybe it was wise to prolong the idyllic unawareness of childhood a while longer. Until now, I had been just a string-puppet manipulated by others. Then, suddenly, I was crammed onto a train with 200 other young girls, heading toward a foreign country. With an open mind and a very vibrant undercurrent of anxiety, I faced the challenge, trying my best not to conjure up presentiments of fear.

The train journey was smooth and once I settled down, I was able to refocus on this new chapter of my life. As the train slowed to a crawl, I heard the conductor announce, "Berne Railway Station." Passengers scrambled to gather their purses, hand luggage and brief cases, and prepared to leave the train. Fidgety children were taken by the hand and escorted into the station.

Once outside, I spotted an endless line of hefty double-decker buses, ready to transport us to the hospital. Despite the clear, blue sky and rather cool mid-sixties temperature, the pungent odor of gasoline made it almost difficult to breathe.

Boarding was orderly, almost regimental. In silence and in single file, we entered the bus from the open platform in the rear. Walking past the seated conductor, we filed into our seats. When the first level was filled to capacity, the remaining girls were guided up the narrow, spiral staircase to the second level.

Curious to preview my surroundings, I positioned myself in the window seat, eager to become acquainted with my new home. After Ktismata, Ioannina and Saloniki, with their very diverse panoramas, I was unprepared for the quaint beauty of this medieval city built around the Aare River.

Gothic sandstone buildings loomed proudly, their foundations firmly settled on quaint, cobbled walkways. Bay windows, fancy arcades and intricate gables enhanced the picturesque portrait, bringing to life a long-declined era. I was mesmerized as fountains sprang to life. The rhythmic trickling of water created an almost tuneful echo.

As the bus made its way through the city, toward Bremgartenstrasse 117 and our Lindenhofspital destination, I was enchanted by Berne's unparalleled ambiance. The fountains and magnificent dome covering the House of Parliament left me enthralled by a different cultural extravaganza, yet somewhat intimidated by the grandeur.

Following a twenty-minute tour of the city, the bus stopped in front of the hospital. Several staff members were standing at attention, ready to greet the new crop of student nurses.

A young woman in her later forties introduced herself as the program coordinator. Of medium stature, she was more overweight than average, though certainly not unattractive. Her dark hair, severely twisted in a bun, accentuated an expressive pair of dark, almost almond-shaped eyes that seemed deprived of any graciousness.

"Guten morgen und willkommen—good morning and welcome," she said without even a faint smile. Though the day at Lindenhofspital had hardly begun, I was immediately cooled by her aloof manner.

A sudden downpour of pelting rain created an unexpected pause in the conversation. I gazed at the window just as scudding overhead formations obscured the light of day. Pedestrians scrambled for cover as if a bomb had been hurled from the skies. Was it a presentiment? Was the sudden reversal in the atmosphere, from a calm, sunny morning to an ill-natured summer squall, a message?

We were escorted to our quarters and each girl was assigned a living space. How strange it seemed to be invited to sleep in a bed complete with a pliable mattress wrapped in crisp white linens and a pale blue wool cover. On top sat the softest pillows imaginable.

"Is this actually happening?" I questioned to no one. "Is this a dream? It took me all these years to spend an evening in a real bed!"

"Avyrini," the woman said, removing my attention from my thoughts, "this is where you will live while you're working and studying at the hospital. There will be three meals a day. Lunch will be served in about thirty minutes, so freshen up and come to the refectory."

I couldn't believe my ears. My eyes followed her as she excused herself and took absence from my company. Was this a dream? A comfortable bed, three meals a day and best of all, no nuns to administer horrendous punishments or shout demeaning insults. Maybe I had served my time for being born an illegitimate child. Perhaps my punishment was completed.

I had to admit that the food at Lindenhofspital was poles apart from what I had been accustomed to at Aunt Cynara's and in the orphanages. Although the monks had shared their decent rations with us, and even though I had tasted fresh eggs after stealing them from the poor chickens, I had never before treated my palate to a feast of scrambled eggs and bacon. This was a whole different culinary experience. To keep from disrupting the diners, I gathered every morsel of self-control I had accumulated throughout the years to keep from screaming with delight.

Mornings no longer revolved around witnessing the crimson sunrise melt into a radiant, yellow fireball while gagging on a minute crust of soggy, stale bread.

After breakfast, we were given an itinerary of study-work events. Wake-up time was 4:00 a.m. We had several hours of classes, followed by eight hours of hospital work, administering bed bans, changing and making beds, medicating wounds and sponging the patients. Upon completion of this tour of duty, we headed over to the sweatshops for sewing and tattering, under dimly lit lamps, until 10:00 p.m. It was a grueling day that seemed to drag on endlessly.

I slithered through the day, working beyond exhaustion, complimented for my extraordinary needle and thread talents. Deemed the best seamstress in the sweatshop, my extraordinary creations were destined for the shah of Persia and many European royals. Eventually, I had built quite an outstanding reputation not only as a seamstress, but as an embroiderer. I also made vestments, cassocks and clerical street garments. Having learned how to thread a needle at an early age, I eventually assumed the role of teacher, demonstrating my own techniques and patterns.

Although it was tiring to sew with my energy unfurling in spurts after a long day in the hospital, I much preferred it to the nursing with all the open wounds, blood and emotional and physical unpleasantries associated with caring for the sick and suffering. However, still unable to govern my own life, I was forced to abstain from any illusions of happiness, except for my dream of going to America. Like a lit candle, this reverie illuminated the darkness around me.

One afternoon, I was summoned by the head nurse.

"Ayvrini, we have an emergency," she blurted. "I need you to stop what you're doing and come with me immediately. There's a patient just admitted who will require emergency surgery."

I excused myself after placing a bedpan under a young soccer player who had been badly injured in a car accident, and treaded along the imaginary footprints of the head nurse.

"In there, Avyrini," she said, pointing her index finger toward a light cream-colored door. "She's in there."

Pausing to fix my hair and straighten my white cap, which had tilted askance during my accelerated journey on the tail of the quick-footed head nurse, I knocked.

"Entrez, s'il vous plait—please, come in," a soft voice responded. Obliging, I carefully pushed open the door and walked over to a beautiful woman reposing in bed. Dressed in a long, red silk robe, she looked as if she were filming a movie scene.

"Hello," I said, "I'm Avyrini. How are you feeling today?" At first glance, I recognized the fine bone features, glowing dark eyes and alluring charm of Madame Lutz, renowned Swiss actress.

"I'm not doing so well," she whispered. Her still-smooth brow furrowed when the pain became excruciating. Although she was thirty-five and enjoying a splendid prime, I could see she was suffering.

"What's the matter, Madame Lutz?" I asked, walking over to fluff her pillow. "Are you in pain?"

"Yes, Avyrini, I think my appendix has to come out."

Madame Lutz was in fact scheduled for an appendectomy. I, on the other hand, was assigned to care for her post-op. Attentive and diligent about my responsibilities, I did my best to ensure the most comfortable convalescence possible under the circumstances.

Visiting her room often, I extended added courtesies, enjoying the company of this gorgeous actress whose name danced on the tongues of every Swiss cinema buff. She possessed a certain self-assurance I almost coveted. Perhaps, in time, I would learn to be more self-accepting. However, I would have to find and define my self before I could decide if I was going to accept or reject my findings.

The day-after-day contact seeded a warm relationship between us. Madame Lutz was vulnerable, and I was uncompromisingly gracious in her regard. A creature dedicated to fiction and flights of the imagination in film, she intrigued me. For so long, I had lived in my own whimsical mind's eye, escaping the sadness and anguish of my life through role playing. It must be refreshing to be able to turn to a make-believe world at will, I thought to myself.

After meeting Madame Lutz's husband during his numerous bedside calls, I was eventually invited to the couple's home. Although I was just two years shy of adulthood, I embroidered fancy daydreams in which Madame would star as my adoptive mother. They invited me for overnight stays, and I relished the attention and the family-like setting in which I found myself. They were warm, open people who treated me with kindness.

Often, after an endless, exhausting week, I would spend my time off at the Lutz residence. It was a delightful interlude and I was beginning to regard the couple as a refreshing and regenerating interlude in my downcast life.

Nonetheless, after a while, Madame's husband became a bit overly affectionate with me. Taking a fancy to my youth and inexperience, he demanded certain liberties I was not willing to concede. Angered and frustrated by my repeated rebuffs, he crossed the line without my approval, pushing me into a nonconsensual relationship.

Upset and disillusioned by the lack of allegiance Monsieur Lutz demonstrated to his beautiful wife, I wallowed in self-pity, like a bee in a cup of honey, questioning why this continued to happen to me. Why me? Why, when things were going so nicely for once in my life? Why was I always prey for someone's uncontrollable appetite? Was this still a befitting punishment for being born illegitimate?

"Avyrini, are you unhappy at Lindenhofspital?" Madame Lutz asked one day, apparently honing in on the sudden onset of my bouts of melancholia. Sparring with myself for a brief moment, I debated how I should respond to the question. Turning awkwardly from her gaze, I nodded affirmatively, sparing the embarrassing details.

"Yes," I mumbled, lightly biting my lower lip. "I don't like working at the hospital. I'm really not happy there."

"Would you like to go to Germany?" she asked, searching for my lowered gaze.

"I'd like to finish my classes here and then leave," I responded.

"OK," she said. "I'll speak with the head physician. He will take care of the transfer."

I felt a weight lift from my chest. Questioning if the move to Germany would bring me closer to my dream of going to America, I focused on another chance for change and the possibility it promised. Still faithful to my prayers, I asked God if this transfer was perhaps the beginning of a new chapter.

I began studying German, since it was one of the official languages in Switzerland, along with French and Italian, and I continued my training at the hospital. Eventually, I immigrated to Germany along with numerous other nursing students.

Once again, we were offered room and board in exchange for continuing our nursing courses and a hard day's work. However, in contrast to our Swiss responsibilities, these tasks were not focused on bedpans, injections and attending to the patients' needs. Instead, we were treated with a demeaning attitude that no measure of patience on my part could tolerate. Given large, cumbersome boxes crammed with personal hygiene products—soap, shampoo, toothpaste—we were ordered to deliver them to impoverished families living in dilapidated buildings situated along the periphery of the city.

Since elevators were nonexistent in this part of town, we were obliged to carry the hefty, bulky packages up and down badly damaged staircases, sometimes eight or nine stories high, risking a fall. My arms and legs ached at day's end and my back felt taut, especially when I tried to sit or bend over to retrieve something I had dropped.

My optimism became dour, summarized by a vacant silence. I seemed to float around ungrounded, heavy-hearted and exhausted, unable to visualize even a tiny ray of light in the bleakness that was my life.

Several weeks after my arrival, I learned that the US had a military base in the vicinity of the hospital. Thrilled with the news that I was sharing a neighborhood with die Amerikaner, I opened my mind to the possibility of crossing that threshold and perhaps actually having the opportunity to speak with an American serviceman.

Together with two other girls, I decided to head over to the base, scout around and try to locate the mess hall. In the orphanage, the nuns had frequently spoken of finding suitable things to eat by rummaging through the refuse bins when the soldiers had finished dinner. After all, nourishment was vital to keeping up one's forces, and who could ever denounce someone for fighting against the threat of starvation? It was a matter of survival. This was the religious women's rectification with God and the orphans for preaching and practicing trash stealing.

We arrived at the base just as the huge, red orb of day's light was sliding behind the horizon, casting the rear of the mess hall into the dimness of dusk. No sentinel was visible; therefore, the scene was set for us to approach the lengthy line of trash bins placed askance.

Nearing the designated area, I noticed that the overlong blades of grass were burnt and flattened. Probably in the sunlight, multiple boot prints in various dimensions would be in evidence—an explanation for the severely trampled ground covering.

"Avyrini," one of the girls whispered, cupping her mouth with her hands, "look. This dumpster is wide open—I bet we could find some good things in there."

"Let me take a look," I said, imitating her softer tone as I inched over to the garbage container.

I grabbed on to the edge of the dumpster, stood on my toes and leaned over to catch a glimpse of whatever treasure could be hidden among the rubbish. A capricious, ill-timed wind swirled around me, carrying the rancid aroma right to my nostrils. Gagging, I refused to relinquish my purpose for trespassing on private property.

"It seems to be filled with empty cans," I said, withholding my breath to keep from retching. "I'll climb in and see what's buried."

Slipping in head-first, I was fortunate that a huge pack of newspapers buffered my tumble. Rummaging among the bags and empty bottles—mostly beer, scotch and soda—and heavily dented tin cans, I searched for the much-coveted cache of an unopened canister of food.

Focused on accomplishing my goal, I did not hear the advisory whispers of my friends, who, spotting a soldier approaching, gave fair warning before dashing behind the dumpster to conceal their illicit presence.

Like the quick and often erratic downpour following an earsplitting clap of thunder, I felt first one then a second bag smash down on my head. What is happening? I asked myself. When the only logical answer popped into my head, I realized that I had to make myself known, whatever the consequences or risk of being smothered to death.

"Arrêtez! Je suis ici. Anhalten! Ich bin hier. Stop! I'm here," I shouted in French, German and English, once I understood the serious nature of the attack I was under.

"Who's in there?" a husky, male voice responded, peering into the dumpster.

"I'm calling the MPs," he said, not waiting for my response. "I'm going to summon the Geheime Feldpolizei," he repeated in a heavily accented French and German that squeezed a chuckle out of me, willingly or otherwise, despite the delicate situation at hand.

"No, no," I squealed, overcome both with the nauseating fumes of trash and the fear of being caught red-handed, "don't call the police." It was apparent that I was soon to come face to face with an American.

Gazing up, I connected with a creased forehead and a pair of bright blue eyes expressing bewilderment. "I am," I said, rising slowly to my feet without the slightest hint of embarrassment, "I'm Avyrini, a nurse at the hospital. And these are my two friends," I blurted, pointing to the girls who were still crouched near the trash bins. "We were just looking for something to eat."

Reaching for my hand, the young serviceman helped me leave behind the day's rations of military garbage. Tall, athletic and handsome in an all-American way, he appeared somewhat intimidating in his khaki uniform. I couldn't remove the words "he's an American" from my mind.

The look of confusion and surprise that splashed across his face was far too authentic in my opinion to even remotely consider questioning its validity. Consequently, taking the unexpected encounter as serious business, I dropped to my knees. Seeking confirmation I asked, "Are you American?" refusing to remove my eyes from his sharply chiseled features.

"Yes," he said, a bit staggered by my humbling position. "I'm American. But what are you doing on your knees?" he continued, pausing after each word, perhaps to determine in his own mind the answer.

"W-w-what's y-y-your n-n-name?" I stuttered, deliberating with myself over what action to take.

"I'm Al," he said as the taut contours of his broad jaw softened into a smile.

"Take me to America," I blurted. "Al, please take me to America! I want to go to America!"

I dared not breathe. My heart raced. My stomach rumbled. Beads of sweat ran across my forehead and down my cheeks. What did I just do? I questioned silently.

"What did you say your name was?" he asked.

"Avyrini," I mumbled, barely able to speak.

"Well, Avyrini," he said, digging in his hip pocket, "why don't you give me your telephone number." Pulling out a crumbled, rough-edged piece of paper, his long, thin fingers reached for the pen in his shirt pocket.

"Al, I don't have a phone at the hospital."

"OK, I'll give you mine—how does that sound?"

I watched speechlessly as he sat the paper in his open palm, scribbled his number and handed it to me. For one fleeting second, our fingers brushed against each other, sending a tingling chill up and down my back.

"You can catch me here," he said. "It's best to call in the evenings. Avyrini, you and your friends better get back to the hospital now. It's getting pretty dark out."

"OK, Al," I said. I hope to see you soon."

"Listen, Avyrini," he continued after a brief hesitation, "will you have a drink with me tomorrow?"

A rush of heat ripped through my body. Before he could change his mind, I both nodded and answered "yes" in perfect synchrony. I had to be absolutely certain Al understood I was accepting his invitation.

"OK. Should I pick you up at the hospital?"

"Yes," I whispered with whatever voice I had left.

"How about seven o'clock? Is that OK?"

"Yes, Al, that will be fine."

I felt my knees weaken. Swarms of butterflies invaded my stomach. Realizing I was trembling, I prayed, Oh, God, please don't let me faint—not now, not in front of Al. Not in front of my American.

Al was my hope, my dream, my life—the answer to my prayers.

Like Caesar, who in 49 BC crossed the Rubicon, reaching the point of no return, I too had walked across my own river, arriving at my own point of no return.

> *The die was cast for me that evening. There would be no turning back!*
>
> *"Jacta alea est! The die is cast."*
>
> —Julius Caesar

TWELFTH EPISODE

"But once they reached the springs for the fourth time, then Father Zeus held out his sacred golden scales: in them he placed two fates of death that lays men low—one for Achilles, one for Hector breaker of horses—and gripping the beam mid-haft the father raised it high and down went Hector's day of doom, dragging him down to the strong House of Death."

—Homer, The Iliad

Although in the early '60s, the "second wave" of feminism had not yet expanded its sails to full mast, precocious and emotionally keyed up beyond belief, I took the initiative, picked up the receiver and dialed Al's number to confirm our first date. I had to be certain that the tall, handsome, young American with the blonde, cropped hair and the magnetic glint in his eyes was not just the figment of a lonely teenaged girl's creative imagination.

When he responded, my heart skipped a beat. "OK, Avyrini—I'll be there at seven," he crooned after I posed my question. Silently, I mimicked the adorable way in which he mispronounced my name until, no longer able to contain my delight, I shouted it over and over, risking serious vocal chord strain.

With the energy of a three-year-old powered by an overdose of sugar, I settled the receiver in the cradle and scampered about, wondering what I could possibly wear to look halfway attractive to my American.

The options were scarce and not very alluring. Nevertheless, I slipped into a simple, black skirt and red blouse, rolled a tube of shocking pink lipstick along the contours of my lips and waited for Al.

Promptly at seven, a blue Volkswagen Beetle pulled up in front of the hospital, stopping short in the entry. Athletic of build with strong shoulders, sculpted, muscular arms and a pair of legs that seemed to run from his feet to his forehead, I wondered how he could possibly fit into such a miniature vehicle.

Not giving him time to exit, I ran out, yanked open the door and climbed inside. The sun had retired, nullifying all traces of daylight, and evening had settled in without waiting for the moon to cast even a dim glow. It was a romantic setting and my thoughts were in harmony with the dreamy mood.

Al switched on the light to make my entry less complicated. From the corner of my eyes, I spotted what seemed like am endless stack of boxes piled one on top of the other. Turning to get a better view, I realized that he had five cases of beer.

"That's a lot of beer back there," I said, grinning sheepishly in his direction.

"Do you like beer, Avyrini?" he asked in response to my comment.

Although I had tasted it, I really was not accustomed to much more than powdered milk and water. "Yes, Al," I responded, "I like beer." Concerned more with getting the correct answer than telling the truth, I thought it best to reply affirmatively. Maybe if I said "no," Al would not like me, I thought, nervous about this stranger who could eventually redirect the course of my life.

We had a fun evening, drinking beer and talking about our lives in the present moment. Al told me about his life in the military and I reciprocated with my hospital and professional events.

At evening's end, he leaned over and kissed me on the cheek, jumped out of the car, dashed over to the passenger's side and opened the door. Turning, I met his gentle, blue eyes. Sparkling in the moonless night, they reassured me that he had enjoyed our first date.

Both feet planted on the ground, I was confronted by my military man, gallantly bent in a salaam. Gradually rising, he encircled me in his arms, involving me in a long, passionate kiss.

"Thank you, God," I whispered soundlessly.

Gently, Al positioned me in the crook of his arm. "Can I see you again, Avyrini?" he asked softly, like a small child doubting permission would be granted.

"Sure, Al," I blurted. The words sprouted before I had time to even draw a breath, fearful that any hesitation would create even the tiniest speck of doubt.

"OK, Avyrini, I'll pick you up at seven tomorrow. Is that suitable for you?"

Is that suitable? I repeated in my mind. Is he serious?

"Yes, tomorrow at seven would be perfect," I muttered, momentarily sliding off the cloud upon which I had spent the evening. He turned sideways to catch a better glimpse of his watch, swinging his arm under the dim streetlight. I took the opportunity to focus on his profile—the perfectly formed nose, the strong, resolute jawbone, the thick row of sandy blonde lashes. Undoubtedly, he was handsome.

Unknown to Al, I had already made long-range plans, certain that God would put his imprimatur on the blueprint I was designing. Oblivious to the fact that I could not act alone in this drama, I proceeded to set the scene. What intricate plot was I candidly weaving in my mind?

For a long time that evening, I twisted and turned in my bed, far too overwrought by it all to sleep. Although I hoped otherwise, the symphony of squeaking bed springs revealed my agitated state. My mind was brimming over with wishful scenarios of Al sweeping me off my feet and away from Germany and the life of misery I had known until today. Finally exhausted, I drifted off.

The following morning, I awakened with a throbbing headache. An unquiet and restless evening with only a couple of hours of sleep, in addition to the three beers I'd drank, was at the root of my malaise. Groaning, I made the decision to find an aspirin as soon as I reported for duty.

By midday, I was feeling better and anxious about my second date with Al that evening. I knew what I had implored the Lord for. I knew what I so desperately wanted—but I did not know if Al would be a part of it. Would he make my dream come true?

Al was waiting me for me when I walked through the hospital's massive entry door. To keep the pelting rain from saturating me, I made a mad dash for the car. Al's head was turned slightly toward the street; however, I caught his hand lifting a cigarette to his mouth. Letting go, he lit it, hurriedly exhaling two puffs of smoke while cuddling the cigarette between his lips.

The all too familiar scene conjured up painful memories of Uncle Evan—his nicotine-stained fingers and discolored teeth as well as the awful odor of tobacco, which found permanence on his breath, in his hair and on his clothes. I shuddered just as Al spotted me. Bolting from the car, he saved me from reliving a miserable moment. Maybe Al was truly my savior.

"Hi, Avyrini," Al said, giving me a quick peck on the cheek that sent a bolt of lightning careening through me. Removing his jacket, he put it over my head while we ran for the car. Protective, I thought to myself.

Until then, no one had ever bothered to worry about me. Perhaps Al really did like me. It was an alien feeling, but I could get used to it without much difficulty. Actually it felt nice—warm and endearing.

We had dinner in a crowded restaurant patronized predominately by military men and women engaged in boisterous discussions and heavy drinking. The setting was not exactly designed for a "getting to know you" conversational experience, but I was thrilled just to be in Al's company.

Shouting above the din, he told me about his family and his life in the USA before his enrollment in the military. I listened attentively, my gaze never wavering from his. Al's eyes lit up as he spoke, regarding me with such sweetness, filling my eyes with tears.

"Avyrini, do you want to go to America?" he asked, pausing to light a cigarette.

A wave of disbelief smothered my breath. I couldn't feel my legs—my thoughts seemed stifled. All I heard was "go to America." It played in my mind like the refrain of a song repeated for the sake of rhythm. I knew that if I stood, I would come crashing down to the floor. My voice was muted; everything seemed to shut down.

"Hey, Avyrini," Al, said, reaching across the table for my hand, "did you hear what I said? Do you want to go to America?"

"Oh, yes, Al—yes, I want to go to America. I've wanted to go to American since I was a small child. Can you really help me?"

Al witnessed my ecstasy with mounting enthusiasm. Frisking through his pockets, he searched for a pen. "Ayvrini, do you have something I can write with?" he asked. "Maybe a pen or pencil?"

Reaching for my purse, I let my trembling fingers push the contents around until I found an eyebrow pencil. "You can write with this," I said, handing it to Al.

"Give me your napkin," he blurted. "I soiled mine." Lifting the napkin off my lap, I shook it twice to set free the crumbs, and passed it to Al.

Uncapping my eyebrow pencil, he began writing on the napkin. Puzzled, I held my breath. Capping the pencil, he handed it back to me. "OK, I'm done."

Still mystified by his strange behavior, I returned the pencil to its place in my handbag, next to my lipstick. What now? I thought.

"Avyrini," Al said, smiling wryly as he returned my napkin, "this is the address and phone number of my parents. If you wish, you can write them a letter expressing your wishes to come to America. They will be happy to help you."

Gazing down, I saw the key to my dream scribbled in bold, brown letters across the surface of the napkin. Gulping for air, I locked eyes with Al almost incredulously. A steady stream of tears spilled down the contours of my cheeks, dampening the front of my blouse. My unsteady hand tried in vain to interrupt the flow. The quicker I wiped away the tears, the quicker they came drizzling down.

From her distaff onto the spindle, Κλωθώ—Clotho—was slowly spinning the thread of my life. Undeniably, the Fates were at work!

After a tender goodnight kiss, Al accompanied me back to the hospital. I walked up the one flight of stairs two steps at a time, my feet treading on air. Once there, I undressed quietly so as not to awaken my roommates and dropped down on my knees. "Oh, God," I prayed, "now I know You are there. Now I know You are listening to me. Oh, God, thank You. Oh, God, please make this dream come true—do whatever You want with me, but please let me go to America!" With the name of God on my lips, I fell asleep.

Al and I saw each other on a regular basis. And although I enjoyed his company and sweet attentions, life in Germany was horrendous. Delivering boxes was an exhausting hardship, of little satisfaction. It was also, beyond a doubt, evident that I was not interested in nursing. However, I studied hard, finished the program and graduated.

With the ink still wet on my diploma, I phoned Madame Lutz, gave her the good news and told her I was miserable in Germany.

"Avyrini, why don't you come and stay with us in Switzerland for a while?" she said. "Are you ready to go to England now?"

"Yes, Madame Lutz," I responded. "I'm ready to go to England."

I packed my few belongings, made certain that the napkin with the address of Al's parents' engraved across it was secure in my purse, and departed. Saying goodbye to my American boyfriend was emotional, even if we promised to see each other again soon.

Back in Switzerland, as a guest of the Lutzes I was informed that their British friends, Dr. Weatherly and his wife, would be willing to offer me hospitality. Though both grateful and excited, I felt insecure, still self-conscious about and embarrassed by my illicit beginnings and Greek heritage. In my mind's eye, I was still the λίγοσ μπάσταρδοσ! The little bastard was who I was—it was my identity.

As soon as I arrived in Switzerland, Madame Lutz spoke to me about her friends, Dr. and Mrs. Weatherly. "When you go to England," she said, "you can phone them. They have been informed of your arrival. I'm sure you will all get along nicely."

"Thank you, Madame," I said as she gave me a big hug. "You are most kind to me. I will leave in the morning."

The following day, I bid farewell to the Lutzes and departed for England—another new country, another adventure. It was time to turn over another page. More questions invaded my mind. What's next? I thought as I stepped on British soil, welcomed by a moist breeze. Nervously, I stroked my head, trying to contain my already wind-blown locks

The Weatherlys were a gracious couple who soon took me under their wings. It seemed as if they felt compassion for my trials and the inauspicious evils that besieged my childhood, even if they found the circumstances of my young life inconceivable.

Mrs. Weatherly, a tall, slender woman whose tenacious personality seeped through her determined gaze, greeted me with a firm handshake.

"Avyrini, you'll be staying here with us," she announced. "Come with me and I'll show you where to leave your luggage."

She walked ahead of me. Her long legs, difficult to keep pace with, took her to the destination long before I arrived. I couldn't even dream of outflanking her.

"I think you'll be comfortable here," she said, cracking a smile that vaguely disturbed the still relatively unblemished matte finish of her hand-painted, porcelain complexion. Though in her middle sixties, she had been treated gallantly by a time that wrecks havoc on most, demonstrating little if any pangs of conscience. Except for a few crow's feet and fine lines around her eyes, she looked younger than her chronological years.

In the room, there was a pair of twin beds, dressed in matching green-and-white floral spreads.

"You can choose which bed you prefer," she said, opening the blinds to let in the last bit of sunlight, still visible at midday.

That evening, I met Dr. Weatherly, a worthy mate for his amicable wife. Tall and slender, he was elegant in his grey, double-breasted, cashmere suit, white–on-white shirt, bordeaux-and-silver-striped tie, and oxblood, wing-tipped oxfords.

"This is Avyrini," Mrs. Weatherly said, presenting me to her husband.

"Hello, Dr Weatherly," I whispered, extending my hand. His dark, deep-set eyes, initially shaded by the downturned brim of his grey fedora, came alive.

"I hope you will be happy here," he said, smiling. Gazing into his weather-beaten face, I noticed that time had not shown him the same gallantry as his wife, though he was a very distinguished gentleman with what remained of his well-coiffed silver locks and his gold-rimmed spectacles.

Always complacent, benevolent of heart and willing to bear goodwill in my regard, I was left in amazement. Few if any had ever shown such courtesy and respect. No one had ever treated me with such dignity. The joy in my heart was a new experience; until then, I had shared familiarity only with sorrow and pain.

However, after a short, idyllic visit, I began to feel as if I was intruding on their privacy. Unwilling to reciprocate their generosity by being a burden, I decided to move to the hospital in Wimbledon, where I was working.

The accommodations I was offered included a flat, meals and a roommate who answered to the name of Maureen. An Irish girl with curly, red hair and freckles, she soon confessed that she was gay and made it known that she had an interest in pursuing a relationship with me.

"Maureen," I said one evening, "I'm not interested. I have a wonderful boyfriend in Germany and I'm going to America."

The truth was, I was not on the prowl for any romantic liaisons. After all the sexual abuse I'd suffered, I was just grateful to be left in peace.

Although room and board were provided by the hospital, a strict set of rules and regulations dictated a wake-up time and an unwavering curfew at 10:00 p.m. Any infringement of the laws resulted in termination of employment at the hospital.

Shortly thereafter, Dr. Weatherly introduced me to another physician, Dr. Green. A surgeon in charge of the medical nursing staff, Dr. Green was a mature gentleman with an appearance revealing every aspect of a full life, from joy and delight to disappointment and challenge to struggle and triumph. On his wide-bridged nose sat a pair of low-lying reading glasses. The dark, black frames contrasted with his pale complexion, so typical of a person who spent every waking hour under fluorescents instead of sunlight.

Summoned to his office at the conclusion of the workday, I wondered what he could possible want. Knocking, I heard his voice: "Avyrini, come on in. I'll be with you in a moment." Gathering his papers, he closed the folder, pushing it off to the side of his desk. "I'm going to assign you to the operating room. I think you'll do well there. We will teach you about all the surgical instruments."

The following morning, per Dr. Green's instructions, I reported to the OR. Once crossing that threshold, I discovered that my task as a peri-operative scrub nurse would be to disinfect the instruments, swipe the surgeon's brow and hand him the appropriate implements for his surgical work. In return, I would have room and board plus a stipend of twenty pounds a month.

Realizing I was obliged to stand beside the gurney in full view of the patient while he was being cut through, I cringed. Though I was unaware, it was a premonition. During my first surgical experience, I stood firm, watching as the physician made the incision across the patient's abdomen. I winced, even if logic told me he would feel no pain. I stood there glaring at the font of crimson blood that sprouted from the wound like the ejection of lava from an erupting volcano. Splattering the surgeon's scrubs, it spilled over onto me.

A woozy, queasy feeling was the last thing I felt before crashing to the floor, unconscious. Opening my eyes seconds later, I saw the physician's face staring down at my defenseless, prostrate body.

"Avyrini," he said, somewhat amused by my totally ungainly fall from grace, "you will get used to the sight of blood." I didn't.

Reporting to Dr. Green, I mentioned I was nauseated by the sight of blood and disheartened by the constant reminder of human suffering. Though he tried to reassure me that I would get acclimated to nursing life, I knew differently.

The agonizing litanies of moans and groans depressed me. They spoke of my own pain and suffering. I was traumatized, forced to witness in others, the very same horror I had endured. But this time, as an idle spectator, I was completely powerless.

Confused, I deliberated my life choices, which were dramatically less than few. Then, one day, Dr. Green, decades my senior, declared his love with a marriage proposal.

Shocked, I wheedled my way out, eager to start anew. My resources were practically nil but I placed myself in God's hands. That evening, I fell asleep with the napkin Al had given me clutched in my hands.

THIRTEENTH EPISODE

"Let me not pray to be sheltered from dangers but to be fearless in facing them. Let me not beg for the stilling of my pain, but for the heart to conquer it. Let me not look for allies in life's battlefield but to my own strength. Let me not crave in anxious fear to be saved but hope for the patience to win my freedom."

—Rabindranath Tagore

Though a bit surprised by the thoughts and feelings tottering in my head, a second reflection gave me the jolt I needed to put them into a different perspective. The anxieties, until then, had been far too strong and encompassing, hindering my ability to move forward, casting me instead into an unfruitful lethargy.

However, I understood that if I continued to oppose my inclinations to change my professional choices, I would lock myself into misery—something I was rather tired of dealing with. Although sadness, anguish and pain were all-too-loyal allies, I knew I had to distance myself from this toxic trio.

Frequently, between fainting spells and bouts of nausea from the odor of blood, my thoughts lapsed, jostling my spirit into the false and short-lived serenity of denial. Then, suddenly, like a bolt of lightning, it crossed my mind to just admit that it was time for me to take the reins of my own life in hand.

I had no one, anyway, either to support my choices or step into a parental advisory role. No one really cared one way or another. In a sense, I was my own parent. Either I stepped out of the box now, or I would have to pay the consequences for shutting myself in the familiar but despondent cocoon.

Accepting my findings, I eventually learned to appreciate the common sense of my thought process. Mind made up, I walked over to the window, drawing open the drape just in time to catch a glimpse of the colorful rainbow waxed to full radiance. Was it a sign from God? More importantly, was it a message or just an uplifting moment?

The following morning, I was summoned to assist the surgeon in the operating theatre. Scheduled to perform an appendectomy on a young girl right about my age, he instructed me to scrub in and be ready to satisfy his demands for a positive surgical outcome. Conscientious about my professional obligations, I did as I was told.

The appendectomy went smoothly. I tried to suppress the nauseous, unsettled feeling in my stomach once the incision was made in Barbara's abdomen. Blood sputtered from the open wound like a Strombolian eruption, pooling clotted blood into small puddles near my feet. Though it was not my maiden surgical experience, my green complexion could have fooled everyone in the theatre.

Barbara was an ideal patient and taking care of her post-op lead to an engaging friendship. Three times a day I visited to change her bandage and medicate her incision, deliver her medicine and check her vitals.

During one of my visits, soon after her anesthetic wore thin and she was sufficiently clear-headed, Barbara asked, "Avyrini can you stay a while and chat?" Rolling her tired eyes, she paused, smiling though it was apparent that the pain was often a hardship to bear.

"Sure, Barbara," I responded, attracted to her open, gracious personality and filled with compassion for her suffering. "I have a few moments to spare before I continue my rounds."

"Avyrini, do you like nursing?" she asked, staring across the room at me. "You sure look nice all dressed in white. It brings out your beautiful olive skin."

"Thanks, Barbara," I said sheepishly, somewhat embarrassed. Compliments were an unknown occurrence in my life. "But no," I muttered, trusting my new friend with the confession I was about to make. "I don't like living and working in the hospital. Many times, I've wished I could leave all this behind and just get out on my own—maybe even find another job. Something unrelated to nursing and hospitals."

"Really," she blurted, her pained look melting into a light smile.

"Listen," she continued, sitting upright in her bed. "I share a flat with two roommates, Pam and Sharon. You're more than welcome to come live with us." To say the least, the invitation sounded inviting.

"I work for a newspaper," Barbara continued, "but Pam and Sharon work in a factory. They can surely get you a job there. And you can help us with the rent. What do you think?"

"I think I'll take you up on that idea," I blurted, excited at the prospect of actually having an option to choose.

"Good. As soon as the doctor says I'm ready to go home, I'll take you with me."

I was beyond thrilled. At just months shy of eighteen, except for my move to England, I was rarely in a position to make a decision—about what I ate, what I wore, what I studied, where I went or where I lived.

Until then, I was just the product of an unmentionable sin, a pawn, maneuvered according to the whim of the Greek government and their religious cohorts. No questions were ever posed regarding my thoughts, feelings and needs. It was a clear-cut testament to the fact that how I felt, what I thought and what I wanted was irrelevant. In fact, the only time I used the "I" word was in my conversations with God.

Excited about my new plans, I promptly set up an appointment with Dr. Green and informed him of my decision to leave nursing and the hospital.

"But Avyrini," he blurted with almost exasperating annoyance, "after all the years you struggled and studied to become a nurse, you want to quit and walk away from it? I think you should give this more thought before you make such a rash decision."

Despite his protestations, I gave my resignation, bagged my few possessions and accepted Barbara's invitation to move in with the girls. Thanking him for his support and advice, I said goodbye, closing the book on my nursing profession.

Once outside the hospital, a crisp wind teased my hair with the same nonchalance of two puppies engaged in an innocent wrestling match. A sense of impatience and the exhilaration of freedom left me oblivious to the delivery truck that had discourteously spat a malodorous vapor in my face.

Thankfully, I did not have far to go to reach Barbara's flat; it was just a few bus stops away. Seated on the upper level of the double-decker, I gazed out the window, actually noticing for the first time the quaintness of the pubs, bistros and restaurants. People hurriedly walked past, hardly raising their eyes from the ground. Where are they all going? I found myself asking.

When I reached Barbara's flat, I was surprised to see three girls standing in the cold, improperly dressed, awaiting my arrival.

"Avyrini," Barbara said, extending her cold, ungloved hand to take mine, "these are my two friends, Sharon and Pam." Turning to her roommates, she added, "This is Avyrini, the wonderful nurse I told you about." We exchanged smiles and greetings. At that first encounter, I had no idea that we would be friends for life.

"Let's go inside. It's too cold here and we're not dressed appropriately," Barbara said, shivering as a gust of wind made of itself an unwelcomed intruder.

Once inside, I noticed how compromised the surroundings were. Two disheveled beds stood on opposite ends of a room totally devoid of any other furniture except for a small table in the kitchen. Measuring not larger than fourteen by fifteen feet, the four cream-colored walls resembled a woven quilt. Every crack and chip probably represented a part of the flat's history. Though allegedly a property of the royal family, it was far from imposing.

A coin-operated apparatus fueled the electrical power. If we wanted heat, hot water and electricity, we had to repeatedly feed it schillings. Otherwise, we were forced to sit in the darkness until, hungry and exhausted, we crawled into bed, quivering from the cold, simply because we did have the money to switch on the utilities.

Pam and Sharon were gregarious girls given to unprompted conversations on subjects ranging from anything to everything. Pam was Canadian and Sharon Australian. Unreserved and decisive, their opinions were rarely if ever withheld. Consequently, learning of my discontent with nursing, they suggested I accompany them to the molding factor to apply for a position.

Exhilarated by the possibility of a new career, I agreed. I slept little that evening, sloughing through a bundle of emotions and thoughts, and prayed long and hard. In the morning, before Pam and Sharon even awakened, I was dressed and ready to leave.

We hopped on the double-decker, found seats in the same vicinity and remarked how comforting it felt to be warmed up. About twenty minutes later, we reached our destination.

Introduced to George, the factory foreman, I was acknowledged with a smile and a nod. He announced that I was hired after slapping the bowl of his pipe against the wall, sending a dot of partially charred tobacco to a resting place beside my right foot. No apology followed the perhaps unintended discourtesy. Straight-faced, he muttered a few instructions and asked Pan and Sharon to explain the job description. Shaking my hand, he welcomed me as his newest employee.

Unaware of the difficult work involved under grueling conditions, I was grateful to have been hired. The money would be comfortable, and I would be in a position not only to assume responsibility for my share of the rent, but perhaps to pay for a few hours of heat and electricity a week.

The molding factory was scorching. Obliged to stand in front of the mold press while a searing heat liquefied granules of plastic before infusing them into the mold, I often felt as if I were on the verge of losing both consciousness and my job.

Believing the blaze a preview of the fires of damnation, it was a motivational tool to keep me virtuous and in clear conscience. Fearing the Lord, I knew that if I misbehaved, He would seek retribution, even if my life until then had seemed like a continual journey through hell. Perhaps I had paid my dues in advance, even before committing the sins for which I was already held accountable. After all, God was παντογνόστησ, the nuns in the orphanage would say; He's omniscient.

I worked hard not to disappoint Pam and Sharon, who had referred me to George as a conscientious and capable worker. Even though the fumes from the melting plastic were not exactly aromatic, and itch-stimulating beads of sweat caused my clothing to stick to my body as if they had been drenched in glue, it was undoubtedly preferable to the bloody sights and repulsive aromas of hospital life.

However, the day seemed endless and the task at hand tedious, and often unbearable. Joy and enthusiasm eventually returned to suffering and misery. Discouraged, I felt as if I had been pulled back to square one.

Al came for short visits from time to time. He was full of doting attention and always brought cigarettes. But after all the sexual abuse I'd suffered as a child, I was totally disinterested in any romantic relationships. Al was not a boyfriend in my eyes. Al was God's liaison here on earth; the knight in kaki armor who would carry me off to my dream life in America. When the time was right, my destiny would unfurl. I knew I was slipping deeper into sadness.

One evening, while we sat in the darkness of our flat, discussing the day's events, I confided in the girls.

"I want a better a life," I blurted, tears streaming down my cheeks. "I want to go to America. This is not how I want to spend my life. I know there is something better for me, but not here in Europe, and I am certain that I will find it if I leave this all behind."

A wave of melancholy washed through me, rendering me inconsolable. Barbara, Pam and Sharon looked on in disbelief.

"But Avyrini, how can you go to America?" Sharon asked. "You don't know anyone and you don't have any money. Why don't you come to Canada with me when I return home?"

Pam took over the conversation, asking me to go to Australia with her. Moved by their endearing friendship, I thanked them for the kind invitations but mentioned that my heart was set on my dream: America. Ever since I was a tiny child, I'd envisioned myself crossing the Atlantic to create my fortune. Was it just a puerile folly? The ridiculous, wishful thinking of a despondent child seeking asylum in fanciful daydreams? Truly, I thought not.

"I have Al's parents," I said. "He told me to write them when I was ready and they would help me. And that is what I am going to do."

Al had sent me many letters declaring his passionate love for me. Along with the letters, he sent me cigarettes from the military base, which I happily shared with Pam and Sharon.

The following day, I drafted letters to both Al and his parents, mentioning my intention to go to America. After I checked my spelling and signed my name, I dropped down on my knees, begging the Lord to "please deliver me from my misery." Just listening to my prayer brightened my mood as I felt God would not disappoint me.

Two weeks later, I received a letter from Al.

"My dear Avyrini," he wrote, "meet me in Germany and we will go to America together. My parents are expecting us. Don't worry about the plane tickets. I will take care of all the arrangements. Call me when you arrive."

Delirious, I read the letter over a hundred times. I ate with it. I slept on it. I carried it in my handbag everywhere I went. It proved that God was listening—that He really was there.

I informed Pam and Sharon of my decision to leave. After thanking George for his kindness in giving me a chance to work in the factory, I broke to him the news that I was resigning. Packing his pipe with fresh tobacco, he said, "Avyrini, I'm happy for you."

I scurried about with the letter Al's parents sent me, confirming their agreement to sponsor me. At the American Embassy, I applied for a visa after getting my passport. I was instructed to get the necessary immunizations required by law for entry into the United States.

I packed my belongings, slipped my diary into my suitcase, tucked both Al's and his parents' letters into my passport and slipped it into my handbag. Finally ready, I bid farewell to Pam and Sharon, promising to always keep in touch—a promise I never reneged on.

Boarding the train for Germany, I couldn't help questioning if I was being redeemed without repentance—without a confession, sacramental or otherwise. What sins had I committed, anyway? Mistreated and abused sexually, physically and emotionally, I was, in a sense, the sins of others.

The afternoon air was crisp when I landed in Germany. Instead of phoning Al, I went directly to the base, since he assured me he would be there to meet me. Three hours later, tired and worried that perhaps he had fallen on a misfortunate circumstance, I phoned to see what the delay was about.

"Ayvrini," a baritone voice responded, "Al is not here. He was discharged—he's gone back to the United States!"

Devastated, I realized that I had been stood up. With little money and no Al, I had but one option: to return to England.

Like a winter sunset casting the day into bleakness with hurried impatience, my mood darkened. How could Al do this to me? We were supposed to go to America. This was my dream; this was my prayer. Maybe there was an error. Could Al have forgotten our appointment?

I returned to England, disappointed but certainly not a defeatist. I was going to America—with or without Al. Pam and Sharon were sympathetic, trying their best to console me.

"I'm going to America," I sobbed. "I will go by myself. Al's parents are waiting for me."

"Why don't you ask George for help?" Pam suggested. "He likes you."

The following morning, tearless but with puffed, red eyes, I accompanied the girls to the factory. George took one look at me and realized that the situation was doom-and-gloom dramatic.

"He stood me up," I cried, running into his arms. "Al left without me. He went home to America."

"Avyrini," George whispered, gingerly patting me on the back to calm my thundering outburst, "don't worry. I'll help you."

Kind and compassionate as well as relatively wealthy in his own right, George said, "Listen, calm down. I'll give you 500 pounds. That should get you to America."

I couldn't believe my ears. It was the voice of God speaking through George's lips. The will of the Lord was unraveling my destiny—I was going to America even if I went alone. That evening, I wept until exhaustion pushed me into a deep sleep. But for the first time in my life, the tears that drenched my pillow were tears of joy.

FOURTEENTH EPISODE

"Now, I say to you today my friends, even though we face the difficulties of today and tomorrow, I still have a dream. It is a dream deeply rooted in the American dream."

—Martin Luther King, Jr.

I had recently turned twenty-one, an event that proclaimed my official graduation from childhood, leaving me the sole proprietor of my life. Without a family, I had no support system, no roots and no anchor to keep me docked. Consequently, I was under obligation to remain neither in my native Greece nor in any of the European host countries that had been my home for the past seven years. Although the umbilical cord had been severed, I experienced neither the melancholy of homesickness nor the nostalgia of a vanished culture. My goodbye, even if aloof and emotionally unruffled, was life-altering.

It was April 4, 1968. Awakening well in advance of dawn, I tried my best not to disturb Barbara, Pam and Sharon. The lilting echoes of their slow, steady breathing told a tale of girls lost in deep, untroubled sleep.

On tiptoe, I pirouetted across the room, careful not to disturb the serenity of the slumber they enjoyed. Nearing the window, I gazed out, peering into the blackness before elevating my eyes to the heavens to offer a prayer.

Crowded with sparkling stars, the sky was in sharp contrast with the darkness beneath. It was the expression of an emotional potpourri—the dark, discerning side of melancholy and the exhilarating shimmer of happiness. I went from invoking God's help to escape a misery arising from the mistiness of life to a feeling of proximity and communion with my Creator. I felt His presence and the tenderness of His smile. I knew He was truly with me.

Tiptoeing back, I searched under the bed for my shoebox of treasures. Retrieving it, I took out, one by one, my passport, a pack of cigarettes, a book of matches, a small mirror, a tube of lipstick and my treasured photos of America cut from newspapers and magazines. Hurriedly, I slipped the treasures into my handbag. Then, reaching again under the bed, I grabbed my cherished diary and a handful of possessions and dropped them into a suitcase. I continued until I had crowded my life into several suitcases.

With the entirety of my belongings packed, I glanced one last time over my shoulder, bidding a whispered farewell to my wonderful friends who had cared enough to have given me a chance for dignity. Thanks to their loyalty and solidarity, they would always have a special place in my life, regardless of how the Fates would spin for me.

Drawing a long, deep breath, I shut my eyes for a brief moment. In the pre-dawn stillness, I crossed the threshold. Though nervous with anticipation, a budding serenity confirmed that I was totally in accord with my decision. Behind closed eyes, the darkness was illuminated with the radiance of hope, a sparkle fueled exclusively by my faith in God.

Outside, the air was brisk and moist. While the rain had stopped, the evening gloom did not permit the puddles to dry up. Stretching a leg, I settled my foot on a dry patch of sidewalk and waited for the taxi, hoping the driver would be sufficiently gallant to help with my luggage.

I was lucky. Seeing my bags piled on the sidewalk, he jumped from the vehicle and as if he were reading my mind. In total silence, he placed each bag into the trunk and what did not enter was settled on the back seat. Several minutes later, I was heading toward Paddington Station to catch the Heathrow express train to the airport.

This time, the mishmash of careening thoughts accompanying me on my life-altering journey was different. A quick slide through the years whisked me from Ktismata to Ioannina, Saloniki, Switzerland, Germany and England. Like a pawn on a chess board, I had been uprooted and moved from square to square according to the whims of others. However, I promised myself I would try to substitute emerging dreams and objectives for the memories I so desperately wanted to exile from my mind.

The scuttle of cerebral activity, together with the theatrical rush of flashback images playing in front of me, left me without time to ponder the new unknown—until the taxi came to an abrupt halt. Noticing the sign for Paddington Station, I grabbed my purse and exited, waiting for the driver to unload the bags. I had several bags to tote around and quite a way to walk to reach the terminal.

Luckily, the driver found me a luggage cart. Pointing me in the direction of the train, he reassured me that someone would be waiting to take care of my bags. I thanked him for his consideration and handed him an extra well-earned tip. No one except George and my friends, Pam, Sharon and Barbara, had ever graced me with a kindness. Consequently, whenever I was blessed to receive such attention, I had to show my appreciation.

I trailed behind the endless line of people heading in the same direction. Somehow, unlike me, they looked as if they knew where they going. It was a certain non-hesitancy that convinced me that these were not novices on a maiden journey. They had surely traveled this route before.

Once settled on the train, I sat quietly, with my hands folded on my lap, as crowds of men, women and children of all ages, sizes and variations crammed into the coach, clumsily knocking their carry-on bags against the aisle seats with little concern for the passengers already seated.

Some were anxiously clearing their throats and blowing their noses; others dabbed at red, puffed eyes—probably the results of what I imagined were heart-wrenching goodbyes, an agony unbeknown to me. I had no loved ones to pine for and no sense of patriotism. My love was for America—even if until then, we were total strangers.

Realizing that this was a trip of just minutes, I did not remove my sweater, though I began to feel a moistness along the back of my neck. Once the sun rose above the horizon, dragging bursts of pink and red splotches across the sky, the day had warmed.

Penetrating chugging sounds, almost rhythmic, in harmony with the echo of rail crackling, were distracting. I was unable to focus my own thoughts until a sharp blast of the diesel horn and an abrupt stop cleared my mind.

"Heathrow," the tall, slender conductor shouted in a thick, Cockney accent. Passing my seat, he glanced at me inquisitively—a young woman alone heading for the airport. Perhaps I tweaked his curiosity.

Leaving the train was as chaotic as entering. However, despite the tangle of hurried passengers, I was able to make my way into the airport. Heading over to the TWA check-in window, I pulled out my passport and plane ticket. "I'm going to America," I said, almost disbelieving my own words. "I'm going to live in America." The clerk smiled, checked my ticket, tagged my bags and told me I would be boarding in two hours. I was delirious.

Onboard, I was welcomed with broad smiles. The stewardesses were colorfully dressed in red, brass-button suits with collarless jackets, A-line mini skirts and multicolored knit tops with green, red, white and gold stripes. Similarly patterned berets, slightly tipped to the right, snuggly hugged their heads. Equally radiant, their eyes were warm and glowing as they tried their best to please during the long, tedious flight form London to New York.

Even if I can't recall just how long the flight was, I can surmise that it probably took about eight and a half hours, considering the tail and head winds' effect on the speed of the aircraft.

Alone and apprehensive about an unknown future, I settled into my seat and tried to enjoy the wonderful meal I was served. I had not yet touched US soil, yet I was already in love with Americans.

"May I get you a drink?" a pretty, blonde stewardess asked, exhibiting a full set of pearly white teeth.

"What can I have?" I asked in response.

"Are you twenty-one?" she said.

"Yes," I replied, grinning. "I was twenty-one in February."

"OK then you can have a drink if you wish."

"Thanks," I blurted. "I'll have a beer please."

Several minutes later, she returned with an ice-cold beer and a little bag of nuts. Numerous sips later, I felt a bit relaxed, though whenever I gazed out the window at the downy mass of gliding, white clouds, I wondered where this new journey would take me. What kind of path was I following? Lowering my eyes on the massive expanse of ocean, I felt my heart flutter. However, focusing on the present moment and the reality of actually realizing my dream to go to America, I was able to overcome the annoying doubts surfacing at random intervals. Instead, I entertained flights of fantasy to appease the hordes of questions sprouting in my mind.

Two beers later, I drifted into a semi-wakeful state. Refusing to resist the heaviness of my eyelids, I let them drop and eventually dozed off. Unfortunately, the serenity of the unconscious was short-lived. An unexpected air pocket jolted me back to an upright position, recharging my cerebral activity. Fearful the plane would tumble, I prayed, "God I'm finally going to America, please don't let me die before I arrive!"

A voice from the cockpit reassured the passengers that the instability was just a bit of turbulence due to strong winds that had suddenly manifested. Nevertheless, it took me a while to slow my heartbeat and calm down. Glancing at the top of the air-sickness bag protruding from its pocket behind the seat, I promised myself I would not have to snatch it and use it. This was my dream and nothing was going to spoil my euphoria.

The rest of the flight was rather uneventful; therefore, I utilized the quiet interval to imagine what Al's parents would be like. I wondered if they would be willing to accept me even though I was Greek and born illegitimate. Would I finally be able to bury these awful sins of my past and move on with my life? Would the Americans be more pardoning of my yesterday?

Once again, a voice cut through my thoughts, announcing our arrival at JFK Airport in approximately twenty minutes. My pulse raced; was this truly happening? Did he really say, "Arrival at JFK?"

Scared I would fall into a swoon from the excitement, I tried to control my racing heart with deep, slow breaths. I inhaled, asking God to help me clam down and stop the pounding in my chest. I exhaled, thanking Him for taking me to America. Amazingly, it worked—at least for the moment.

Reaching for my bag, I reapplied my lipstick, pulled out my passport and then unfolded the letter I'd received from Al's parents, and reread the sentence that changed the entire course of my life: "Dear Avyrini, come to St. Louis—we will be happy to sponsor you in the United States."

"Ladies and gentlemen," a firm voice said, silencing the passengers. "The captain has turned on the 'fasten seatbelts' sign in preparation for landing. Please put your trays back, make sure your seats are in an upright position, place all carry-on bags under the seat and extinguish all cigarettes. Remain seated until the plane comes to a stop."

I stomped out my cigarette and slid my bag under the seat in front of me. My heart was racing again. I actually feared it would explode in my chest.

"We are making our descent into JFK International Airport," the voice continued.

I was beyond thrilled. I was numb—frozen in my seat, unable to think, unable even to blink. My feet were gone, nonexistent. My hands, icy and motionless, settled on my lap.

However, my stomach would not quiet down. Flocks of butterflies chased each other in a reckless game of tag, inconsiderate of my feelings. As the plane took a sharp nose dive, they became more and more daring and defiant until it seemed as if they were seeking an escape through my mouth. Coughing a few times, I actually fantasized that I could perhaps forcefully evict them. But such a luxury was not destined to be—at least, not just yet. Although I could discipline my thoughts, I was an impotent warrior, unable to dominate my emotions. Undisturbed by a prayer seemingly fallen on deaf ears and consequently a request unanswered, I focused instead on the present moment, believing that if I didn't think about the butterfly battle, perhaps they would call a truce.

Gazing out the window, I caught sight of a dazzling blaze of lights as dusk began to enrobe the city in a shawl of shadows. The closer we came, the brighter the lights gleamed. It was as if the sky somersaulted from above my head to beneath my feet. In a few moments, I thought, I would be walking in heaven. It was absolutely breathtaking.

I heard a rumbling sound as the landing gear was released; it would not be long now. A few bumpy jolts and the plane was racing along the runway. My eyes shut tightly. My breathing stopped. I dug my nails into the armrests of my seat.

"God, please let me land safely."

When I opened my eyes, I was on American soil. It was no longer a dream—it was my new reality!

FIFTEENTH EPISODE

"We will only say to the people, 'Let your conscience be your guide.' Our actions must be guided by the deepest principles of our Christian faith... Once again we must hear the words of Jesus echoing across the centuries: 'Love your enemies, bless them that curse you, and pray for them that despitefully use you.'"

—Martin Luther King Jr.

Unconsciously emulating pontifical behavior, I fell to my knees and kissed the ground belonging to the United States of America. Brushing away the granules of soot that stuck to my lips, I gave thanks to God for redeeming me one more time. Astounded by new and overwhelming emotions, I tried to give a worthy voice to my prayer, failing to utter more than an essential monosyllable: "Thanks."

Believing I was journeying to a land of utopia, where life was an idyllic extravaganza of unbroken, perfect moments, I never expected the absolute mayhem and confusion that greeted me when I entered JFK Airport. Starry-eyed, exhausted, anxious, scared and happy perhaps beyond all reason, I stepped into a flashing scenario of shouts, cries and people in all shapes, sizes and colors scurrying about as if lost in a tangled maze with no possibility of exit.

What struck me hardest was the distraught expression on the faces of the men and women I thought smiled from dawn to dusk.

"This is America," I whispered. "Why is everyone so sad and angry?" Clutching on to my passport and handbag, I braced myself, determined to follow a straight path while trying to avoid getting trampled on by this maddening crowd.

Pausing a moment to get my bearings, I surveyed the scene. I noticed that Americans were so different from Europeans—so much more colorful. My fantasy was intrigued with this kaleidoscopic panorama of multihued people. So many men, women and children were black, and they all had black tightly curled hair. I had never before seen such dark skin. Yet it was only April, and still rather cold. Could the American sun have turned their skin such a rich chocolate color?

I moved along, following the other passengers, en route to the luggage pick-up station. Still infatuated with the diversity of Americans, I wanted to reach out to see if black skin felt any different from white. I was far too young and naïve to realize that the dissimilarity was limited exclusively to the color.

A scream interrupted my thoughts. "Someone killed him. They shot him… Why would anyone want to murder one of the greatest men of our times? Who would pull the trigger on a hero?"

Confused, I stood waiting for luggage that never seemed to arrive. The inconsistencies between my initial expectations and the reality of this moment were even more confusing. I couldn't understand the prevailing grim mood. It just seemed so out of character with my personally designed profile of the happy American.

But I was in for a rude awakening. Walking over to the baggage claim counter forty-five minutes later, I caught the attendant's attention amid the chaos.

"I've been waiting almost an hour for my luggage," I said, irritated, "but it never comes. Can you help me?"

"Let me check to see if some of the bags maybe missed the flight or are arriving with another load. I apologize for all the confusion."

"What's going on?" I asked. "Why is everyone shouting and crying?"

"Dr. Martin Luther King, Jr. was assassinated!" he responded. "It's a terrible tragedy and a big loss for this country."

"How did it happen?" I asked, interested to learn more about this apparently great man whose demise had such a devastating impact.

"He was standing on the balcony outside his motel room in Memphis when he was killed by a sniper's gunfire to his neck and jaw. They say the bullet traveled right through his spine."

"Who was he? Did he have a family?" I pursued, gaining interest.

"He was a phenomenal man and a charismatic leader in the Civil Rights Movement, a visionary who never gave up on his dream. He has a wife and kids. I think he won the Nobel Peace Prize in 1964. This vile act will have awful repercussions."

Confused, I had no idea what he was speaking about. However, my dream had just come true; I had never given up on it, either. Almost instantly, I felt a mysterious complicity with this Martin Luther King.

"What's the Civil Rights Movement?" I questioned.

"It's all about equality between the races—you know, the blacks and the whites."

Now I was beginning to understand what he was referring to. That explained the dark-skinned people—they were of another race. It had nothing to do with sun tanning!

"You're a bit too young to remember," he continued, clearing his throat, "but there was a time, before Dr. King, when a black person was forced to sit in the rear of the bus in certain places. It's called prejudice—people think they are superior to others. Where are you from?"

"England," I lied. "I'm from England and I never saw a black person before today," I blurted with the naivety of a six-year-old child.

His grin was wide, exposing a perfect set of huge, white teeth that glistened against his dark, creamy skin.

"Why does prejudice exist?" I continued, trying to learn more about this strange, new word.

"It's just ignorance," he muttered, looking askance. "But it's so unfair and certainly causes a lot of unnecessary pain and suffering."

What I did not understand was why there should be inequality. Why did skin color dictate certain ideas and behavior patterns? Didn't God make all human beings in his image and likeness?

Thinking back, I reflected on all the intolerance others had exhibited in my regard—the hurtful insults, the beatings and the severe punishments as well as the rejection and abandonment. This, in a sense, was prejudice also. Since I was born illegitimate, I was considered inferior to other children—but instead of being coerced into the back of the bus, I was ostracized, abused and exiled from my family. Yet I had absolutely no responsibility for the crime responsible for my condemnation.

"Miss," the clerk called, reeling in my attention. "I'm sorry to tell you this but I think your luggage is lost. You do have your purse and documents, don't you?" he inquired, his dark eyes dwelling on mine. Somehow, it was a gaze of understanding and compassion, a soft, moist glance that spoke of a desire to personally atone for the wrongdoing at my expense.

"Yes, but all my belongings, my diaries and my money are gone," I sobbed. "Everything I own has been stolen. All I have are the clothes on my back."

A new consciousness was seeded in me in that precise moment.

Amid the hustle and tension, I realized that I was penniless except for the bus fare safely tucked in the letter Al's parents had sent me. It probably was an act of God that guided me to keep this lifesaver in my handbag instead of the suitcase.

Thankfully, I now had enough money to get to St. Louis. I would worry about the rest when the time came. At present, I would overcome one hurdle at a time.

After saying goodbye to the gracious baggage clerk, I walked over to the Greyhound window and purchased a bus ticket. Several minutes later, I was settled in an aisle seat. Waiting for the rest of the passengers to board, I couldn't help reiterating in my mind what I had learned earlier: Skin color determined where a person sat on the bus. Could I have mistakenly interpreted what I'd heard?

I almost couldn't or perhaps didn't want to believe that some Americans behaved in that prejudicial manner. They were my heroes, my salvation—after Christ, of course. How could they possible regard God's creatures with such unjust bias and coldness of heart?

I made a mental note to ask Al about this issue. Surely, as a military man, he would be able to explain this peccadillo named prejudice.

The trip was long, tedious and stressful. Along the way, I witnessed violent uprising, blazing cars and property fires, aggressive rioting and random acts of vandalism, committed in retaliation for the murder of Dr. Martin Luther King, Jr. He had to have been quite a special man to warrant such heinous outbursts.

As the bus sped along, I felt trapped in a horrifying nightmare. The scenes unwinding before my eyes were tumultuous, emotionally explosive and bloody—only I was sadly not asleep. It was not just a nightmare.

In fact, very much awake, I was devastated by the vengeful reprisals sprouting from the new sin I had learned about. But I was the object of prejudice also—yet I felt neither vindictive nor committed to settling the score. Neither did I intend to harm anyone nor cause undue misery to others. My mission, my raison d'être, was to be happy, to be free and to enjoy a dignified life in the USA—and maybe even to become successful like the multitude of immigrants who had preceded me there. After all, it was the American dream.

Although darkness had fallen like a curtain signaling the conclusion of a drama's final act, it was not thick enough to cast the antagonists into oblivion. The screams were too ear-shattering, the delinquency too rampant and with city after city engulfed in wings of fire, there was no escape.

Exhausted, emotionally and physically, I shut my eyes, preferring to remain in my own world a bit longer.

Doubts sprouted. I was lonely, famished, penniless and terrified not only of the murky unknown, but of the initial glimpse that created my first impression of America.

Misgivings multiplied. Did I err in immigrating to the USA? Would I have been better off remaining with Pam, Barbara and Sharon in England, even if I awakened heavy-hearted each morning, miserable, and retired every evening lusting for a better life? Was I foolish to listen to the voice in my head that whispered from time to time throughout the two decades of my life, "Avyrini, go to America"?

When the Greyhound stopped, I sat upright in my seat, wondering if we had arrived in St. Louis. Unaware of the long trip ahead, I had no idea I was on a bus programmed to make a stop in every city along the way.

"We are taking a break," the driver announced. "We'll stop here to get some food and drinks, use the restrooms and stretch our legs."

The passengers yawned as if waking suddenly from a long sleep, and exited in silence. I remained seated.

"Miss," the driver said, observing me through his rearview mirror, "aren't you going to get something to eat?"

Realizing that without money, satisfying my hunger and quenching my thirst were certainly not options, I replied, "I'd love to have a bite to eat, but all my luggage and money were stolen at the airport. I can't even buy a pack of gum."

"Don't worry, Miss, come with me. I'll get you something to eat."

Kind and generous, the sandy-haired man with the ruddy-complexioned, round face made certain I had food and water for the duration of the trip. Noticing his large, dark-rimmed glasses visibly set askance on his head, I tired my best not to giggle.

Once inside the rest stop he ordered two hamburgers, some fries and two Cokes.

"One of each is for you," he said, grinning, handing me a bag with a burger, fries and Coke. The aroma of charred meat wafted past my nostrils, teasing my palate even before I bit into the juicy burger. After the airplane fare, it seemed as if I was about to consume a gourmet dinner.

"Thanks," I said hurriedly, eager to enjoy the feast. Smiling, he nodded and accompanied me back to my seat on the bus.

Crammed in beside me was a middle-aged, portly woman whose exaggerated girth caused her to unwittingly trespass on my territory. Though unconscious, this intrusion rendered the trip excruciatingly uncomfortable. Squashed like articles of clothing in an overstuffed suitcase, and unable to move without jabbing her, I was forced to adopt a limited movement strategy to maintain a peaceful relationship for the duration of the journey.

However, as with all decisions taken freely, I was obliged to suffer the consequences—spasmodic, brow-crinkling leg cramps accompanied by a distressing accumulation of fluid in my ankles and feet.

To say I was uncomfortable fails to accurately depict the moment. I was simply miserable and yearning for my destination, whatever it might bring.

The idea of standing was inviting; the thought of a home and a bed was almost bewitching and the feeling that someone was waiting for me—someone who actually wanted me—was beyond rapturous.

Again, I shut my eyes. Pausing for an adequate interval, I cleared my mind of all expectations. Then, breathing deeply, I began to set the stage for my arrival at Al's house.

"Gather your hand luggage," the driver announced after clearing his throat several times. "We're pulling into the St. Louis bus terminal."

From the window, I saw a huge sign—N. 13th Street. However, I had no way of knowing that one of the cross streets to the station would in time be renamed Martin Luther King Drive. Yet despite all the unknowns, I knew I was home.

SIXTEENTH EPISODE

"Where there is no struggle, there is no strength."
—Oprah Winfrey

Although the unforgiving circumstances of Dr. Martin Luther King's assassination gave free rein to a confusing outpouring of violence, flooding my heart with fear and apprehension, I tried to redirect my focus on putting the surprising aspects of my new country's culture into perspective. This was a whole different world, with situations I had never before encountered despite the fact that I had lived in four different European countries.

Leaving behind the rash, judgmental opinions I could have given life to, I opted to concentrate on seeing my knight in shinning armor and meeting his parents. What seemed like an exotic maze of asymmetric shapes rendered more distorted once caught in the mass of twinkling lights, as the plane left behind the anonymity of the heavens, was now part of who I would become.

Quietly, I gave thanks, moving my mind back in time to the inspiring stories I had read about pioneering immigrants of generations past who had packed their meager belongings to head for America and the hope of a better life. Today, deserting my native land, I too had stepped into the history books. Furthermore, like those who preceded me, I also was filled with expectations, hope and the allure of living my dream.

A tall, blue-eyed gentleman with blond, curly hair interrupted my thoughts.

"Hi, Avyrini," he said, clumsily entwining his long arms around my tiny waist. "Welcome to St. Louis."

He had absolutely no idea just how happy I was to see him. A familiar face was exactly what I needed not only to calm my racing heart, but to appease the fear that had twisted my stomach into knots.

"Hi, Al," I responded noticing how different he looked out of uniform and with his rather un-military curls. He certainly was handsome.

"Where is all your luggage?" he asked, his brow crinkling into the deep lines that speak of perplexity. "Didn't you bring your belongings with you?"

"I packed several suitcases before I left England, but they were all stolen at the airport in New York."

"All?" he responded almost in disbelief. "Avyrini, how could all your bags be taken? I could understand perhaps one, but all! Did you make a missing bags claim?"

"No, Al, I was so scared."

"Scared? What were you scared of?"

"Al, I never saw black people before, and they were all shouting and crying and running wild through the airport. I didn't know what was happening but I knew it had to be something bad."

"Avyrini," Al said, taking me by the hand, smiling, "there is nothing to be afraid of. Black people are just like us. They eat and drink, smile and cry, go to sleep and awaken and experience happiness and sadness like we do. They go to school as children, grow up, work and eventually marry and have their own families. Their accomplishments and failings are equally noteworthy as are ours. There is no difference except for the color of their skin. You will see."

What Al said made sense to me. I knew that we were all created by God in His image and likeness. Yet I had a difficult time understanding why some people were treated better than others.

"OK, Avyrini," Al said, sighing, "let's go home. Don't worry—my mom will give you some clothes until we can buy new ones for you."

Al's words seemed reassuring and by now, struggling with exhaustion and a host of other human weaknesses, I was only to joyful to let him take over. Considering what I had been through, emotionally and physically, during the past twenty-four hours as a young woman crossing the ocean alone, I felt encouraged by the presence of this welcoming American in counterpoint to the dismal environment into which I had landed.

Once outside the bus depot, we walked over to Al's car. He opened the door and I climbed in. A flashback scene took me to Germany and our first date. Remembering his rear seat stacked with cases of beer, I chuckled silently. It was different this time. On his seat were several newspapers and a baseball cap.

To my inquires and accusation of abandonment in Germany, the now firefighter explained that he had received his discharge from the Army and gone home immediately, fully secure I had his parents' address and the assurance of their willingness to sponsor me in the USA.

Though I nodded my head, I emphasized how scared I was to discover that I had been stood up.

"Well," he said, "what matters now is that you are here with me."

We drove for an undetermined span of time until a paved driveway enticed him to abruptly pull off the road. Flanked on either side by a lush, well-manicured lawn, the scene was almost cinematic, especially in comparison to my past residential destinations. Dew had spread its moisture like soft honey running down the crispy quarter of a freshly pared apple. The blades of grass reflected under the evening light, glistening.

We were in Affton, Missouri, a small community in South St. Louis County. I later learned it had several historical landmarks, including Grant's Farm and Oakland House.

Tiny buds with the vaguest suggestion of color promised a flourish of multicolored flowers in late spring. Swaying languidly in the evening breeze, they were illuminated under a row of amber garden lights.

"Here we are, Avyrini," Al said, taking a deep breath. Stepping out of the car, I surveyed the area to get a better perspective on my new surroundings. If first impressions are an opinion determinant, mine was decidedly favorable. The house was a large two-story, imposing and stately—obviously well maintained. I had not expected such a luxurious residence. To date, I had lived in less than Spartan dwellings including years in rundown Quonset storage huts with neither water nor electricity. This was in net contrast to my past experiences—at least, my first impression gave that opinion.

"Let's go inside—my parents are expecting us," Al whispered nervously.

Fumbling in his pocket for the key, he seemed a bit agitated. When the front door flew open, his search ended. Greeted with a smile and a handshake, Mr. and Mrs. Becker motioned for us to enter.

At first glance, the interior seemed to be in perfect harmony with the exterior. Upscale, traditional furnishings spoke of wealth and sophistication. An elderly woman seated in a huge, wood-framed armchair neither acknowledged our presence nor upset her pose upon our entry.

After the introductions, the Beckers led us through the living room to a multi-veined oak door. Al quickened his pace, overtook his parents and pulled the door open. It squeaked like a mouse caught in a trap. In retaliation, it discharged two slender splinters that fell beside his left foot. With the pointed tip of his shoe, he sent them spinning across the room.

"Ayvrini, we live downstairs in the basement," Mr. Becker said, catching my puzzled look.

Tall and somewhat stockier than his son, he was by all definitions still an attractive man. His sandy hair was heavily frosted with silver strands. Deep lines and dark circles drew attention to his bloodshot eyes.

At the time, I had no idea what constituted a basement. But making my way down the narrow, iron staircase, I soon discovered it was an area about the size of the first level of the house. Devoid of any room delineations, the Beckers' living quarters were undecorated and anchored by a gray concrete floor and matching cobwebbed ceiling.

The underground room was a gloomy, humid space, not much of an improvement over my previous lodging conditions. An all-too-familiar odor of mold permeated, painfully offending my olfactory sense.

Sparingly furnished with what appeared to be previously discarded pieces, I questioned why three people would live in such an undignified manner, crammed in the basement, while one played queen of the realm, living solo in a big, two-story house. Something was not quite right.

"Where do I sleep?" I asked Al after surveying the room with a quick turn of my head.

"Avyrini," Mrs. Becker said, gesturing with an extended index finger pointed across the room, "you'll sleep on that couch." Both Al's mom and dad had the ruddy complexion and unsteady gait of serious drinkers who repeatedly exceeded their limits.

Small in comparison to father and son, Mrs. Becker was a typical, overweight, middle-aged woman who tried unsuccessfully, with poor make-up techniques, to eliminate the effects of time. However, in lieu of camouflaging fine lines and a marred complexion, she highlighted her imperfections under a thick layer of heavy foundation that resembled a cracked mask.

Humbly acknowledging my gratitude, I walked over to the couch and sat down. It was obvious that Al's parents had consumed a few cocktails before our arrival. Nonetheless, I was unaware of the full extent of their alcohol problems, and the deleterious effects it could have on their lives.

No longer alone, and relieved to be in a safe environment, I longed for a good night's sleep and the hope that I would awaken to a sumptuous American breakfast of bacon and eggs, like in the movies. Too exhausted to think of much else, I did not question why Al and his family were relegated to the basement when the actual living quarters were rather spacious.

The following morning, I did enjoy the breakfast of my dreams. Afterwards, I tried to acclimate myself to my new family. It was not easy to build a relationship with the Beckers because of their continual inebriated state. Al didn't seem concerned and often ignored the signs of his parents' drinking problem. Denial is a convenient tactic but fragile and certainly no match for the power of truth.

Life seemed rather monotonous, just sitting around waiting for Al to finish his shift at the Affton fire station. Since household chores seemed a rather futile endeavor in such a dreary, neglected environment, there was not much to keep me busy.

When Al worked the day shifts, he would take me out in the evenings for some burgers and a beer. We would chat about the day's events—mostly his—and try to make some plans for the future.

One day, he inquired about my alien status.

"Avyrini, your visa will soon expire," he said. "If we don't do something, you'll have to return to England."

I felt my heart take a sharp nose dive down to my feet.

"I don't want to return to Europe. I want to stay in America," I blurted. "Isn't there something we can do? There has to be a way for me to stay here. I'm not going back!"

"Yes, there is a way," he replied. "You can marry me. Then, as my wife, you can remain in America forever. You can even become an American."

Although I was not in love with Al, I loved the words "you can remain in America forever" and "you can become an American."

I agreed to be Al's wife despite the lack of romance both in his proposal and in our relationship. However, as the wife of an American, I would be assured a permanent stay in the USA.

Before the "I do," I discussed with Al my desire to change my name. Since Avyrini was difficult to pronounce, and given that I wanted to eliminate all traces of my Greek identity and the misery it triggered, I decided I would answer to the name Angela from this day onward. It would be on all my documents. In that manner, I would bleach out my heritage. I would be Angela Becker—an American woman.

Our marriage was overseen by a justice of the peace at a simple civil ceremony. Two weeks later, a religious rite was performed in church. Without mutual love, the vows were meaningless words spoken to attain a specified end. It was certainly not an occasion inscribed in the memory for safekeeping, to be reminisced over with misty eyes and a warm heart in later years. Instead, for all purposes, it was merely a marriage of convenience.

The Beckers were in attendance, to offer their support and impart their blessings on our union, though I often questioned if they were truly in tune with what was actually happening. Did they really understand that their son had taken a wife?

My conversations with them were restricted to isolated phrases and polite formalities. They didn't demonstrate any interest in getting to now their daughter-in-law, regardless of our close living arrangement. Daily, they would sprawl in front of the TV, guzzling one drink after another, hardly communicating even between themselves.

Several months later, while in a drunken stupor, Mr. Becker lost his balance, took a nasty tumble and en route to the ground, slammed and scraped his head against the concrete wall. The blood-curdling screams of husband and wife literally knocked the wind out of me.

"Angela! Angela!" Mrs. Becker gasped. "Hurry! My husband tripped and fell. I think he's seriously hurt."

"Call an ambulance," I screeched, glancing at his unconscious form. Pools and splashes of glistening, crimson blood were everywhere, transforming the staid, gray basement walls and floor to a post-battle combat zone.

"Is he dead? Is he breathing?" Mrs. Becker yelled breathlessly. I noticed how swollen her jugular became—gorged with the blood-rush of hysteria. It seemed intent on popping out of her neck. Her gaze, laced with panic and desperation, regarded the motionless body of Mr. Becker. Mine, ablaze with fear, searched for a pillow to rest his head on.

The paramedics arrived just in time to prohibit me from joining Al's father in a loss-of-consciousness state. Much as my years in the operating room should have acclimated me to the visual experience of blood, I was never able to tolerate the outpouring of vital body fluids. As if an explosion of blood were not ghastly enough, this time, the ruby-red liquid was splotched with clumps of brain matter.

Mr. Becker's fall brought serious consequences. His fractured skull was far too detrimental to his survival. On the way to the hospital, in the serenity of his comatose state, he passed away.

Immediately following the funeral, Al's grandmother evicted his mother from the basement. She was told to pack up and remove her presence from the premises as soon as possible—an order not open for discussion either by her grandson or his wife. Grandma Becker's word was an indisputable law.

Realizing a life change was imminent, I decided to seek employment. Browsing the classifieds, I discovered an insert advertising a position at Target. I applied, and was thrilled when informed I was hired. I had now joined the American workforce! Proud of my accomplishment, I told Al.

"The extra money," I said, "will let us get a place of our own."

"That will certainly help with the rent," he replied, "and it is certainly time for us to move out of Grandma's basement."

Once in a while, beside the hope of dreams, it is necessary to incorporate a sprinkle of realism. I had to become responsible—I had to fully participate in my own life.

Checking the "for rent" ads, we found a couple of small efficiency apartments—one for the now-homeless Mrs. Becker and one for ourselves. They were space-restricted and uncomfortable for two people, but it was a definite improvement over the basement—and it was our home.

Furnished sparingly, it was easy to maintain. However, living came with a price tag. Bills kept rolling in and we did have to nourish ourselves. I knew it was time for me to supplement my meager wages with a second job.

This time, the classifieds brought me to an ad requesting a caregiver for an elderly woman. Certain I would be able to take on this challenge, I applied. Nevertheless, unbeknownst to me at the onset of my commitment was the fact that my employer, the lady's husband, was an influential and affluent builder and philanthropist, renowned and respected in the community. To protect the innocent family heirs from any slander or unjust repercussions, I never referred to the couple by name. From day one, they were simply Mr. and Mrs. V.

My job description called for feeding, medicating and assisting Mrs.

V., to make certain her personal needs were tended to in a secure and satisfactory manner. Remembering my experience from the past as a trained nurse, I anticipated neither conflicts nor hardship—just an additional stipend to make life easier.

Not long after I was officially employed, Mr. V. notified me of a revision in my duties. I was now required to assume all the domestic responsibilities—from housecleaning to cooking to laundry and shopping—plus there were two adult children in residence.

The house was large, almost too spacious for the couple, who had witnessed over ninety summers and were no longer very agile. Furthermore, the middle-aged daughter Mr. V. had fathered with his wife was a pathological kleptomaniac who shoplifted with clock-like regularity. Born with Down's Syndrome, her brother also lived under their parents' roof. Therefore, in reality, I was hired to take care of a problematic family of four, though I was not compensated accordingly.

The kleptomaniac daughter had filled one of the vacant bedrooms with merchandise she'd lifted from various neighborhood shops. Odd in her look and manner, the shouting temper tantrums characterizing her personality were in sharp contrast to her brother's outgoing and overly affectionate nature. Having a crush on me, he demonstrated his amorous feeling by pinching my derrière and upper arms until I was black and blue.

Mrs. V., on the other hand, in spite of her frail stature and advanced age, often changed from a placid and reserved lady into a barmy Jekyll, chasing her husband, shrieking and waving a butcher's knife wildly in the air.

My role in this bizarre scenario was mediator. I was expected to keep order in the house and peace among this eccentric menagerie of unconventional if not totally dysfunctional individuals.

Parsimonious beyond reason, despite his exorbitant wealth, M. V. brushed his teeth with bleach because in his opinion, it was more economic than squandering money frivolously on toothpaste.

"Angela," he'd vehemently say in defense of my frequent recriminations, "no… No, toothpaste is expensive, a waste of hard-earned money. Bleach is better. It whitens your teeth and all for pennies. You really should give it a try."

With that, he sighed, dipped his yellowed, wasted, long overdue to be replaced toothbrush in a handleless, chipped cup, half filled with bleach, and stuck it in my face.

"Go ahead, give it a try," he said, smirking.

"No thanks Mr. V.," I blurted. "I already brushed my teeth."

I returned home in the evenings mentally, physically and emotionally exhausted. However, the extra money, even if an inequitable compensation for the full range of services rendered, was an asset in our time of financial scarcity. For this reason alone, I persisted. It had nothing to do with loyalty and everything to do with personal convenience.

Underpaid and overworked, I could not help feeling exploited by a wealthy man who showered his grandchildren and the generation thereafter with substantial bank accounts and houses while still in their teens.

Though I worked for Mr. V. every evening and on weekends, I took my job at Target seriously, since it was my main source of income. Even if I was diligent and conscientious, and somewhat diplomatic in handling several disturbing and persistent instances of sexual harassment initiated by the manager, I felt discouraged.

"Angela," he crooned, undressing me with his glance, "if you go out with me, I'll give you more money."

"Listen, I'm a married woman and a Catholic," I replied. "I'm not interested in cheating on my husband—not even for more money."

I mistakenly believed that it had ended there until months later, when I was surprised to discover that when I got the same job for a friend of mine, she was hired at triple my salary. Apparently, I was penalized for my moral standards and cast in an unfavorable position.

However, my employment trials did not end there. One afternoon, during a lunch break, I purchased a birthday present for a friend of mine. At the conclusion of my shift, right before punching out, I surveyed the stock room for discarded articles, as I had been instructed to do. Gathering the tattered paper, boxes and cord, I bundled them together and shoved them down the incinerator.

Noticing a piece of trashed wrapping paper with more wrinkles than the brow of a centenarian, I took it to embellish the present I had purchased earlier, then shut the light and left the store.

Approached by the security guard, I was accused of shoplifting, handcuffed and arrested in front of all the employees and customers in the entry of Target.

"Sir," I said through quivering lips, "there must be a mistake. I didn't steal anything."

"Miss, I saw you take something—I was watching you in the monitor. You took the paper. We have pictures of the whole thing."

"But it was just a sheet of discarded, wrinkled wrapping paper," I gasped, unable to breathe. "It was supposed to be disposed of."

I phoned Al. "Al" I stammered, "I've been arrested for stealing a sheet of paper from the trash at Target."

Al came rushing over to clarify the situation, believing it was my heavily accented English that permitted me from defending myself. Twenty minutes later, after Al's explanations, I was released.

The following day, under my husband's tutelage, we engaged the services of an attorney to sue Target for unjust accusation. I was awarded the sum of $10,000, which I immediately turned over to Al.

By now an incorrigible alcoholic like his parents, Al squandered the money on booze and expensive clothes. Upset with his extravagant behavior, I scolded him repeatedly: "Al, stop that foolish spending," I said. "We don't have enough money for food and utilities and you're wasting it all. We could use it to buy a house and perhaps get a better car than the old Buick you drive."

"OK, Angela, you win—no more booze and clothes. But I have to go out now, I ran out of razor blades."

Several hours later, I heard a boisterous rumbling sound—Al had returned home on a BMW motorcycle!

"Get ready, Angela," he shouted, coming through the door. "We're going to Vegas."

Too tempted to resist, I agreed. I mounted behind Al and we rode off, heading for Vegas. Riding through the Death Valley desert under the sweltering June sun was brutal. The piercing rays burned right though my shirt, scorching my shoulders. By the time we arrived at the hotel, I had huge blisters that made any clothing an agonizing experience.

At the casino, the clamor, the variegated diversity of people, the clang of chips, the gasps and hurrahs were exhilarating, until I realized that Al had lost money with his reckless gambling at the tables. I, on the other hand, played the coin slots. He persisted, foolishly believing he could recuperate the loss and win big. Though it was my maiden casino adventure, something told me it was not going to happen. Of course, my feeling was correct.

However, what we did not expect were the flash floods. The deluging waters invaded like Attila the Hun, fierce and inconsiderate, creating ruin and havoc. In the outburst, Al's BMW was swiped away by the whirling torrents, leaving us little option but to return home by bus.

I was beginning to understand that life in the United States was not a carousel spin at a local amusement park while awaiting an opportunity to grab the brass ring. Yes, I was free, but I was starting to learn just how exorbitant a price I would have to pay for this gift of freedom.

SEVENTEENTH EPISODE

"I will neither give a deadly drug to anybody who asked for it, nor will I make a suggestion to this effect. Similarly I will not give to a woman an abortive remedy. In purity and holiness I will guard my life and my art."

—Hippocrates, the Hippocratic Oath

The return trip to St. Louis was uneventful until we actually arrived at our font door. Noticing that Al's Buick was no longer parked in the driveway, our thoughts automatically turned to a criminal scenario.

"The car," Al blurted. "It's gone. Someone stole the car. I'd better get the police over here quickly."

"Let's ask the neighbors if they saw anyone prowling around," I interjected, giving him time to calm down and catch his breath. "I'll go over and talk to them while you take the bags inside."

Walking over to the house next door, I anxiously knocked several times to announce my arrival, badly bruising my knuckles. From the porch, I could hear the TV blaring, giving me the confirmation the couple was in residence.

The noise subsided, proving my flesh-scraping knocks were not endured in vain. A fifty-ish, slightly overweight man with thinning, dark hair came to the door. His black-rimmed glasses were wrapped around a pair of forward-tilted ears, producing an almost comic effect. The deep stains decorating the front of his shirt hinted that he may have been at the table for the evening meal, or perhaps folding his napkin and sliding his chair back after finishing dessert.

Apologizing for my intrusion, I inquired if he had seen anyone snooping around our property.

"We just got back from Vegas," I said, "and we discovered our car is missing. It must have been stolen while we were away."

"No, Angela," he responded, clearing his throat. "It wasn't stolen, it was repossessed."

"What do you mean it was repossessed?"

Pausing to light a cigarette, he continued, "Your husband didn't keep up the payments and the car was seized."

"But we were in Vegas for a week."

"This is not about a week, Angela. Your husband was not paying as he should—that's why you lost the Buick."

I thanked him for the education and went back to find Al guzzling a beer in front of the TV.

"Al," I said, "the car was not stolen—it was repossessed because you failed to keep up the payments."

"No big deal" he mumbled. "I'll get us another car in the morning."

"I'm going to bed, Al. I think I may have caught a bug in Vegas. My stomach is upset and I feel a bit woozy."

"OK, Angela, I'll be there in a little while."

Several days later, when the nausea continued to haunt my days, Al encouraged me to seek a medical solution instead of just waiting it out, moaning and groaning annoyingly and needlessly. Taking his advice, I did.

A kind and emphatic man, the physician was approximately two decades my senior. His soft gaze and questioning nature left me somewhat astounded—no one had ever cared enough to ask me how I felt either physically or emotionally. Nobody was ever interested in listening to what I had to say. Labeled an insignificant person, I was practically invisible except when either a punishment or evil deed was to be executed on my behalf.

Answering to the best of my knowledge, I vocalized a brief summary of my life, including the traumatic tonsillectomy at the hands of the nuns. From the look of disdain on his face, I realized it was his turn to be surprised.

"Angela," he responded, "that's quite a saga. I'm sorry to hear you had such a traumatic childhood." Once again, it was amazing to be in the presence of someone who seemed interested in my well-being.

"I'd like to run a few tests and give you a thorough examination," the physician said, jotting down notes as I spoke. "We will get to this root of this malady."

Prodded and punctured with an understanding but clinical approach brought to full swing the rule of reciprocity. Encouraged to recall the words written in the Gospel of St Luke 6:31—"Do unto others as you would have them do unto you"—I realized that the tables were turned. Flashing in my mind like bolts of lightning during a tropical storm were vibrant images of my nursing days, during which I perforated the flesh of patients while they moaned and frowned in pain, real or imaginary.

Later that evening, I told Al about my exam and mentioned that I was still not feeling well.

"I hope the doctor can help me," I said, weary and distressed. "I want to feel well again. I'm so tired and listless."

Two days later I received the diagnosis: "Angela," an animated voice resounded, "you are pregnant. Congratulations!"

"Pregnant? I'm pregnant!" I shouted. "I'm going to have a baby?"

"Yes, that's the general idea," the doctor said, chuckling. "I'll refer you to a wonderful obstetrician and have my nurse set up an appointment right away."

Thrilled by the news, I expressed my approval and wrote down the doctor's name. "Thanks," I whispered, having a difficult time fueling my voice. "I'll wait for the appointment."

However, much as I danced with merriment, trampling in my mind over every puckered cloud in the heavens, I never anticipated Al's heated reaction to my joyful news. Annoyed and visibly displeased, he rose from the chair; the force of his furor toppled it to the ground. His eyes spilling over with disgust, he regarded me with contempt.

Dashing to the bedroom, he slammed the door and locked himself in, refusing both company and nourishment.

The following day, upon his return from work and prior to returning to his reclusive sanctuary, Al made it known, without any hint of doubt or gallantry, that he was not happy to tackle parenthood. Like a spoiled toddler vying for his mother's attention to satisfy an egotistical whim, he sulked, sprinkling periods of self-imposed exile with moments of fulminating eruptions.

Of course, my thoughts and feelings were neither solicited nor, if volunteered, ever meant to play any role in the decision taken. His opinion took precedence; his feelings were the priority.

A disgruntled man, physically and emotionally disheveled, stumbled to the dinner table that evening.

"Angela," he stammered, "you knew from day one I did not want children. We can barely pay our bills, and just lost the car. You earn $1.82 an hour. There is no way we can support a child. It is out of the question."

Turning, his bloodshot eyes caught my tearful glance. Lifting his hand, he pointed a trembling index finger in my direction.

"Angela, we will not have a child. I don't want one. I'll get you an appointment for an abortion."

"Al," I sobbed, patting my stomach, "there's a baby growing inside me—a human being with a heart and a soul. How can I agree to abort? That's murder Al. Do you understand? Thou shalt not kill—it's a sin."

"Angela, don't defy me. I don't want to be a father. I don't want this baby. I don't care what kind of sin it is. If you want to keep it, I'm leaving. You will raise it alone. I want no part of this."

Pleading for my life and that of my unborn baby, I begged him every morning and each evening for a week. With a litany of desperate implorations, I tried to appeal to his heart.

"Al, we can do this. We can raise our child together. I'll get a better job. Maybe we can start our own business."

"You'll get an abortion, Angela, and that's my final word. Otherwise you'll be alone and probably sent back to England."

Heartbroken, I realized that Al was right. Without his presence in my life, I would be deported as soon as my temporary visa expired. Consequently, turning against my ideas and principles, I agreed to the abortion, even if reluctantly. Convinced I was being coerced against my will did little to alleviate the guilt brewing within.

Mine was a mandatory decision based on Al's intimidating threat. Deep down, I knew I was the victim of emotional blackmail. However, I also realized I had no other option, as an alien without secure status, but to comply.

"OK, Al," I sobbed, burying my face in my hands, "I'll have the abortion."

"Good, Angela, I knew you would see it my way." His cruel words cut through me like a stiletto, turning an innocent bystander into a martyr in the blink of an eye.

In 1969, abortions were illegal; therefore, apart from the moral dilemma, I also had to wrestle with my own fears. Would something go wrong? Would I undergo a botched procedure, compromising my well-being? Disturbing questions kept churning in my mind—questions I did not really want answered.

"Don't worry, Angela," Al said, as if he were actually reading my mind. "I know where to take you. Everything will be just fine."

Two days thereafter, Al accompanied me to a dingy brick building on St. Charles Rock Road. Hesitantly crossing the threshold, I noticed a pungent aroma of disinfectant. Trapped within four soiled and faded walls, the silence was echoless, eerie. Trembling, I held on to Al's arm, terrified to focus my gaze on the actual surroundings. If I experienced it with my eyes, I had to believe it. Somehow, the sense always molded fantasy into reality. I resisted as long as I was permitted, until circumstance ended my game.

The waiting room was tiny, dark and vacant. A poor ventilation system was responsible for the stale, difficult-to-inhale air. My heart raced. Gazing at my feet, I caught sight of the badly stained floor. Surely, the once-white tiles had not been mopped in weeks.

The negligence was overpowering. Horrified, I questioned the validity of this medical facility. It seemed more like a battalion of germs waiting to attack a prey. Powerless, I had to succumb. A returning bout of nausea forced me to head for the door.

"It's OK, Angela," Al said reassuringly. "It'll be over and done with soon enough. Just have a little patience. The doctor will be here shortly."

With precision timing, the echo of new leather shoes, still squeaking with every footstep, announced the "doctor's" arrival. A slender man of undetermined descent walked through the door. Slovenly dressed in wrinkled, oversized clothing and stern of face, he had the insecure vagueness of demeanor and manner characteristic of a fugitive intent on maintaining anonymity.

Ignorance is a true asset in certain moments. However, sometimes, like a deserter, a ray of light escapes even after the sun has retired. In the flickering glow, I did not like what was uncovered.

Shocked by his standoffish bearing, I wondered if I was in the company of a physician or a charlatan. After my flight into the hearth at the hand of my grandmother without the courtesy of a medical follow-up, I was prone to losing my balance and falling, and walked with a limp, never able to enjoy a pain-free stroll. Therefore, all that could go wrong under the knife of an unprofessional was limitless.

Removing his round, horn-rimmed glasses, he extended his hand, reaching for my arm. It was a purely mechanical gesture, programmed without any sense of gallantry or compassion.

"Come with me," he lisped in heavily accented English while tugging at my sleeve.

Immediately, Al dropped my hand. Taking a few steps back, he mumbled, "Angela I'll be here when you're finished. Everything is going to be OK."

His words, a pair of dissecting scissors, cut me apart like a frog in a biology lab. Here I was, about to let this spooky stranger execute my innocent child, and that's all the father could say. It was his child also! This cold, distant man—this man who had handed me my dream, this man who was responsible for my baby's heartbeat—was asking me to silence it.

Furious, I followed the "doctor" without any further acknowledgment. In silence, we walked thorough a narrow, wood door into another empty space. Equally dismal as the entry foyer, it was hurriedly identified as the "operating room." The pungent scent of disinfectant returned, more overwhelming—an odor that carried the guarantee of neither a sterile environment nor meticulous personal hygiene.

A sinner, fully aware I was angering God, I was ashamed to offer any words in prayer. Instead, closing my eyes for a brief moment, I hoped a pardoning sympathetic angel would keep me safe, maybe nestled under a big, golden wing, though in my heart, I knew I was deserving of no such favor. Fate had flipped my dream into reality only to later refuse my wishes to spare the life of my child.

"Take off your pants and underwear," the "doctor" ordered, rudely interrupting my thoughts. "When you're undressed, get down on the floor." His was not exactly the comforting bedside manner of a caring professional who, proud and teary-eyed, had taken the Hippocratic Oath, promising to respect and preserve life.

Shaking like a season-old leaf, coiled and burnt, that had outlived its natural lifespan, I obeyed. Soon, a mere puff of wind would bring the former bloom down to a graceful end.

My child was not given that gift. There would be no fulfilled lifespan and no dignified calling to final rest. For me, there would be no comfort, no serenity and no anesthetic. With the agonizing pain of labor, a child is embraced by the light of day. With the excruciating suffering of an untrained hand invading my privacy, a child was cast into the darkness forever—a cruel destiny sealed by merciless scraping and one swift tug.

Mea culpa. Mea culpa. Mea maxima culpa. I had infringed upon the Divine Law.

Al helped me to the car in silence. During the drive home, there were neither questions pertaining to the procedure and my well-being, nor comments. It was as if we were returning from Sunday Mass, each lost in our own reflections.

I was sick for over three months, hemorrhaging intermittently between bouts of relentless cramps. Exhausting and depressing, life became a nightmare—oppressive, pointless and worthless. Realizing that I was sinking into a murky abyss, I tried to overcome my emotional, psychological and physical frailty, and pulled myself out. Acclimated to years of despondency and survival, I sucked on my experience, hoping it would provide sufficient nourishment to overcome this tormenting moment.

Al fell into his parents' footsteps, drinking heavily while developing an offensive personality. Squandering hard-earned money, he was often self-absorbed and rambunctious. The excessive alcohol consumption turned him ill-natured, evil-minded and humiliatingly abusive.

However, working two jobs, I was more absent than present from home. Nevertheless, in the evenings he forced himself on me, demanding that I oblige in keeping with my duties as a wife.

Several months later, the nausea returned. No longer ignorant, I realized I was possibly pregnant again. Having recently obtained my permanent green card, I felt secure and no longer menaced by threats of deportation.

As soon as the doctor confirmed my suspicions, I broke the news to Al.

"Not again, Angela," he growled. "You'll just have to have another abortion."

"Absolutely not, Al," I snapped back, enraged. "I'm not having an abortion—I will die first. I'm keeping the baby. If you want to leave, that's fine with me."

An abrupt shoulder turn followed by a staggering stride removed his presence from the room. Pleased by my assertiveness, I phoned the doctor for an appointment and prepared myself for motherhood.

In keeping with the general tone of my life, the pregnancy was not without obstacles. Four months later, I started bleeding and was put on full bed-rest. Twenty-two weeks into the pregnancy, my water broke. Terrified, I screamed, begging Al to take me to the hospital.

Following a painful and complicated labor that lasted for forty-eight hours, Shannon Maureen was born. Dangerously premature, she was frail, with malformed feet and arms. But when the nurse placed her in my arms, I gazed down at my baby. In my eyes, she was the most beautiful creature I had ever seen.

Though not a full-term baby, she weighed almost seven pounds and was growing too big too soon. This was why I had gone into early labor.

Like all newborns, Shannon cried and fussed when she was in distress. However, I was quickly informed that severe pulmonary insufficiency compromised her chance to live.

Immediately, she was placed in the NICU, the neonatal intensive care unit. Al visited regularly and seemed supportive, though I knew he was dependent on alcohol.

I prayed for Shannon Maureen every waking moment, but born after a five-and-a-half-month gestation period, she was not developed for survival. Her fragile, paper-thin lungs stopped inflating; her muffled heartbeat was quieted. God had given and God had taken, and my baby girl had become an angel. Devastated, I slipped into depression once again.

Unable to fund a funeral for Shannon Maureen, Al and I entrusted the tiny, mangled corpse to Jewish Hospital. Kind and empathetic in their manner, we felt reassured that she was safe from harm.

I returned to work and my life with Al, though the sweet face of my little angel remained in my mind. It was there every morning when I opened my eyes and at night, it was in my dreams. But despite the inner torment, I did the best I could to be a model employee and devoted wife. It was not easy—but nothing ever was for me.

One day, I awakened with excruciating cramps and severe bleeding. Believing it was part of my cycle, I waited for the pain to subside. However, the pattern was repeated month after month. The cramping became more unbearable and the hemorrhaging was difficult to deal with. Unable to work, I was penalized with pay cuts, which put us in a very precarious financial position, angering my husband.

Al became more aggressive, forcing me to see a doctor. Too distraught to oppose, I went for a check up. Following a barrage of diagnostic exams, I was contacted.

"Angela," the doctor said, "you have fourteen fibroid tumors in your womb. They are the reason for your monthly problems."

"Is there a medicine I can take to cure them?" I said, not understanding the nature of my malady.

"No, Angela, I'm afraid you will require surgery."

"Surgery," I responded anxiously. "What kind of surgery?"

"We'll have to do a hysterectomy. We'll remove your uterus but leave your ovaries intact. Angela," he continued, clearing his throat, "you do realize that you will never be able to bear children."

"Never be able to bear children"—the words crushed me. I felt as if a bus had run over me. First an abortion, then my baby died, and now I would never become a mother. Maybe this was divine retribution. Perhaps God felt I should be punished for killing a child.

I agreed to the partial hysterectomy, which, surprisingly, was executed with minimal pain. Recuperating at home, I gradually regained strength and returned to my jobs and household chores.

Shortly thereafter, I was bombarded with racking, convulsive abdominal pains. An indomitable fever followed. Seeking medical advice, I was told that the physicians were baffled. I was immediately admitted to the hospital, and my fever escalated to 108 degrees, bringing me to the edge of delirium.

Though seesawing in and out of consciousness, I overheard the nurses deliberating bedside: "Maybe the surgeon left an instrument in her abdomen when she had the hysterectomy," a high-pitched voice said.

"Well, if Angela does make it, she may suffer brain damage," another nurse chirped in.

Brain damage? What could they possibly mean? I thought, seconds before conveniently losing consciousness.

Placed in an ice machine, I awakened shivering and freezing to death. My teeth chattered at breakneck speed, jeopardizing the safety of my tongue. Until my fever had subsided, a young nurse, gentle and nurturing, sat beside my bed like a loyal sentinel guarding a treasured dignitary.

Once my prognosis was reversed from critical to stable, the dedicated nurse encouraged the physician to remove me from the freezer.

Thanks to the doctors and the exceptional commitment and persistence of the amazing nurse, I recuperated from the dangerous Staph aureus infection that almost took my life.

I was administered amphetamines to combat the exhaustion I suffered as a consequence of my life-threatening ordeal. Although the prescription drugs quashed the mental and physical fatigue, ingesting the meds led to chronic insomnia. Excessively energized, I was incapable of winding down or relaxing sufficiently to get a good night's sleep at day's end.

Reflecting, it seemed as if there were a lengthy checklist of problems and dilemmas I had to endure along my journey. But every time I resolved an issue, another sprouted like a spring bud that in time would turn to full bloom.

EIGHTEENTH EPISODE

"Success is not final, failure is not fatal: it is the courage to continue that counts."

—Winston Churchill

After the tragic passing of Shannon Maureen, life seemed to unexpectedly switch gears. Instead of moving forward in my land of dreams, I was returning to the dark days of yesterday, filled with frustration and abuse.

Al's drinking escalated, and as if one vice were not sufficiently detrimental, he added another—an addiction to marijuana. Living in close-confined quarters made the potpourri of alcohol, tobacco and pot a stomach-turning experience. In addition, the toxic substances negatively reprogrammed his behavioral patterns.

Depression and anxiety attacks fought for dominance in his life. Between the drinking and the weed smoking, his mood swings mimicked with precision the manifestations of bipolar disorder. One moment he was manic with euphoria, optimistic, and arrogantly self-assured, and the next he was buried in depression, irritable, pessimistic and entertaining serious self-destructive thoughts.

Conversations were no longer possible. Al was intellectually absent and emotionally stuck on a careening roller-coaster. Eventually, a lethargic fluctuation of concentration, imprecise perception and erratic thinking gave way to abusive, angry outbursts.

Still mourning the loss of my baby, once again, I found myself starring in a victim role. When Al wasn't mistreating me, he was aimlessly cruising around for days, philandering with women, oblivious to his marital vows and responsibilities. Of course, I was clueless about his whereabouts. When he walked through the door, I knew he was home and when his presence was lacking, I knew he was on a rampage, carousing with reckless abandon.

Money became a rare commodity. Consequently, tiers of unpaid bills gathered height and dust. Without any resources to satisfy our mounting financial obligations, I realized that I had to get a higher-paying job.

Relying on my nursing diploma and hospital experience, I applied for a position as a nutritionist in a nursing home. Working as part of a team, I planned and prepared meals for the residents. Though the salary was somewhat higher than the Target wages, with Al taking my checks to fund his vices and addictions, it was far from sufficient to cover expenses, let alone start a savings account.

"Al," I said one day, realizing that my wallet was empty long before my wages were due, "this is not working. My money is gone. I'm not going to let you manage my paychecks any longer."

"Why, Angela?" he grunted. "I'm the man of the house. I take care of you."

"Al, you use my money to fund your drinking and pot smoking habits. At this rate, we'll never be able to buy a house. This place is small and uncomfortable. We barely have space for ourselves. Don't you want to have a house of your own?"

"OK, Angela, we'll start saving for a house. Maybe we can even rent one while we wait."

Surprisingly, Al kept his word this time. Within two weeks, we had located and moved into a house. Interestingly, our contract contained an option-to-buy clause. In a sense, it was a ray of hope, a tiny, flickering light in the long tunnel of darkness.

Gathering our few possessions, like two gypsies with our lives packaged in cardboard boxes, we left the cramped efficiency apartment and moved into the house. Though undersized and Spartan in décor, it was a definite upgrade from my residences of the past.

Crossing over the entry, my eyes roamed around the freshly painted walls, pausing on the large window, never before having witnessed such brightness in one room. Even if tiny, the house was more spacious than any other dwelling I had ever lived in. Thanking God for my blessings, I unpacked our meager possessions.

Several months later, Ken, a friend of Al's, offered me a night job.

"Why don't you work here in the tavern?" he asked one evening while we were enjoying drinks together with his wife, Carol. Insecure of my table-waiting skills, I was somewhat hesitant to give an immediate head nod. However, the money was attractive bait, far too alluring for me to reject.

"OK," I agreed. "I'll give it a try. We could certainly use the extra money." Carol and Ken seemed genuinely pleased with my new commitment; Al, though not in opposition, remained stoic.

The decision proved to be financially lucrative. Perhaps my Greek accent, or perhaps my extroverted personality and willingness to please, were incentives for open-handed tippers, encouraging them to dig into their pockets. This generosity allowed me the luxury of amassing sometimes as much as over a hundred dollars an evening. Though considered a decent amount, it was not sufficient to satisfy all past debt, pay the rent and utilities, and take care of our nutritional needs.

Therefore, financially unable to enjoy the blessing of any leisure, I accepted another position: caring for George, a handicapped, alcoholic gentleman. As a consequence of a nearly fatal accident in which the truck he was driving slammed into a bus, he had undergone a double leg amputation.

Although George had engaged the services of a maid to take care of the household chores, I was hired as a companion. We played cards and often spent hours deep in conversation. Apparently, I filled a void for companionship. He was interested in my beginnings, and I told him about my life in Greece, neither mentioning nor expounding upon the events and circumstances of my tragic childhood.

In response to his interrogations about my current situation, I confided my husband's drinking and drug issues, and his resulting abusive behavior.

"Angela, why do you stand for such nonsense?" he said, extending his hand toward mine. "Why don't you leave your husband? I have a big house with many empty rooms. I'd be happy if you moved in and stayed here with me. And when I die, I'll leave the house to you."

"Thanks, George," I stammered, meeting his gaze coyly, as if in disbelief. "I'm deeply touched, but I have to refuse your kindness. I'm here in America because of Al. He rescued me from my misery in Europe and married me to assure my position in the US. Regardless of his abusive ways, I will honor my marital vows and stay with him."

"Well, Angela," he responded, flashing a semi-smile, "all I can say is that Al is one lucky man who doesn't deserve you. But if you ever change your mind, or if the situation becomes unbearable, my offer will still stand."

Dabbing at an escaping tear before George caught sight of it, I reconfirmed my gratitude, feeling the invasion of a wave of warmth sweep through me.

Putting aside some of my tavern tips and part of George's big-hearted salary, and adding it to Al's savings from his firefighting and construction jobs, we finally gathered sufficient funds to exercise our option to purchase the house we were leasing. Having the means available, it was now a question of setting the plan in motion.

When Al wasn't ranting from the after-effects of alcohol overdose, he was a quiet man, not given to any exchanges of dialogue. Therefore, when I chanced upon his silhouette in the dimness of dusk, I decided it was time to discuss buying the house.

"Al," I began sighing softly, "I think it's time to make an offer on the house. We have enough cash between us to put a down payment, and our combined salaries are enough to qualify for a mortgage."

"That sounds like a great idea," he said, awakening from his stupor. "We'll go to the bank in the morning and then notify the owner of the house about our decision."

Satisfied, I turned on my heels, directing my stride toward the door.

"Angela, you're putting on weight." Al snickered before his hurtful words were drowned out by the increasing volume of the TV.

The jingle—"When you say Bud, you say you care enough to want the best"—played in my ears. Reversing my course, I noticed Al gulp down a stein of beer without even a pause to breathe. Beside his feet were three crushed cans of Budweiser.

"Al, how many beers have you had?" I asked, realizing that my answer was in his mounting level of intoxication.

"When you say Bud," he sang off-key, slurring his words, "you say you want the king of beers."

"Al, you're drunk," I shouted. "Did you understand what I said about buying the house?"

"Yes Angela, I'm not deaf. I heard what you said. Did you understand what I just told you? You know, about getting fat? You look awful, really old and ugly with all that weight. You better stop eating and get rid of it because I don't want to sleep with you anymore. You're disgusting. You eat too much. You eat all the time."

Like a stampeding herd of buffalo, all the humiliation, embarrassment and pain of my abusive childhood boomeranged, crushing my chest. The impact was overwhelming. Hurt and offended, I ran from the room, bruising my arm in the doorway. The sudden drip of tears clouded my vision.

Having been reared on over-boiled rice, powdered milk, over-ripe berries and stale bread, the American diet, rich in meat, potatoes, fresh vegetables and bread as well as delicious desserts, was too tempting to refuse. Perhaps I consumed a bit more than I should have, but Al's cruel recriminations were heartless and unwarranted. From dawn until dusk, he assailed me, his words attacking my flesh like a contagious bacteria, curtailing my previous enjoyment of culinary delights.

I started skipping meals, then gradually diminishing the portions I consumed until I was nourishing myself on the rations of a recently weaned baby. My weight started to drop. Pound after pound seemed to evaporate, producing a euphoria that further seeded my aversion to food.

The more I lost the more I wanted to lose. It was no longer a question of regaining my girlish figure. Instead, it was a quest to be irrationally thin. Beauty and sex appeal were irrelevant. No longer about how I looked, it all focused on what I wanted, irrespective of any and all consequences. I was dragged into the pit of obsession.

Often listless and exhausted, I intermittently switched to binge eating, believing I could eliminate the drawbacks of my weight-loss regime and regain my strength with one overabundant meal. However, imagining in my twisted mind an immediate recuperation of pounds lost, I ran to the bathroom, terrified and disgusted, and forced myself to regurgitate.

Besieged by a haunting guilt, which sent me spiraling into depression, I became aggressive and angry. Hunger gnawed at my insides. I awakened famished and retired with painful contractions. My immobile digestive system was fighting for survival. Self-hate surfaced, encouraging me to deprive myself even further. When my imposed famine was too painful be bear, I binged and vomited with a ferociousness that eventually damaged my stomach and esophagus.

Not even the silent disappearance of weight was able to calm the anxiety swelling within. A skyrocketing bulimia became my reason to be—a way of life. My distorted body perception disallowed me from accepting the truth. I was just skin and bones and literally destroying myself.

In spite of my anorexia-bulimia roller-coaster rides, I continued working and tending to Al and the house. He became increasingly more difficult to tolerate, but indebted to him for my life, I took his violent harassment as reparation for sins committed, almost with monastic silence—until God came to my rescue once again.

Finally drifting off to sleep after several hours of restless twists and turns, I awakened the following morning to an absence beside me. Believing that Al had been disturbed by my reckless bed gymnastics and had moved to the sofa for a peaceful rest, I slipped into my slippers and headed for the living room.

The room was vacant. However, the stench stimulating my gag reflex betrayed the two ashtrays brimming over with ashes and a couple of still-smoldering butts. In addition, lowering my eyes to encourage denial, I spotted several beer stains on the carpet.

Hypothesizing that Al had gone out to buy cigarettes after an apparent night of chain puffing, I went into the kitchen to percolate some coffee, realizing it would take about fifteen minutes to get it strong. Exhausted, I was heavily dependent on the energizing power of my morning brew.

Al did not return that evening. Checking his closet and drawers for a clue, I discovered that they had been emptied. Two pieces of luggage were missing. Al had packed his belongings and taken off. With the same hocus pocus manner in which he had appeared in my life, he had disappeared. Al was gone.

I later learned that the selfish man who was unwilling to give the gift of life, the bully husband who forced me into aborting my first pregnancy, had deserted me for a barmaid with three children. But despite it al, in my heart, I had granted him forgiveness, though it was unsolicited. Al would remain forever in my memory as my earthly savior who had rescued me from certain death, giving me my dream to come to America. Al Becker, the former soldier, would always be special. He was unforgettable.

NINTEENTH EPISODE

"What man actually needs is not a tensionless state but rather the striving and struggling for some goal worthy of him."

—Victor Frankl

The hardships and obstacles that had defined my life until this point were in a sense the building blocks of my character, as well as a means to test and strengthen my dependence on faith. Each hurdle, every drawback and all the tormenting impediments served to lengthen the cross I was carrying.

What I was not yet able to understand was the power of the cross settled on my shoulders. Still too young to recognize the merit of suffering, I accepted it as my lot in life, repeatedly begging God to help me endure and overcome.

Time and anguish developed my survival tactics, which by no means implied that the battle was always without serious injury. However, I faced every challenge with the courage and determination powered by the struggle to keep my head above the water line.

Faith encouraged me to continue seeking a wick for my candle, as I sparred with Satan's obsession to hold me oppressed in the darkness. Plucking my wick, his evil intent left me disadvantaged and sightless to the darkened path before me.

The unwinding of events reflected my recurring trials and signaled my prayers for deliverance. Life was a network of scorched tussocks that never quite lost their ability to regenerate, moving me to hope for an eventual bloom.

Being abandoned by Al, I had no idea just how my today would unwind, or if I would ever have a tomorrow. Living exclusively in the present moment, my plans extended hour by hour; I looked no further.

When the bank arrived to inform me that Al had defaulted on the mortgage payments, I was taken aback, though I should have known better, judging from his erratic behavioral history.

However, instead of trembling in desperation, I took the news of an imminent foreclosure with resignation. There was no purpose and certainly no benefit to be derived from trying to alter the inevitable, over which I had absolutely no influence.

Heartbroken to have lost my only possession after much sacrifice and hard work, I phoned Ken to give him the news. Listening with a sympathetic ear, he said, "Angela, you can come here and stay with me and Carol until you get your bearings."

Graciously accepting his invitation, I was thankful and comforted by the realization that the Lord was keeping a vigilant eye over me. Whispering my gratitude, I breathed a sigh of relief. If it weren't for the kindness of Ken and Carol, I would have been alone and homeless. Yet through it all, I never lost faith, certain of naught but God's constant presence in my life.

My tips at the tavern seemed to double overnight. Surprised, I noticed I was actually earning a pretty decent wage. Maybe the tide was turning, I thought. Perhaps I would have enough funds to be able to thank my dear friends, pack my bags and get a place of my own.

I realized I had to keep a stiff upper lip despite the ill-wind and the gathering clouds hovering over my head. But more importantly, I knew I had to continue believing in God's assistance and mercy.

The following evening, I dressed and headed over to the tavern to begin my shift, unaware that Fate was knitting a new shawl to shield my shoulders. Crowded with patrons in search of distracting diversions from the weight of life's compelling responsibilities, I was quite busy taking orders and making certain that every customer was served and satisfied.

Pausing a moment to speak to the bartender, I noticed a young, attractive man seated at the bar, nursing a beer. He seemed involved in his thoughts yet very much present in his surroundings.

A coincidence lifted and locked our glances. Smiling, he nodded, beckoning me to come over. Another coincidence set the chemistry brewing. "He's attractive," I said to myself, making my way over to where he was seated.

Rising to his feet, the young man extended his hand. "Hello, I'm Gary Mattox," he said, introducing himself. "And you are…?"

"Angela," I responded, finishing the sentence, immediately resolving the identity mystery. "I'm Angela Becker and I work here."

Gary was tall, with strong shoulders and a firm hand grip. His complexion had the sun-baked glow of an athlete whose life was lived more outdoors than in. Thin, spider-like lines ran across his young forehead, perhaps betraying the anxiety of man unable to streamline his calamitous life.

Green, his eyes sparkled, failing to conceal the attraction he felt for me. An affable man, this interesting individual did little to conceal his enthusiasm to pursue my friendship.

Confiding in the alluring stranger whose charming glance had the power to accelerate my heartbeat, I told him that I had recently lost my house. In return, he unburdened his soul, confessing his bipolar disorder and the series of mental breakdowns that had kept him confined in a psychiatric hospital for two years.

Emotionally downtrodden, he won my compassion and attention. Every evening after our initial meeting, Gary came into the bar. Our conversations became more personal and intimate as we tried to get to know each better, sharing our respective tragic circumstances.

I learned that Gary was a Vietnam vet on disability because of his psychological challenges. My weakness for US servicemen was in full swing. I admired men with the patriotic zeal to stand up for and defend their country. Convinced there was something very special about the American military, I revered being in the company of the men and women willing to give their time, energy and in some instances, lives to defend my much-loved, new country.

There was no denying the fact I was drawn to the armed forces like a mother to her newborn infant. In my mind, these individuals were valiant heroes, regardless of the circumstances surrounding their individual missions and tours of duty. Consequently, I looked at both Al and Gary through biased eyes.

Several weeks after out initial meeting, Gary and I had a serious discussion minutes before the Tavern door closed, clearing out the last tipsy patron.

"Angela," he said, directing his gaze to meet mine, "instead of living with Ken and Carol, why don't we move in together?"

"Gary," I blurted, "I'm still married to Al. He deserted me but he's still my husband."

"Angela, maybe we can save your house. I'll settle the back payments and we can move in. How does that sound?"

"How does that sound?" I shouted. "It sounds wonderful—almost unbelievable."

Gary had deforested the wilderness into which I had been thrown. An earthly savior, he was willing to redeem my home and my bruised life.

Soon after, we took possession of the little, nondescript house Al and I had purchased. But this time, I shared it with Gary. Divorced from his wife, my new life partner was not without baggage. He had partial custody of the estranged couple's nine-year-old son, Jason. Therefore, every weekend, the young boy packed his bag after school and came to stay with his dad—an arrangement that did not sit well with Gary.

Life was far from idyllic, even though I developed a warm relationship with Jason. Depressed over the short visits allotted, and heavily medicated with Thorazine to control his disruptive thought and perception issues, Gary either vegetated, sitting around in a stupor, blatantly unresponsive, or spent the day and evening snoring uninterruptedly.

Upset with his wasteful expenditure of energy, I took his medication, rushed over to the toilet and flushed it down, watching like a sentry guard until all traces had disappeared.

"Gary," I said, walking over to where he sat almost comatose, "don't you think it is time to get off your derrière and get a job, to help with some of the bills?"

His green eyes, lifeless, stared into space unfocused. However, I knew things would soon change. Gary would swing to unbelievable emotional heights; he just didn't realize the effect his condition had on those with whom he shared his life.

Two hours later, Gary had risen from the dead. "Angela," he shouted, "start packing. We're moving."

"Moving?" I blurted, shocked. "What do you mean moving? Where are we going?"

"I'm renting a U-haul truck and when Jason comes on Friday, we're all going to Oregon. I don't like the custody agreement. Weekends are not sufficient for me. We can raise the boy ourselves."

Never in a position to object, I agreed, working hard to pack our belongings in the few days I had before the weekend. I neither questioned Gary's decision nor experienced any sadness over walking away from my first home in the USA.

Looking forward to a new adventure, I yearned for serenity. But more importantly, I desired a balance in my life, a serenity that would finally settle my thoughts. Tired of adversity and the repeated crescendo of troublesome overtures, I was ripe for a bit of overdue happiness. It just had to be in the plan for me. But was it?

Vulnerable and afraid to fill my mind with optimistic thoughts, I silenced my reflections during the drive, momentarily postponing any and all expectations. If I didn't plan a bright, sunny day, I would not be disappointed by the pelting rain. The pain and suffering I had known until then seemed to surface from time to time, almost as a reminder of my purpose there on earth. Would this eventually change? Or was it really my destiny?

The ride was long and tiresome but I passed the time in the company of my reflections—a powerful and inescapable influence in my life.

When we arrived in Oregon, I was awestruck by the beauty of Klamath Falls. The day was clear. A magnetic, blue sky and blazing sun welcomed us with extraordinary warmth. Mount Shasta, a snow-capped, 14,162-foot-high volcano, loomed in the distance, its majestic stature giving the impression of a false proximity. It was certainly a breathtaking first impact.

Gary had rented a house in Klamath Falls and we busied ourselves unpacking, and adjusting to the new surroundings. In this scenic and peaceful environment, we focused on registering Jason in a Catholic school. However, even this seemingly simple task was not without a glitch.

Pulling up to the school, I was impressed by the orderly group of well-behaved children, regimental in their dark uniforms. Black leather oxfords glistened in the noon sun. Apparently, last evening's shoe-shine ritual had not been in vain, despite the sand-kicking tag-playing. It was obvious that trousers and skirts had been pressed at one point of the early morning, even if energetic children with an allergy to sitting still set a new pace for mobility behind a desk.

I assumed that it was recess and that the students were out for a brief, twenty-minute break before the start of the afternoon session. Several nuns, comically penguin-like in their long, flowing, black habits, vigilantly monitored the boys and girls. Childish giggles spoke of a carefree youth, so different from my own.

Once inside, we headed for the administrative office. The principle, a small, middle-aged nun with thick, rimless glasses welcomed us with a soft, almost understated smile, sweetly maternal.

Her long, black veil and starched, white fluting accentuated a minuscule, alabaster face. Trapped within her somber habit, the religious woman had an air of pious discomfort. A pair of slender, child-sized hands rested, folded on top of her desk as if she were deep in prayer. Only the intricate network of deep green veins running from her knuckles to her wrists betrayed her age.

"Good afternoon," she said, greeting us with a timid nearly withdrawing gaze. My mind flashed back to the orphanage horrors. How very different she was from the cold, distant nuns who had undertaken my upbringing for so many years—the unforgettable, religious ladies who had tested and exasperated my patience almost nonstop. "May I be of assistance to you?"

"Yes, sister," Gary said, mimicking the soft purl of her words. "I want to enroll my nine-year-old son, Jason Mattox, in your school."

I observed, hushed by the embarrassment of my English, still heavily threaded with a strong Greek accent.

"Mr. Mattox, I'm glad you are considering a Catholic education for Jason. I assume he will be in the fourth grade."

"Yes, sister," Gary murmured.

"Mr. Mattox, we will need Jason's birth certificate and a copy of his transcripts from the previous school."

Gary gazed down at his feet in silence.

"Is there a problem?" the nun asked, sliding her glasses along the narrow bridge of her nose.

"No, sister," he blurted, far too defensively to be convincing. "We just moved and I have to find the papers. They must be packed in one of the boxes." Nervously clearing his throat, he continued, "can he attend classes in the mean time? I'll bring you the birth certificate and transcripts as soon as I find them. I don't want him to lose any more time."

"Well, bring him here so I can meet him and we'll see about starting school—but I need the documents as soon as possible."

We agreed and returned the following day with Jason. A shy, quiet lad who spoke only when addressed, he presented no motive for refusal.

At first unsuspecting of any foul play, the principle eventually became suspicious of the "missing" papers, which even the passage of time could not locate.

Eventually, the bubble burst. The nuns became apprehensive, realizing Jason was not where he was supposed to be legally. It didn't take much cerebral energy to resolve the mystery—Gary had breached his custody agreement. By then, it was already December.

Since it was nearing the holidays, I mailed greeting cards to my friends in St. Louis, wishing them a merry Christmas and telling them about my new life in Oregon. However, unbeknownst to me, Gary's ex-wife, adept at playing Sherlock Holmes, devised a plan to discover our whereabouts.

Making a list of all my friends, she went from house to house, pulling open the mailboxes and trespassing through their correspondences, in search of a letter or card with my return address. Admittedly, it was a pretty clever crime, which bore sweet fruit.

Then, one afternoon, following a painful root canal, I trudged through the mounds of mid-December snow to pick up Jason at school. Upon our return, I was shocked to find three police vehicles parked in front of the house and two others on each side of the property. Puzzled, I noticed that the house was surrounded! The glare of flashing, rotating beacons sent a message of trouble.

Scared that a tragedy had befallen Gary, I ran from the car, leaving the motor running.

"Wait here, Jason," I shouted, breathless. "I'm going inside to see what's happened to your dad. Don't touch anything."

Anticipating my thoughts, three police officers darted over to the vehicle, opened the door and reached in.

"Come on out, son," a robust, ruddy-complexioned officer said, bending in front of the window. "You have to come with us."

One minute later, Jason, ashen and obviously terrorized, was seized and escorted to a squad car. Following his course across the yard, I spotted the open entry door. Soon, Gary appeared, in handcuffs. Two officers with the statures of professional quarterbacks held him under the arms. It was obvious that my husband had been taken into custody.

After Gary's arrest, I found myself alone, and without financial resources. Panic-stricken, I questioned, What now?

Gathering my wits, I invoked the name of God, begging for assistance in my predicament, and phoned Gary's parents. Crying, I related the events of their son's arrest and asked for money to return to Missouri.

Granting my wish, Mr. Mattox senior wired me the funds needed to hire a transport crew to pack and move our belongings back to Missouri. My neighbor volunteered to help load the truck.

Accepting his kindness as a token of friendship, I thanked him for his time and efforts. While he, together with another friend, carried out my furniture and possessions, I busied myself with cleaning up and wrapping some smaller, more personal objects.

"Angela, we've loaded the truck," he announced, wiping with his bare arm the rivers of sweat running down his brow. Working hard and perspiring heavily, the two men smelled like a couple of neglected swine.

"You're all set to go, Angela."

I locked the door to the house and began the long drive back to Missouri with my furniture, belongings and a small car attached to the back of the U-haul. Despite the onset of torrential rain, undaunted by the rumblings of nature, I continued my journey, lips moving in constant prayer.

Thankfully, the rain ceased as quickly as it had started; dark clouds slipped past to unveil a splendid sun. Just over the horizon, a radiant, multicolored rainbow designed a breathtaking exhibit in the sky.

"How could anyone not believe in God?" I whispered. But what was so evident to me remained possibly a mystery to others.

Once I reached my destination, I was shocked to note that my car was missing. Apparently, while driving through the mountains during the torrential downpour, it had broken loose and remained behind.

Upset, I retraced my journey, found the abandoned car and had it towed to a local garage. Returning to Missouri, I purchased an early-morning greyhound ticket to Oregon, crawled into bed for a few sleepless hours and departed the following day.

When I arrived, I slipped behind the wheel of my almost-lost car and drove back to Missouri. However, the curtain was not yet lowered on my latest drama.

Once back in St. Louis, the U-haul was unloaded. I was dismayed to see that only a few of my possessions were on the truck.

"What happened to all my things?" I shouted. Disturbed by the ruckus I was creating, Gary's father yelled from the doorway, "Angela, what's all the fussing about!"

In tears, I walked over to where he stood.

"Mr. Mattox, most of my furniture and possessions are missing," I sobbed. "My neighbors fooled me—they said they would remove and load my furniture and instead, they stole it. I will return to Oregon and see what happened."

"Well, Angela," he replied, shaking his head, "you know you really should never trust strangers."

I assumed there was some truth to what he was telling me; however, I was alone and at the mercy of others. Furthermore, experience had taught me differently: One stranger had generously given me the money to come to America, and another had made it possible for me to remain here. Even Gary was a stranger. Strangers were my support system, my family.

After settling down a bit, I took inventory. Sadly, I realized that most of my furniture, my sewing machine plus my washer and dryer were gone. And if that was not devastating enough, even the cash I had sorted and left on my dresser was stolen.

Furious, the following morning, after another restless night, I drove to a gas station, filled the U-haul and drove back to Klamath Falls to confront my neighbor. Unprepared for what I was about to discover, I steered up the driveway, jumped from the U-haul, dashed to the font door and slammed the knocker several times. The sheer force of my adrenaline-stimulated strength left me with shooting pains traveling up to my elbow—but no response.

I scurried over to the window and peered in. The house was dark and vacant—no people, no furniture. Like a bolt of lightning, it hit me: The scoundrels had taken possession of my furnishings and property and moved away!

I sought verification of my theory. Speaking with another neighbor two doors down, I received confirmation of my suspicions. The evildoers stole my belongings and moved away before I could take action.

Recognizing that it was foolhardy to squander time and emotion over circumstances beyond my control, I turned my attention to Gary. Bail had been set at $55,000. Thankfully, one of his nine siblings, a sister who lived in Illinois, posted the $5,000 to get him out of jail. En route to her house, accompanied by a physician, Gary was advised by a Dupo police officer to consult Clyde Kuehn, a noted Illinois criminal defense attorney.

Following the officer's advice, Gary engaged Mr. Kuehn to defend him from the child abduction charges. possibly carrying a ten-year prison sentence.

Subsequent to a three-year custody battle and the expenditure of $25,000, Gary was exonerated of all charges. Furthermore, ignoring Angela's warnings about his serious psychological history and issues, Mr. Kuehn advised him to fight for full custody of Jason. Listening attentively to all the facts, the attorney devised his strategy.

"You must get married before I can make recourse for full custody," he said nervously tugging on an imaginary goatee. "Are you willing to do that?"

"I can't marry Gary," I blurted. "Legally, I'm still Al's wife!"

"Angela, you have to get a divorce."

"How do I go about getting one?" I asked.

"We will put an ad in the paper, summoning Al. He will have thirty days in which to present himself for the divorce proceedings. It's called 'divorce by publication.'"

"What if he doesn't show up?"

"If he fails to appear, Angela, you will be granted a divorce in absentia, for abandonment. This frees you to marry Gary."

We published the ad for the allotted time. When the date expired and Al failed to appear in court, I was granted the divorce.

As soon as Mr. Kuehn phoned to deliver the news, Gary was ready to say 'I do.'

"Angela, let's get married now," he said, smiling. "I want you to be my wife."

I agreed and before the justice of the peace, we promised to love, honor and cherish each other form that day forward, until death did us part.

Thus, on November 28, 1980, I became Mrs. Gary Mattox, twelve years after my arrival in the United States.

PART III

Αναστολή καταδίκησ
Reprieve

"Do not be misled by the fact that you are at liberty and relatively free; that for the moment you are not under lock and key: you have simply been granted a reprieve."

—Ryszard Kapuscinski

TWENTIETH EPISODE

Feeling empowered as Mr. and Mrs. Gary Mattox, we pursued our battle for full custody of Jason. Arguing that Gary and I had established a serene routine, giving the young boy the stability required to grow into a well-adjusted adult, the judge scrutinized our competency as parents, interviewing Jason in his private chambers prior to rendering a verdict.

Once all the evidence was collected and the testimony heard, the honorable judge decided that Gary would be awarded full custody of his son. Though the twelve-year-old Jason was no longer covered under the tender years doctrine that guaranteed a maternal victory except in cases of abuse or unfit status, it was still rare in Illinois for a father to win a custody dispute. Therefore, Gary's accomplishment was somewhat of a landmark decision.

"Mr. Mattox," the judge said after the hearing, "your triumph today is due to your wife, Angela. She is a stabilizing influence in your life and I feel certain that she will be a wonderful parent to Jason." Glancing in my direction, he continued, visibly moved, "Angela, I'm impressed with all the hardships you have overcome in your life. You are a decent and respectable woman and will do a fine job raising Jason."

"Thank you, Your Honor," Gary said, flashing me a smile. "Angela and I will take good care of this young man."

When informed of the court's decision, Jason was delighted. Having made new friends at school, he was scholastically and socially acclimated to his surroundings. Furthermore, we bonded almost instantly. Both in court and at home, Jason made it unquestionably clear that he preferred living with me and his dad.

The media carried the event and the following day, Gary's photo and court victory were headline news in the morning newspaper.

I wept for Gary's victory and my own, trying to understand the full intensity of a father's joy in witnessing the happiness of his son, returned to the fold. Unable to speak from the overbearing emotion, I whispered, "Gary, this is a blessing from God." Catching his moist gaze, I understood that he was far too excited to respond, though he agreed wholeheartedly.

"We should celebrate," he stammered nervously, pulling a cigarette from the pack nestled in the breast pocket of his striped shirt. "Let's go for a sno cone," he said, offering me a cigarette.

"What's a sno cone?" I asked, nodding my head in agreement.

I had absolutely no idea how Gary's few words, spoken in rhapsody, would change the direction of our lives forever.

Gary flicked his lighter twice—once to light my cigarette, and a second time to light is own. Taking a long drag, I filled my lungs with nicotine, oblivious to the consequences I would later pay for my self-destructive habit.

Gary ran ahead to get the car while I waited under cover. The sky had darkened—an omen of nature's outburst just moments away. However, perfect timing kept me from being drenched once the clouds opened. A horn tooted as Gary pulled up. I jumped in, feeling a few teasing rain-drops tickle my shoulders.

"Looks like a storm is hitting us," I said, settling myself in my seat. "You got here just in time."

"No, Angela," he blurted, "the sky is clear on the east side, it's just a quick shower."

My own doubts were tucked away as I watched Gary's prediction come to be.

Several minutes later, we drove up to a sno cone stand.

"Wait here, Angela, I'll get one for you. It doesn't make sense for you to wet your shoes. There are deep puddles everywhere."

I had never before had a sno cone and actually looked forward to the adventure of tasting something different. New experiences carried a special promise of excitement, regardless of the eventual outcome. They presented an opportunity for learning and growth, even if they sometimes threatened survival, forcing me to yank out my hair in distress. Yet, I had to acknowledge the truth: With every tormenting experience, I became more deeply rooted in my faith. More importantly, I seemed to grow an additional layer of skin, which rendered me less vulnerable to the hurtful spins of Fate.

Gary's knock on my window cleared my mind, shutting down the memories, immediately ushering me back to a decidedly more comfortable plateau.

"Here, Angela," he said handing me a sno cone. "The place is jammed. They have a fantastic business—I've never seen anything like this! Look at all the people lined up to get sno cones."

I had to admit, it was pretty amazing. People of all ages and sizes stood waiting for sno cones. Caught in the downpour, many were soaked to the bone, their clothes literally stuck to their flesh. Fearful of forfeiting their place in line, no one sought refuge; apparently, there was little if any concern about a good drenching.

Extending my hand, I grabbed the sno cone. Bringing the bright red mound of glistening snow to my lips, I bit down with the same gusto I would have used to dig into a crispy apple.

Neglecting to anticipate the impact of shaved ice hitting against my front teeth, I was unprepared for the shooting pain darting from my upper jaw straight to my head. To my painful cries and face distorting winces, Gary responded with a hearty laugh.

"Angela, you're not supposed to chomp on it like an apple. It's frozen. You have to either lick it or eat it with a spoon."

Covering my mouth with my hand, I waited for the burning to subside. Another lesson was learned at my expense.

"Angela," Gary said as soon as I was pain-free, "I'd like to open up a sno cone stand. Did you see how great their business was? I think we can make a lot of money."

Continuing to devour my shiny mountain of red watermelon snow, I wondered what all the fuss was about. The sno cone tasted OK, but I really couldn't go into a paroxysm of delight over it. Such enthusiasm was unwarranted, in my opinion. Although refreshing and cooling, the sno cone did not have the appeal of an alluring sweet dangled in the face of a child in exchange for good behavior.

"Am I right to assume you'll agree to starting our own sno cone business?" Gary asked, excited.

"Well," I responded, patting my frozen lips with a stiff paper napkin, "tell me a bit more about the sno cones. How are they made?"

"It's rather simple, Angela," Gary said. "There is a machine that turns out mounds of shaved snow. Afterwards, a sugary syrup is squirted over the clear snow. Gradually making its way down through the grated substance, it gives the sno cone a distinguishing color while adding a sweet, distinctive flavor."

"I could make my own flavors, Gary, right?"

"Yes, Angela. We will open the stand and buy the shaving machine. Then, you can bring the syrups from home."

"OK, Gary" I blurted, excited. "Let's do it. Let's open a sno cone stand."

Without procrastinating, Gary literally broke into a trot the following morning, contacting his attorney to get the necessary paperwork and satisfy the funding requirements needed to start the business. I busied myself getting the signs, billboards and shelves to be installed in the trailer. We also needed plumbing and electrical power to run the machines.

Working nonstop we finally opened our sno cone stand. Placing an order for flavor concentrates, I awaited their arrival, studying the ratios I would utilize to produce optimal flavor results.

Unimpressed with the watermelon sno cone, I devised a different formula to heighten the taste and enhance the sweetness factor of the product, determined to supply customers with the absolute best sno cone available.

When the flavor concentrates arrived, I incorporate them into the sugary water. The standard sno cone called for a four-ounce concentrate recipe. Modifying the proportions, I added an extra ounce and a half of concentrate to the mixture, which intensified the flavor.

With my own concoction ready to be tested, the stand furnished and our excitement brimming over, we opened our sno cone business, optimistic but unaware of the adventure ahead.

If our debut was a premonition of success, it was right on target. Six hundred customers walked up to the window and purchased sno cones the first day. We were delirious, and motivated to improve our product.

At home, either after-hours or in the early morning, before I opened, I made seventy-five different flavors with my concentrate-reinforced recipe. Thrilled, customers were grateful, lauding me as having the best sno cones in the world. Their return and referrals were reassuring endorsements of customer approval.

Happiness and self-satisfaction were my new companions. Seeing the bright smiles and receiving the applause, praise and compliments from my delighted customers did wonders for my repressed and demolished self-esteem.

Was I dreaming? Would I awaken to find myself painfully curled in a doughnut on the cold dirt floor, barefoot and in a tattered dress? Was the abandoned, repudiated Greek girl Avyrini really a successful entrepreneur, loved and admired by many?

Nothing could threaten my climb to success. Customers became friends and I, their confidant. The fourteen-foot trailer, settled on a parking lot, was decorated with photos of my customers and their families. Ceilings and walls were filled with smiling faces of men, women and children. On the outside was a large sign: SNO-BIZ.

A people person, I loved each customer for who and what he or she was. They were all special and each was deserving of the best sno cone imaginable. Learning their names and their life stories, I listened compassionately as they unburdened their souls. Some were angry, others tearful, but they all found solace and comfort in my sno cones and in my willingness to dispense advice.

I cared about pleasing their taste buds, and I cared about alleviating their troubles. Teenagers approached me with their questions, doubts and concerns, either feeling embarrassed or misunderstood by their parents. Even though my seven-day, 11:00 a.m. until 1:00 a.m. work schedule was grueling, I made time to address the needs of all who came to my SNO-BIZ sno cone trailer.

This new role came as a surprise. Alone and withdrawn most of my life, I was suddenly sharing myself with others. But more astonishing was the fact that my customers thought that I actually had something worthwhile to share.

Inferior feelings of unworthiness were transformed into self-assurance. People in trouble came to me—the little urchin, born illegitimate in shame.

I addressed issues and dilemmas with the same dedication and seriousness of a trained psychologist, taking to heart all their sorrows and pain. My customer base multiplied from hundreds to thousands—I was now the Sno Cone Lady and my earnings were a testament to my success.

Although three or four other sno cone stands had sprung up within a three-mile radius, my lines grew longer as my customers multiplied.

Motivated by our end-of-season calculations, we decided to broaden our business venture and profitability quotient with the acquisition of a

Dairy Queen franchise in Arnold. We cut the opening ribbon with enthusiasm, expecting the same extraordinary results. However, the Dairy Queen business did not prove to be as lucrative as SNO-BIZ sno cones.

After the first year, we discovered an employee stealing scheme that left us depleted of $5,000 a month. Added to the exorbitant insurance fees, it forced us to close the year in the red. Determined to reverse the tides and make the business successful, we persisted, continuing to lose money.

"Angela," Gary said one evening after working on the books, "this Dairy Queen is not working out. We lost $20,000 this year. I think it's time to let it go."

The following morning, discouraged, Gary ripped off the Dairy Queen sign and returned it to the franchisor, taking a loss on the investment. Focusing on the sno cones, I donated all my waking hours to delivering a top-of-the-line dessert to my loyal customers, who continued to arrive in droves.

Perhaps we did not feel challenged enough; perhaps we were restless, eager to spread our professional wings and curious to see how high we could soar. Or, perhaps were out to break our previous earning record.

Whatever the motive, it mattered little when we made the decision to undertake another venture. This time, we opened an ice cream shop on Cherokee Street, a busy, commercial area in St Louis.

The seven-block neighborhood was comprised of retail and grocery shops as well as diverse eateries. On paper, it looked like a winner. However, in the 1980s, Cherokee Street was not always well-frequented. Instead, it was patronized by prostitutes and drug dealers.

Amid the chaos of starting another new business, Gary paused one afternoon while browsing through some documents.

"Angela, you should become an American citizen," he said. "It's time. You love America and you should be an American."

"I'm afraid about passing the test, Gary. What if I can't do it?"

"No, Angela, you'll do just fine. They give you a book to study. I'll help you."

Gary brought me the book and I made certain that I knew every fact about my beloved America. When I was pronounced an American citizen, I stood, eyes brimming over with tears, and recited the Pledge of Allegiance. I knew nothing could ever duplicate this moment—neither financial success nor glory. For the first time in my life I was proud of who I was: Angela Mattox, American.

Shortly thereafter, Gary's psychological health began to decline. A lackadaisical attitude toward taking his prescribed medication resulted in a bipolar disease flare up, causing havoc in our lives. From a semi-comatose, useless individual, he suddenly sprang into a bionic man, with spurts of irrational energy fueling his movements for as long as seventy-two hours. Often, he would disappear for days or weeks, giving neither notice nor a forwarding address.

The professional stress, in addition to my personal upheavals, worsened my bulimia. Tipping the scale at barely sixty-four pounds, I was in constant pain from an irritated esophagus and the production of unabsorbed stomach acid. Just skin and bones, I subsisted on nervous energy.

Soon after, unable to deal with his irrational behavior patterns, Gary recovered in the psychiatric ward at Jefferson Barracks VA Hospital for three years.

Left alone to run the two businesses, I had to deal with some rather ornery customers, some on the prowl for trouble. One man came every day asking for straws. After a while, his daily visits multiplied. Although his repeated interruptions while I was serving customers became irritating, I was willing to be of assistance until I discovered that he was using the straws to snort cocaine and sniff glue.

Distraught by my refusal to grant his requests, "Glue Head" tried to steal from the cash register. However, thanks to the vigilance of the barber across the street, the drugged thief was caught and apprehended.

Returning to work the following morning, I noticed Glue Head's prostitute girlfriend, scantily clad, advertising her wares in front of the ice cream shop. Her face, hardened by a sloppy, heavy-handed application of make-up and the physical abuse resulting from her professional endeavors, took on a much older appearance in the early-morning daylight.

From the sneer curled on her brassy, red lips, I knew she was up to no good. With a derisive laugh, she approached. "Wait until you see what happens to you!" she blurted, flashing a set of stained teeth.

Paying no heed, I opened the shop. At the close of day, she had returned to her post. Scoffing, she repeated, "You may not believe me, but you will see what is going to happen to you."

I realized that she was probably not bluffing. In fact, her threats were an attempt to seek revenge for my part in pressing charges and sending Glue Head to jail. Undaunted despite it all, I avoided her gaze, locked up the shop and went over to my sno cone business.

Returning the following morning, I discovered that the shop had been brutally vandalized during the night. The door was smashed in, the window shattered, the counter thrashed and the ice cream machines thrown on the floor. The furniture was in pieces. It was apparent that the place had been ransacked and willfully defaced to express contempt and vengeance. There was no doubting the message.

Running outside to seek police assistance, I spotted Glue Head's girlfriend. Smirking and giggling like a delighted child handed a stick of colorful cotton candy at an amusement park, she strutted her bare legs up and down the street, flaunting her sheer enjoyment of the scenario.

"Good morning, ice cream lady," she sneered, breaking into a hardy laugh as false as a three-dollar bill.

"God will punish you one day," I responded, actually taking pity on her. Continuing my journey, I walked with my head held high, like a person of merit, deserving of respect.

The sad reality was that I could neither excuse nor rectify her morally and ethically delinquent behavior as a consequence of a probable traumatic upbringing, since I myself came from the depths of abandonment, physical and emotional abuse, rejection and all levels of deprivation. But I fought my demons, one by one, never allowing them to stifle either my spiritual growth or moral conscience. I worked and I worked, long and hard, for whatever I accomplished.

There was never any doubt in my mind; I knew I would never end up on the streets, like this callous, heartless girl. This was neither who I wanted to be, nor who I was.

A week later, the young prostitute's lifeless body was found on the highway, stuffed in a box—a truly tragic conclusion to the life of a very disturbed young woman. When I received the news, I bowed my head and said a quiet prayer, asking God to have mercy on her soul.

TWENTY-FIRST EPISODE

"Being unwanted, unloved, uncared for, forgotten by everybody, I think that is a much greater hunger, a much greater poverty than the person who has nothing to eat."

—Mother Teresa

Focusing on my *sno cone* business I eliminated all else from my life. Pleasing my rapidly increasing customer base and watching it multiply at break-neck speed was my one and only priority, not to mention enjoyment.

I woke up in the morning planning new exciting flavor variations and went to sleep at night dreaming up new recipes and perfecting the classic ones that would continue to keep my *sno cone* in the number one category.

Not only did the taste experience have to thrill, but the product had to far exceed any other on the market. In my mind I had made a commitment to satisfy and please, and I promised myself I would only succeed. There was neither time nor place for failure in my life—that was my yesterday.

Today, tenacious and determined,I vowed to continue experimenting until I was beyond a reasonable doubt certain I had the absolute best *sno cone*. Dedicating twelve to fourteen hours a day to my business, I spent the time preparing flavors, collecting grated snow from the machine, and carefully pouring the syrups over the flawlessly spherical crystal clear mounds.

Like children fascinated by an inexplicable phenomenon mysteriously unfolding before their eyes, I marveled, unable to blink as the glistening colorful liquid meandered over the smooth surface, tinting the mound a vibrant hue. Proud of my creations I handed them to men, women and children, holding my breath while their eager tongues made contact with the sweet cold dessert.

Their smiles, giggles and echoing sounds of somatic euphoria were both reward and stimulus encouraging me to work even harder to go one step beyond. The customers noticed and admired my determination and passion to please. Returning they brought family and friends to my *Sno Cone* stand.

Faces became familiar, voices recognizable and my love for each and every customer invited openness. I was the *Sno Cone* Lady—friend and confidante.

Throughout the years, my relationships spanned generations. I watched teens grow into adults and return with their own children.

Though not accomplished overnight, success brought me the exhilaration of accomplishment—personal and financial. With my bank account increasing and my customers' genuine smiles broadening I gained a new self-awareness.

No longer shrouded in misery, no longer catching my reflection in a looking glass and observing the despondent dimness of eyes unable to glow, the image of a paltry woman of insignificance began to fade. Bit by bit with the help of my satisfied customers my self-esteem began to generate. Now I was more than just a 'little bastard.'

One afternoon while whipping up *sno cones*, a long time customer walked into the shop. The year was 1998—thirty years since I arrived in the United States. My life went from a harrowing scene in Dante's *Inferno* to a beautiful house in St Louis Missouri in which I starred as a successful entrepreneur in a capitalist country that encouraged free enterprise.

Journeying a long way from the day of my arrival; a date marked by a tragedy resulting in the build-up of many ramifications on twentieth-century America: the assassination of Dr. Martin Luther King Jr.

However, spinning 180 degrees, I was now revered as a renowned figure in my city—I was the *Sno Cone* Lady.

"Hi Angela," a faithful patron said greeting me. "Listen I've always wondered about your accent. Where are you from?"

I was prepared neither for the question nor my reluctance to respond. Apparently my traumatizing past was still pulsating.

"I'm Greek," I replied in barely an audible whisper, "and I grew up in orphanages."

"Greek," he blurted, "that's interesting. I never knew anyone from Greece. What's your maiden name?"

"My birth name is Avyrini Souliou," I said.

"Can you spell that for me?" he asked, pulling a pen from the breast pocket of his shirt.

"Hand me the pen, I'll write it for you."

"OK, thanks Angela."

Too busy to mince this unusual conversation, I didn't expend much brain energy to figure out the why behind this gentleman's odd question. Therefore, when he returned the following day I was caught totally off guard.

"Hi Angela," he mumbled displaying his full set of teeth in one of the broadest smiles I had seen in a long time.

"You're not going to believe what I found. Look here," he giggled, sticking a slip of irregularly torn note paper in front of my face. "I have the phone numbers and addresses of your parents!"

"What" I shouted incredulous. "What do you mean?"

"Angela your mother Maria Souliou lives in Sparta Greece and your father Spiros Judis lives in Montreal Canada."

I felt my knees turn to slush and my face drain of blood.

"Angela, are you all right? You look like you're going to faint."

"I'm OK," I lied, trying to catch my breath. My heart was racing, causing a ruckus in my chest. Spinning in my head like a top just freed of its chord, my thoughts twirled so fast I lost my grip on reality.

'*My parents are alive*!' I repeated over and over, afraid to give any credence to my words. Was it true? Could I believe this gentleman?I had to admit I had a huge dark hole in my heart that nothing could fill. Sometimes it pained me terribly and other times I'd allow my faithful companions, repression and denial to soothe the excruciating inner hurt, neither sharing nor confiding in anyone. But it was indomitable. One of my dark secrets, it always returned to torment me.

That evening after closing the *Sno Cone* stand, Gary and I returned home. He always came in the busy late afternoon to give me a hand and load the car with the empty syrup containers at closing.

"What's wrong Angela, you seem extra quiet. Did something happen at the *Sno Cone* stand?"

"Gary, something strange happened," I blurted still dazed by the uncanny turn of events. "A customer gave me the phone numbers and addresses of my parents."

"Are you serious? Are you going to look them up?"

"Yes, I want to meet them."

Once I had learned the whereabouts of my mother and father, I could not free my mind from the recurring thought of actually seeing them in person. With my imagination desperate to quell the emptiness within, I orchestrated emotionally satisfying scenarios in which my mother and father received me like the return of the prodigal son, greeting me with joy and celebration, *"bringing out the fattened calf."*

Alternating between bouts of fitful sleep and periods of semi-wakefulness, I slipped in and out of confusing dreams in which I stood in front of my mother and father—two complete strangers.

My reverie was interrupted by a disturbing accelerated heart beat. In the throes of a panic attack, I bolted up-right in my bed. Nervous and apprehensive I realized I had to resolve this new unknown, flushing currents of uncertainty into my life. Yet despite the sensation of budding angst, I felt a strange certainty in the confusion. I knew I absolutely had to pursue this path. I had to meet my parents.

All my life I had tried to fill the dark cold void in my heart, fantasizing I was the daughter of Mother Teresa. In my mind, this caring, nurturing woman was the embodiment of a mother. Willing an able to love unconditionally, I imagined myself in her arms during the most painful moments of my lonely life.

Many times in the darkness of night, I evoked her name in tears asking for help. Generous and kind, even the thought of her warmed my spirit, until a feeble hint of light began to flow through the room signaling dawn and the chance to live another day.

The following morning I found it difficult to concentrate. My thoughts kept returning to my parents and the addresses scribbled on the piece of paper near my bed. Dressing I put on one of my vests, a garment heavily embroidered with American flags; an article of clothing that became my uniform throughout the decades. In fact I never left home without one of my patriotic vests.

When Gary came to help me at the *Sno Cone* stand I did not mince words.

"I want to go to Greece to meet my mother," I blurted as soon as he stepped into the stand. "There are a lot of questions I need to have answered."

The conversation lapsed for less than a second before Gary jumped in.

"OK Angela, let's go to Greece." He had just been released from the psychiatric hospital, was on new medication and eager to move around.

Although the moon failed to show its face that evening, there was a certain baffling brightness as I crawled into the car, exhausted from the endless lines of customers.

"When do you want to leave?" Gary asked."

"As soon as we close the *Sno Cone* stand for the season." We'll go to Paris then to England. I'd like to visit my former roommates."

In the fall of 1998 Gary and I boarded a flight for Paris. Unaware of where this new journey would take me, I was empowered with the possibility that perhaps part of my identity puzzle would be resolved when I stood face to face in front of my mother. Unable to bury the past, relics of a long gone era continued to exist. Perhaps I would be able to sort through the remnants and find closure.

En route to Paris I noticed Gary seemed a bit restless, bobbling up and down in his seat like a two year old on sugar overload. Believing it was the excitement of the trip, I did not anticipate any problems.

By the time we landed at De Gaulle International Airport, Gary was having difficulty remaining in his seat.

"Did you take your medication?" I asked, already certain of the response.

"I'll take it when we get to the hotel," he mumbled.

"Gary you must take your pills every day. Remember what the doctor told you."

Turning to face the window, he grumbled, focused on the first sightings of the Paris skyline as the plane began its decent into the airport.

The landing was relatively smooth despite the sudden appearance of disturbing winds. However, unlike my arrival in New York decades earlier this time the baggage retrieval was without any problems.

An hour later we were settled in our hotel room. Tired and in need of a bath, I filled the tub and took a relaxing soak, actually enjoying the hundreds of sweet smelling bubbles forming as the water hugged my neck.

When I came out I noticed Gary was no longer in the room. Thinking he had gone to buy some cigarettes I laid down on the bed, certain a short nap would help me regain my forces. Several hours later I awakened. One quick look around the room told me Gary had not yet returned.

Upset I feared the symptoms of a returning manic state. I knew my husband had been delinquent in taking his medicine. Dressing, I hurriedly left, taking the steps two at a time. Walking up and down every street in the area I prayed, "God please let me find my husband."

As soon as I finished my imploration, I passed a bar and heard Gary's loud voice screaming and cussing. It was obvious—he was drunk. The proprietor had phoned the *gendarme* unwilling to handle Gary's rampage.

"*Madame*," a husky voice echoed when I entered and called Gary's name to get his attention, "your husband is rowdy and disturbing the peace. I cannot allow him to remain here." Distracted and decidedly hyper, Gary looked disoriented.

I grabbed his hand. "Why didn't you take your medication?" I scolded, visibly angered by his stupidity. A muffled apology camouflaged in a grunt was his response.

Thankfully no charges were pressed and released in my custody, we returned to the hotel. Unfortunately the boisterous behavior did not end there. Intoxicated, unruly and disruptive, Gary made himself heard throughout the hotel. His ear-piercing screams and foul vulgarities were far from the dulcet tune of a nightingale's cant.

Clutching his arm I led him down the stairs. "I'm starved," I said, "we have not eaten much today, let's get some dinner." I had to get him out and away from everyone.

We found a tiny bistro just several blocks from the hotel. Settled in our seats, Gary promptly ordered a beer.

"Don't you think you had enough to drink?" I murmured, realizing mine was a loosing battle.

"No just one Angela," he said, taking a full swig as soon as the *garçon* set the tall beer stein on the table. "You could sip it," I said, "instead of gulping it down."

We finished dinner in silence and returned to the hotel arm in arm. By now Gary was noticeably unstable on his feet. His swaggering stride presented clear cut evidence he was beyond drunk.

Nearing the entry of the hotel I spotted our luggage haphazardly cast on the street. Several pieces had broken open and some of our belongings were strewn along the sidewalk. Apparently the bags had been tossed from the window from our room on the fourth floor.

Running into the lobby I shouted; "what happened to our bags? Why are they on the street?"

"*Madame*," the *concierge* said dryly, "you have been evicted from the hotel. *Merci et bonsoir.*"

Guests started to trickle in after a night on the town. "Please leave, *Madame*" he continued, "*Je suis désolé* —I am sorry but we do not want any trouble."

When I went outside, Gary was gone. Alone and terrified in a foreign country I hailed a taxi asking the driver to take me to the airport. There was no point in continuing my journey. Upset, disheartened and unable to think straight I felt it best to return to St Louis. There was no way I could persuade myself to continue after this humiliating catastrophe.

I hated to renounce such an important mission, but I had to accept the fact that circumstances sometimes dictated the course of life. Furthermore, how could I continue my journey to Greece unaware of Gary's whereabouts?

The trip back to St. Louis was difficult. Experience demonstrated that Gary's condition was exasperating, however he was my husband and I loved him, fully intending to honor my marriage commitment. There was something comforting about his presence in my life—naturally when he was appropriately medicated.

My daydreams continued, keeping me company during the flight. Over and over, I choreographed in my mind, the reunion scenario. I would knock on the huge old wood front door. My mom slowed by the effects of time's passage would ever so gently pull it open.

I could actually hear her scuffling footsteps on the marble floor and the crackling echo of the rusted door jam. Surprised to see her long lost first born she would entwine her arms around me sobbing in delight, squashing the breath out of me.

The imagination was a wonderful quick fix for an anguishing reality. Casting director and producer of my reverie, I could plot the scenes to play out to suit my own needs and wants, never once considering the protagonist—truth.

Once back in St Louis, terrified something awful may have happened to Gary, I began a frantic search for my missing husband, summoning the assistance of his sister Sharon, a Chicago attorney with international connections. Even her efforts were spent in vain. There were no traces of Gary and neither a letter nor telephone call to appease my worries.

A month later, I received a phone call late in the evening.

"Angela," a recognizable voice said in a heavily sedated tone, "I'm at the VA Hospital in New York. I've been recovered in the psych ward for the past few weeks. But don't worry I'm OK. They're letting me out tomorrow, and I'm coming home."

Don't worry! If he was that concerned why did he wait a month before contacting me?

Breathing a sigh of relief, I thanked God for keeping Gary safe. God always came through for me. And recognizing my blessings, I always made time for a thank you. I knew that without my faith and the Lord's intervention in my life I would not have survived let alone triumphed.

TWENTY-SECOND EPISODE

"Now I can die in peace. I know you are OK."
—Maria Souliou

Gary's recuperation from another serious bi-polar episode proceeded at an even pace. But much as his wounds healed the effect of his instability was a source of concern.

However, feeling grateful for Gary's safe return, I began making new plans for my journey back to Greece. When his behavior patterns took on a semblance of normalcy and the fretting and restlessness subsided long enough for him to step back into a supporting role, I decided to inform him of my intentions to continue my pursuits to dig into the past.

Though mentally Gary was not a well-man, I saw in him a caring soul-mate and a man who tried to live a decent life, to the best of his abilities. Problematic and difficult to live with at times, he was also a major pinnacle in my lonely life. Despite it all I welcomed his presence beside me as a loyal, loving companion.

"Gary," I said late one evening, as soon as the *sno cone* season ends, I'm going to fly to Greece. I want to look up my mom."

"Angela, are you sure you don't want me to come along with you? I'm OK now."

"No, I'll be fine. I can do this alone."

"If you change your mind, just let me know."

Although I appreciated his availability, I neither wanted nor was willing to deal with any distractions or interruptions. I needed a clear mind and if I had to worry about Gary being careless about his medication and getting into trouble, I would be too anxious and unsettled. Therefore, my mind was made up: I would cross the Ocean alone.

I booked a ticket and made arrangements for a car to be waiting for me at the airport upon my arrival. Realizing that I would be perhaps rendered confused by relentless spurts of emotional energy that could possibly send my thought process into a tilt, I had to be certain that the basic necessities were accounted for. Reservations confirmed, I over-packed and overstuffed my bags as always, and left St. Louis for a life-altering journey into my past.

Many pieces of the puzzle were missing and if I did not explore and investigate my yesterday, I would find neither serenity nor the confirmation of who I was in my today. There were so many unknowns and endless questions begging for answers. It was time to collect the parts of a puzzle I hoped to eventually assemble.

In a sense, I was embarking on an expedition to find myself. Hence, when the plane took off in the gathering dusk, I prayed. I prayed for a safe flight, and I prayed that I would actually live the scenario I repeatedly rehearsed in my mind.

The echo of a bell shattered my thoughts. When the ζώνη ασφάλειασ— the seatbelt sign—lit up, I put my seat in an upright position, quickly fastened the belt and began to prepare myself for a return to my native land after a thirty-one-year absence.

As the plane began its descent toward Ελληνικόν, the Ellinikon International Airport in Athens, I prayed that the landing would be as smooth as the actual flight. Before the landing gear was released, the pilot mentioned that there was a bit of unexpected turbulence in the sudden manifestation of crosswinds. This meant that part of the existing wind was at a ninety-degree angle to the runway centerline, a circumstance that could complicate the actual landing unless a different approach was taken.

Once I heard the thud signaling the landing gear being released, I shut my eyes, clenched my fists and repeatedly chanted the name of God, hardly daring to breathe until, bumped up and down several times in my seat, I realized that the plane had landed.

After I picked up my luggage and cleared customs, I went to retrieve my rental car. As the odor of tobacco was pungent, overwhelming even to a former chain smoker, I welcomed the opportunity to step outside. Accustomed to the American, health-conscious attitude, the lax smoking laws made a vivid impression on my olfactory sense.

Therefore, a bit of outdoor climate was revitalizing, especially after hours of recycled air.

Although far from a harebrained desperado with a rush on destruction, I was pretty much undaunted when confronted with challenging situations. It was a consequence of my upbringing. The crosses saddled on my back from infancy had strengthened me, making me a better individual—more tenacious and certainly courageous. As a result, it was practically a given that I would slide behind the wheel of my rented car, battle illegible road signs and head for my destination.

Exhausted from the flight and excited about the emotional melodrama unfolding before me, I drove out of the airport and onto the main thoroughfare.

"I'm in Greece," I whispered. "I'm going to see my mother!"

Thoughts and feeling vied for dominance, twisted, tangled and meshed together, almost suffocating my air passages. Confused but unwilling to admit any hesitancy or doubt regarding my decision to explore my roots, I let a new scenario materialize in my mind.

I saw the shadowy silhouette of my mom come into view. Yet no amount of creative fantasy could design her absent face. There were no eyes, no nose and no mouth, just a blank slate, and there were no memories to dust off. Although she was a name on my birth certificate, she was a total stranger—just a common Eve.

Tooting horns dragged my attention back to the highway. "Where am I going?" I said aloud to no one. Although my destination was Ktismata, I had absolutely no directions to follow. Pressing my foot on the accelerator, I went as fast as I could, thankful that I was unable to read the speed limits. If I didn't know I was infringing upon a law of the road, I was absolved from blame. Much is to be said at times in defense of ignorance.

Passing the highway signs, I realized that they were all in Greek, therefore undecipherable, since not even one word of my mother tongue found sanctuary in my memory. Blocked, it was buried somewhere in one of the obliterated caverns of my recollections.

Realizing that I could not drive forever, and unwilling to admit defeat, I did not hesitate to stop when I spotted a young hitchhiker frantically waving at me. Pulling over, I rolled down the window. "Do you speak English?" I asked. Judging from his sooty appearance, I guessed he was probably a construction worker. However, though he looked rather slovenly, he regarded my question sincerely.

"Yes," he replied. "I studied it at school." His words were a welcome relief.

"I've been driving for hours," I said. "I must have passed through half of Greece but I'm having trouble with the road signs. I don't read Greek anymore. Do you know where Ktismata is?"

"Yes, κυρία… Yes, madam," he said, nodding his head of thick, black curls. "If you give me a ride, I'll be happy to take you to Ktismata." His words came forth in heavily accented English, rendered charming by an accompanying full-tooth smile. It was obvious he was doing his best to be gallant—and more than succeeding.

"Where are you going?" I inquired.

"Albania, κυρία."

"I'm not going to Albania. I'm headed to Ktismata."

"I don't expect you to take me all the way to Albania. Kitsmata is just about a kilometer and a half away from the border and about eight kilometers from here. You can leave me off wherever you wish."

"OK, come on in," I said, pulling the handle to open the door. Stamping his feet several times, he shook off the large encrustations of dried mud that had settled in circles on the rounded toes of his beige boots, like puppies snuggled at the foot of the bed.

With my new companion and guide, I felt more secure behind the wheel.

"You must be missing a long time from Greece, κυρία," he said, flinging his backpack on the rear seat.

"Seems like forever," I responded, shuddering briefly at the thought of what I had left behind.

"Things are very different today, κυρία. This is no longer the hardship-laden, post-war Greece of the '50s and '60s, fighting for survival. The economy is booming. People are working. That's why I came to Greece. There are lots of good jobs."

I was pleased to hear that the post-war battle had been won in a sense, and that the Greeks were thriving.

Ten minutes later, we came to a residential area.

"We are in Kitsmata," my hitchhiker announced, smiling.

"What are all those tanks doing here?" I asked, surprised to see so many armed soldiers. "It looks like they're preparing for an armed conflict!"

"No—no need to worry, κυρία. There is no war."

As I drove into Ktismata, a thick lump formed at the site of my missing tonsils. Clearing my throat several times did little to alleviate the irritating discomfort. Turning my head, I gazed at the beautiful orange trees, tall, stately and abundantly prolific, like a young girl several years past puberty.

The bright orange fruit glistened in the midmorning sunlight. Minutes later, a passing cloud erupted without warning, spilling a quick brief downpour—a purification rite that left the shiniest, crystalline drops imaginable on the roundness of the bittersweet blood oranges.

There was an implied graciousness along the environs of Ktismata, albeit concealed by my own personal perception. Hitting the clutch, I shifted into second gear and tapped the brake to bring my entry into the town into a more gradual pace.

A white wagtail seemed to appear from the heavens. Coasting around the car, it glided with full wingspan, resembling a free-flying kite caught in an easterly breeze. Soon, two others appeared. In somber silence, they hovered above, monitoring my arrival like a pompous honor guard.

The welcome was poetic. But would it alter the lonely, disconnected feeling that ironically called me back to Kitsmata? Would I be able to discover what if anything was my connection to this ancient world?

I stopped an elderly gentleman whose suffered stride and hunched shoulders were a testament to the endless summers he had greeted. His long, black robe of the church swept the dusty ground as he walked. It had not been tailored to accommodate his curved spine and shrinking stature.

A deeply etched brow, an intricate patchwork of zigzag lines visible through his sparse, ten-inch beard, several remaining strands of silver hair and a toothless smile gave me the certainty that he was old enough to recognize my family name.

Leaning out the window, I introduced myself. "Καλημέρα, good morning. I'm Avyrini Souliou. Do you understand English?"

Glancing at me, his smile returned. "Yes, Avyrini," he said. "I'm 100 years old and I speak English."

Before I could pursue my questioning, he told me he knew my

family and that my aunt and uncle were the proprietors of a huge, heavily frequented store that sold clothing and groceries.

"They also have a truck," he said. "As you can see, there are not many cars in Kitsmata." Graciously, he gave me directions and thanking him, I continued my journey.

I couldn't believe how little Ktismata had changed. Elderly ladies still shuffled about carrying wood, laundry and groceries in straw baskets positioned on their heads. It was 1999—almost the new millennium! But time seemed to float like a directionless boat unhinged of its anchor.

Taking a long, deep breath, I drove to my maternal uncle's store. When I went inside, I was surprised to see one of the shelves stocked with Michelob and Anheuser beers!

"Καλημέρα," I said, approaching an elderly man with dark eyes and a gray mustache. "I'm Avyrini Souliou, your niece from America."

He jumped to his feet and wrapped his arms around me. Tears pooled in his big eyes, spilling down his cheeks. Visibly moved, he muttered, "Avyrini, you must eat something, you're so skinny. Don't you eat in America? You must come to my house."

I agreed and that evening, additional relatives were summoned, among which was a paternal uncle who spoke perfect English. Criticized for my skeletal appearance, I was promised some flesh on my bones and served huge plates of steaming hot pasta drowned in a sea of heavy, almost green olive oil.

As if this weren't challenging enough for my recovering bulimic digestive system, it was spiked with several large cloves of the most pungent-smelling, golden-colored garlic I had ever encountered. I knew immediately that I would not sleep that evening!

After the hearty repast, I was informed once again that my mother, Maria, lived in Σπάρτ, in Sparta. The mere mention of her name sent goosebumps crawling up and down my arms. But would she agree to receive me?

One of my uncles phoned my mother to announce my arrival. The following morning, after thanking my hosts for their gracious hospitality, I left for Sparta, unsure of the outcome.

After quite a harrowing experience with Athens' traffic and less-than-orderly driving conduct, I stopped at a gas station, located a pay phone and dialed the number my uncle had given me. After several rings, a female voice responded.

"Hello, this is Christina."

"I'm Avyrini," I blurted, "and I'm here in Sparta." There was dead silence. "Hello," I repeated.

"Who are you?" Christina asked dryly.

"I'm Avyrini Souliou—I'm your half sister!"

Apparently, she had no idea that I existed. Several gasps, followed by a lengthy silence, told me that my announcement had shocked her.

"Christina, please come and meet me," I said, shattering the uncomfortable quiet. "I'm having difficulty finding my way and it's really pouring rain."

"Wait there and I'll come and get you."

Jumping back into my Toyota 4Runner, I waited. When the downpour subsided, I tried to open the window for a breath of air, only to have to roll it up again to avoid getting drenched as nature teased my patience.

Thankfully, the rain ceased. Christina pulled up in a Toyota, which led me to assume that Toyotas were popular cars in Greece. Leaving my vehicle, I walked over to greet her.

Extending a hand, she said, "I'm Christina." The presentation was a bit cool and aloof, considering we were half sisters. I tried to see if we shared any resemblance. Just under five feet tall, Christina was full of stature. A woman with an enormous bosom, she comically contrasted my lack. Her thick, short nose, wide-set eyes and robust face were framed by a head of short, dark hair.

Unable to see any similarities, I was surprised to learn that she held an important position as administrator in the Sparta hospital. Nursing, perhaps was in our destinies, much as I detested it.

"I don't understand why my mother never told me about you," she stammered. "My dad loves children. He would have insisted you return to us."

I later learned that even Christina was born out of wedlock. However, her father had agreed to marry my mother, eventually legitimizing the child's status.

"Follow me, Avyrini," she said, "and we'll go see Mom. I live in a condo with her."

I drove behind Christina, feeling anxious and restless, not knowing what to expect. Moving back in time toward my roots was not without consequences. The unknown leaves room for fantasy, whereas reality is stark, indelible and uncompromising.

Christina's father was a wealthy gentleman and the family had many acres of fruit- and vegetable-producing land. I was surprised by the beauty of the multitude of orange, peach and lemon trees and tall vegetable plants. There was no doubting that they had the means to take care of another child.

Christina stopped in front of a mid-rise condo on a quiet, residential street. Hopping out of the car, she came to the window.

"Avyrini," she said, gesturing with her hand, "this is where we live. You can park right there."

The butterflies invaded my stomach. Unruly, restless creatures, they thrashed around like a team of blind children chasing each other, knocking into walls and smashing furniture.

Raising a trembling hand to my bosom, I felt the pulsations of a heart unable to control its beats. For a moment, I thought it would explode in my chest. At fifty-three years old, I was about to see my mother for the first time. Wondering if I had the strength to go in and meet her gaze, I questioned if my trip back to my roots was in fact wise or just another painful experience of a life filled with suffering.

Halting my thoughts, I forced myself to breathe; this was not the moment to go into crisis. I knew I could avoid it. I realized that the repeated presence of trauma in my life had prepared me for all eventualities—even the tragic ones. I whispered a prayer for endurance.

Together with Christina, I entered the building. My mother knew we were seconds away after receiving a warning buzz on the intercom. Droplets of sweat crept across my forehead as I prepared myself for the confrontation.

At the top of the staircase stood a varnished, cherry wood door. Slowly, it was pulled open. Long, slender rays of light illuminated the foyer. The hesitation spoke of reflection mixed with a well-proportioned dose of fear. Then, the moment of truth: In the doorway stood the woman born Maria Souliou—the woman who had given me life, my mother.

I felt my eyes fill with tears and my knees tremble. She was such a petite woman, even tinier than Christina. I felt a flush of joy, seeing her for the first time. But when our eyes met, it was like two strangers exchanging curious glances from across a room.

Gone in an instant were my reveries of fulfilling kisses and heartwarming hugs. Silenced was the sweet, endearing dialogue I had scripted in my mind. I did not hear, "Avyrini, my dear child, I love you." I felt neither warmth nor regrets, neither tenderness nor remorse.

Unable to communicate due to the language barrier, Christina translated whatever words we shared. Nonetheless, the dialogue was courteous, strained and insignificant, until I lit a cigarette.

"Avyrini, no good smoking," Maria blurted. A retired nurse, she was apparently concerned about my health. She turned to Christina and asked her to tell me to stop smoking. A tiny glimmer of emotion appeared in her dark eyes.

When Christina was present, my mother remained detached and unapproachable, regarding me as a guest in her home. However, during working hours, when her younger daughter was at the hospital, my mother's standoffish demeanor would melt. It was as if an internal conflict were causing her defenses to crumble at different intervals.

One evening, my mother arrived at the dinner table carrying an armload of old clothes.

"Here, Avyrini, these are for you," she said.

I looked at Christina, who averted her gaze to the floor in embarrassment. Offended by the gesture, I refused the ragged hand-me-downs, angering my mother.

The lack of warmth and acceptance was worsened by the language barrier and the unusual Greek way of life. Its prolonged afternoon siestas and abundant, impossible to digest midday meals complimented by late, snack-like suppers were not congenial to my own customs. Irritated, disappointed and exasperated by it all, I decided to cut my visit short.

"It's time for me to get back to my husband and business," I announced after breakfast.

"Avyrini, when you say goodbye to the neighbors, do not say you are my daughter."

It was shocking! After all this time, my mother was still fearful that society would shun her for an out-of-wedlock child she'd given birth to more than half a century before. Defying her request, I told the neighbor that I was Maria's firstborn.

"Avyrini," she said, smiling. "We always knew your mother had another daughter." So much for secrets!

Much as she tried to be distant, I often caught my mom's eyes glued to my face. She'd whisper over and over, "όμορφοσ, όμορφοσ," unlocking her gaze when I looked in her direction. One evening, curious to unravel the mysterious mumblings, I asked Christina, "What is Mom mumbling?"

"She is saying 'beautiful'—she thinks you are beautiful. Avyrini,"

Christina continued, "this morning, during breakfast, Mom told you, 'I can now die in peace. I know you are OK.' You did not understand but later, she confided that she is at peace, realizing her long-lost firstborn is well and safe."

Tears drizzled down my cheeks. If nothing else, my trip into the past gave my mother the gift of serenity. Reliving all the hurtful feelings and painful memories of my Grecian childhood served a purpose. Perhaps mine was a journey of good will—a scorned child returning to ease the silent pain in the heart of the mother who abandoned her.

TWENTY-THIRD EPISODE

"Go confidently in the direction of your dreams. Live the life you have imagined."

—Henry David Thoreau

Although the long-awaited and much-fantasized reunion with my mother was disappointing and in contrast with the way I had hoped it would unfold, I felt somewhat compensated for my painful trip into the past, knowing I had brought some peace of mind to the anguished woman, most probably tormented by a decision in her early youth that penalized her innocent child.

Reflecting on the past two weeks, I was deep in thought when my paternal uncle phoned to invite me to dinner before my departure to the United States. Since he was fluent in English and apparently willing to talk, I was eager to spend some time with him. After meeting my mother and Christina, I was determined to find to my father. Certain my uncle would be a valuable link and means to achieve my goal, I accepted his invitation.

Although I was unsure about the motives behind my mother's outward indifference, I thought perhaps it could have been nourished by guilt. Seeing me again probably stirred up memories she was unprepared to deal with. Realizing that I had to speak with my father to even begin to assemble the puzzle, I looked forward to dinner with my uncle.

We met in a small, family-owned and -operated εστιατόριο, a restaurant on the outskirts of Ktismata. Thankfully, it was a quiet evening, conducive to conversing. A tall, slender man, my uncle had decidedly more than the beginning paunch of a man perhaps over-enjoying the luxuries of the table. His huge, brown eyes, alert, penetrating and expressive, sparked my curiosity. I wondered if he shared any physical similarities with my father, Spiro Judis.

Ordering an antipasto, he poured several drops of water into his ούζο, his ouzo. Taking a sip, he immediately informed me that my father was no longer among the living. A massive coronary had taken his life.

"Avyrini, your father was a committed Communist who shared ideologies with the party and paid allegiance to Stalin. He controlled thirty-eight villages. Fighting against me, his own brother, he tried to overthrow the Greek government at the conclusion of World War II. See this prosthetic leg I wear? This is a battle souvenir. Failing, your father immigrated to Moscow where he married and had a family. Eventually, he immigrated to Montreal, Canada."

"Canada," I said. "That's not too far from St. Louis. I think I'll look up the family when I return to the USA. Perhaps they can fill in the missing blanks and answer some of my questions."

I told my Uncle about Gary, my booming sno cone business and my life as an American. Listening to my words, he lit up, giving the impression that he was proud of my accomplishments.

We hugged at the end of dinner and he wished me well on my journey. The following morning, I departed. Though I had met my Greek family, I realized that they would probably never be a part of my life. Too much time had elapsed for any loving relationship. Furthermore, there was not enough love to hold us together. However, they would always be an intangible presence, one that would never fade, regardless of how deep the silence would become.

Slumped in my window seat, exhausted both emotionally and physically, I planned my next move as the jet crossed the Atlantic, bringing me back to my beloved United States.

Once back in St. Louis, I instantly phoned my family in Montreal. At the mention of my name, a visibly irate voice shouted, "What do you want?"

"I'm you half sister," I responded. Before I could pursue it further, I heard a click as his receiver hit the cradle. Rudely, he had cut me off. A rush of blood warmed my face. Sweat dampened my shirt. But still stunned, I allowed insult to step aside in favor of curiosity.

After a brief discussion, Gary and I packed a few belongings and drove north to Montreal. The trip was challenging, with speeding vehicles weaving in and out of lanes, often experimenting with some rather dangerous maneuvers. But Gary was vigilant and adept behind the wheel, delivering us safely to our destination.

Once in Canada, we drove to Montreal, right to the address my uncle had given me in Greece. The house looked dark, almost uninhabited. Undeterred, I walked to the front door. Several knocks brought an elderly woman to her feet. Immediately, I noticed that she was barefoot. A quick introduction resulted in a deluge of tears, moistening a pair of dark eyes set in a heavy network of wrinkles. My father's widow had broken into sobs at the mention of my name.

A last ray evading from the evening sunset brought an extraordinary brightness to the pitch blackness inside her house. The elderly woman invited us to enter. A slight odor attributed to improper ventilation permeated the residence.

Stepping inside, I was amazed to see a patchwork of old photos decorating her walls. The stern faces of Stalin, Marx and Lenin glared. Capturing the furor of each man in their harsh facial expressions, the immortalized black-and-white representations did the men justice. Standing guard in full uniform and armed in the midst of this ferocious trio was my father.

Relaxing a bit after the initial emotional catharsis, Madame Judis mentioned her children with Spiros.

"One of my sons is a world-renowned engineer," she said proudly. "He travels frequently. My other son lives here in Montreal, with me."

I quickly assumed he was the man who curtly hung up on me when I phoned. Standing six feet, four inches tall, he was angular and handsome. His dark olive complexion gave him a perennial suntan finish. Almost-black, intense eyes gave him a mysterious aura. I had to admit that he cut a dramatic presence.

A bit more gracious in person, he invited us to sit for coffee. Articulate and multilingual, he acted as the translator.

"Ask Avyrini why she did not look up her father before his death," Madame Judis told her son. Silence—for some questions, there are no viable answers.

I, in turn, asked my half brother if his father had ever mentioned he had a daughter.

"Yes," he said, "but you were always considered a μύθοσ in the family."

"Well I'm not a myth" I blurted. "I'm your half sister. Spiros was my father also. I was his firstborn."

My half brother rose from the chair, excused himself, muttered a farewell and left the room.

Saddened by the cool reception from my family, I regretted making the journey to Canada. Perhaps it would have been best to end the chapter knowing that my father had passed away. In seeking answers to who I was and where I originated from, I discovered that decades later, I was still held accountable for my parents' transgression. At fifty-three years of age, I was still the illegitimate child, the family's shameful, dark secret both in Greece and in Canada—but not in my beloved United States of America.

AFTERWORD

Avyrini is no longer an abandoned, unwanted and unloved child, shunned and abused, always embarrassed of her Greek heritage. Today, Avyrini Souliou is Angela Mattox, a successful entrepreneur, an author, a devoted, loving wife, a respected woman in the community and a humanitarian who dedicates her non-working hours to the veterans at the Jefferson Barracks VA hospital in St. Louis, Missouri, as a volunteer.

I try to nurture the heroic individuals hailing from World War II, the Korean War, the Vietnam War, the Gulf War, Afghanistan and the Iraqi conflicts, listening to their fears and sorrows while giving them all the love, attention and solidarity I was denied as a child.

Despite the prejudicial opinions of my Greek family, today I am SOMEONE. The respected, loved and admired Sno Cone Lady, empowered by adversity, I am a woman who puts smiles on the faces of men, women and children.

Yes, America was and is, for me, the pot of gold at the end of the rainbow. Therefore, it is now time to say "thank you." But more importantly, it is time to give back—to offer others a dream. This is why Martyrdom of the Sno Cone Lady was written: to tell the whole truth and nothing but the truth, to be able to help the veterans at Jefferson Barracks Hospital in St. Louis, Missouri. This is my second dream.

> *"I have spread my dreams beneath your feet.*
> *Tread softly because you tread on my dreams."*
>
> —W.B. Yeats